What Women Want

The Ideas of the Movement

WHAT
WOMEN
WANT

The Ideas of the Movement

Gayle Graham Yates

Harvard University Press
Cambridge, Massachusetts, and London, England

Copyright © 1975 by the President and Fellows of Harvard College
All rights reserved
Fourth printing 1977
Printed in the United States of America

Library of Congress Cataloging in Publication Data
Yates, Gayle Graham, 1940-
    What women want.

    Bibliography: p.
    Includes index.
    1. Feminism—United States. I. Title.
HQ1426.Y38   332.4'4'0973   75-14018
ISBN 0-674-95077-1 (cloth)
ISBN 0-674-95079-8 (paper)

For
Wilson

Preface

This book is at once a personal document, a social commentary, and an intellectual investigation. I have learned in its writing that scholarship in current history is an integration of the questions that drive the self, the issues that shape society, and the evidence available to the intellect.

The work began in the spring of 1969 when, in the course of studying American intellectual history, I raised the question, What is the relationship between historical feminism and the new feminism? But in another sense, it began when I was a child on the farm and was not allowed to raise a calf with my brother, when I was in high school and was required to take home economics at the hour that boys were required to take science. My adult intellectual quest became one with my personal history of rebelling against feminine stereotypes and the social history of my group—women—in American society.

Once started on the scholarly search for an answer to my question, my focus settled on the framework of ideas of the past and present women's movements; and as I read the mimeographed statements, newsletters, essays, and books of contemporary feminists, it became increasingly clear that, despite popular references to the new feminism as one kind of thinking, it actually embraces three distinctive ideologies. What I came to develop here, then, were those three contrasting ideological strands, with some suggestion as to their roots in historical feminism.

My treatment of the intellectual basis of contemporary feminism has, by the nature of its emphasis, left out several other matters well worth exploring. A dozen more books were suggested by my research. One would be a book on the grass roots development of the new feminism. Another would examine the action taken by women since 1963 on specific issues, such as employment discrimination, political discrimination, abortion, advertising, publishing, or education. Still another would deal with the work of the many women who have not been overtly feminist but who have advanced the cause of women's freedom by their social, educational, or literary contributions. Instead, I have developed through a survey of the literature of feminism a framework of the ideas that appear to me to shape contemporary feminism.

My selection of sources was based on a criterion of the deliberately feminist intention of the writers. Even at that, it was impossible to read everything. I relied entirely on written sources, believing that what people had written probably stated their ideas most cogently.

Grateful acknowledgment is made for permission to quote from the following: *Sexual Politics,* copyright © 1969, 1970 by Kate Millett, reprinted by permission of Doubleday & Co., Inc., and Rupert Hart-Davis; letter from Melba Windoffer of the Seattle Radical Women to the Majority in Minneapolis, April 25, 1970, printed by permission of Melba Windoffer—Seattle Radical Women; *The Female Eunuch,* copyright © 1970, 1971 by Germaine Greer, reprinted by permission of McGraw-Hill Book Company; *The American Woman: Who Was She?* edited by Anne Firor Scott, copyright © 1971 by Prentice-Hall, Inc., reprinted by permission; "Family Development in a Changing World," printed by permission of Alice S. Rossi; "Women in Labor," by Marijean Suelzle, from *Women's Liberation,* edited by M.E. Adelstein and J.G. Pival, copyright © 1972 by St. Martin's Press, Inc., reprinted by permission; "Redstockings Manifesto," from *Sisterhood Is Powerful,* edited by Robin Morgan, published by Random House, Inc., copyright © 1970 by Robin Morgan, reprinted by permission; "Goodbye to All That," copyright © 1970 by Robin Morgan, published in *Voices from Women's Liberation,* edited by Leslie B. Tanner, published by New American Library, reprinted by permission; *Language,* by Edward Sapir, copyright © 1921 by Harcourt Brace Jovanovich, Inc., renewed 1949 by Jean V. Sapir, reprinted by permission; "Working Women," by Esther Peterson, and "Equality Between the Sexes: An Immodest Proposal," by Alice Rossi, reprinted by permission of *Daedalus,* Journal of the American Academy of Arts and Sciences, Boston, Massachusetts, Spring 1964, *The Woman in America;* "Poem," by Alta, reprinted by permission of *Aphra,* vol. 3, no. 2, Spring 1972; *The Feminine Mystique* copyright © 1963 by Betty Friedan, reprinted by permission of W. W. Norton & Company, Inc.; "Kinder, Kuche, Kirche As Scientific Law: Psychology Constructs the Female," by Naomi Weisstein, reprinted by permission of *motive,* vol. 29, March-April 1969; "penus envy" and "The Vow for Anne Hutchinson," by Alta, first published in *From Feminism to Liberation,* edited by Edith Hoshino Altback, copyright © 1971 by Schenkman Publishing Co., reprinted by permission of Alta; *The Church and the Second Sex,* by Mary Daly, copyright © 1968, Preface and Introduction copyright © 1975 by Mary Daly, reprinted by permission of Harper and Row Publishers, Inc.; "The Rise of Women's Liberation," by Marlene Dixon, first published in *Ramparts,* vol. 8, no. 6, December 1969; *Man's World, Woman's Place,* copyright © 1971 by Elizabeth Janeway, reprinted by permission of William Morrow and Co.; "The Demise of the Dancing Dog," by Cynthia Ozick, published in *Woman in Sexist Society,* edited by Vivian Gornick and Barbara K. Moran, copyright © 1971 by Basic Books, Inc., reprinted by permission of Cynthia Ozick and her agent Raines & Raines; "The Crazy Lady and Other Feisty Feminist Fables," copyright © 1972 by Cynthia Ozick, published in *The First Ms. Reader,* edited by Francine Klagsbrun (Warner, 1973), reprinted by permission of Cynthia Ozick and her agent Raines & Raines; "Fail: Bright Women," by Matina Horner, reprinted from *Psychology Today,* November 1969, copyright © 1969, Ziff-Davis Publishing Co., all rights reserved.

Many persons gave me invaluable assistance in this undertaking. I did research in the University of Minnesota libraries, the library of the Minnesota Women's Center, and the Women's Liberation Collection of the Social Welfare Archives of the University of Minnesota. Anne Truax of the Minnesota Women's Center and Andrea Hinding of the Social Welfare Archives were particularly helpful. I requested materials and letters from numerous feminist groups and individuals, who responded generously. Many friends and colleagues gave me bibliographical items, saved articles for me, lent me journals, magazines, or pamphlets, and discussed the material with me. Among them, I am especially grateful to Jean Ward, Roberta Gladowski, J. Vernon Jensen, Daniel V. Bryan, Judith Fryer, Jodi Wetzel, Noreen Bagnall, Mary Bednarowski, Betty Ann Burch, Margot Kriel, Joan Mark, and Katie Haynes Thompson.

Several professors deserve thanks for their considerable help from the inception of the idea for this project through its original appearance as a Ph.D. dissertation. Mulford Q. Sibley, my chief adviser, is the true teacher, who helped me to clarify my ideas, encouraged me to move in the direction that my research led, and pushed my questions as far as they would go, by a standard of thoroughness and excellence that was his own and his gift to me. David W. Noble was the teacher whose inspiration and methodological approach to history helped me to initiate and outline my research. Clarke A. Chambers was greatly helpful as an involved second adviser, who read critically and affirmatively each part of the project along the way. Caroline Rose also read my material and encouraged me. Especially deserving of appreciation is Mary C. Turpie, who has been for countless students, as for me, a significant role model for female scholarship and teaching, and who has given herself in both love and academic excellence to the University of Minnesota American Studies students.

Thanks go to Delphine Swanson, whose typing skill and knowledge of manuscript form were invaluable for production of the final copy. Sandra Riekki and Christine Stack also made a contribution of typing.

Thanks are in order for Aida DiPace Donald and Virginia LaPlante of Harvard University Press, whose editorial ability aided the book through publication.

An essential contribution to the book was made by Norma Carlson, who took loving responsibility for my children during hundreds of the hours I spent in the library and at the typewriter.

Finally, I should like to thank my family for their affirmation of my work. My husband, H. Wilson Yates, has given me substantial scholarly support mixed with affection. Calling himself an "anti-sexist sexist," he has taken a full share of responsibility for the maintenance of our mutual life to enable me to write about feminism. Our children, Natasha and Stiles, have sometimes nurtured their mother and have always cared.

Contents

What Women Want

The Ideas of the Movement

1

The History and Framework of the Women's Movement

As the 1970s advance, women are claiming, "This is our decade."[1] The daily newspaper and television are full of references to women's liberation. Positive or negative, "women's lib" is a new term in the American English language. In courts and legislatures across the nation women have been challenging abortion laws, discriminatory practices in employment, and unfair welfare policies. Women are pressing the Equal Employment Opportunity Commission in cases of sex bias policy, with the result that much of the commission's effort is now in this area.[2] Female representatives have increased in number in state legislatures and the United States Congress, elected in 1972 and 1974 at least in part by the force of the women's movement. An Equal Rights Amendment to the United States Constitution is now before the states for ratification. On January 22, 1973, the Supreme Court struck down abortion laws in forty-six states,—perhaps because the time was right, perhaps in consequence of new constitutional interpretations of privacy, but perhaps in part because of the new feminism. On university campuses, in suburban living rooms, foundation conference rooms, industrial cafeterias, and newly established women's centers, women are meeting in both loosely structured and highly organized groups to participate in consciousness-raising or to organize protest over inequities against women. There are women's marches in major cities, women's strikes or protests in industry, and conferences on women all over the country. Women's studies classes are being offered in numerous colleges and universities, as well as in scores of YWCAs, local school district evening classes, and church groups—courses on feminist literature, women and religion, self-defense for women, auto mechanics for women, women and the law.

Writing about women has reached the point of constituting a new literary genre.[3] Dozens of underground newsletters published by women about women are flourishing, and the establishment press has responded with slick new journals with titles like *you* and *New Woman*, while traditional women's magazines are updating their image and content for the "new woman."[4] The new feminist commercial magazine *Ms.* has been phenomenally successful. Feminist books are pouring from the presses.

Women of exceptional accomplishment are suddenly in demand as speakers, writers, and leaders, while unexceptional women are acquiring new pride in the awareness of their potential. A galaxy of new "stars" of feminism has emerged, who are being interviewed, making appearances, writing, and organizing on the scale of popular entertainers or politicians.

Some women are ceasing to shave their legs and discarding bras and makeup in the name of women's liberation. Others are moving into women's communes. And a few are refusing to have any social interaction at all with men.

In the feminism that has broken out all over America in the last decade, nothing short of full emancipation of and total equality for women has been demanded—not only the change of one kind of law or one kind of employment practice or one kind of marriage style, but a complete transformation of American society. Predictably, a backlash has occurred. One example is Midge Dector's publication of *The Liberated Woman and Other Essays* and *The New Chastity,* in which she criticizes the movement and extols the old sanctity of motherhood in the home. Another example is the organization by such eminents as Sidney Hook, Nathan Glazer, and Bruno Bettelheim of the Committee on Academic Non-Discrimination and Integrity to fight university hiring of "unqualified women," which they claim prevents "bright white males" from getting jobs.[5] Sometimes in backlash and sometimes as coliberationist, men's consciousness-raising groups have been formed. In some of them, men whine about threats to their sexual identity; in others, men try to grapple with the meaning of sexual stereotyping.

A new women's movement is abroad in the land, profoundly affecting the shape of current history. Part of its vitality comes from its diversity, which has been a strong factor in its recent brief history.

The Women's Movement, 1959-1973

The new feminism began to arise in the early 1960s, coming to wide public attention in the last two years of the decade. After World War II, when the war effort was no longer the singular concern in American life, requiring women to take outside employment and to engage in public life, women had returned in great numbers to the home as the central focus for their identity. This was a period of conservatism, during which the role of women was regarded as primarily domestic.[6] Yet more than one-third of American women still worked full time, and such women were made aware of discrimination in status and pay as they saw their male colleagues in the labor force advance more quickly and receive higher remuneration for performing the same work as they did. At the same time, interest in higher education for women whose careers had been interrupted by homemaking was indicated by the development of special programs in more than three hundred universities, among them the University of Minnesota with its Minnesota Plan for Continuing Education for Mature Women, and Radcliffe College with its Radcliffe Institute for Independent Study.[7] There also emerged a general sense of disenchantment with the idyllic image of female fulfillment in domestic life.

In 1959, Eleanor Flexner's *Century of Struggle,* a history of American feminism, was published and well received. This reminder of feminist activity probably acted as a small spur to the new feminism. Also in 1959, Mabel Newcomer published *A Century of Higher Education for Women,* in which she showed that women's involvement in academic life had declined over the past generation. In that same year Robert W. Smuts published *Women and Work in America,* documenting the fact that little change had taken place in this century in women's work outside the home.[8]

Such information, along with pressure from leading professional and political women in the nation, led President John F. Kennedy in 1961 to appoint a President's Commission on the Status of Women, "to set forth . . . the story of women's progress in a free democratic society."[9] The commission's specific task was to study and make recommendations regarding employment practices and legal treatment of women in the federal and state governments and to suggest services needed for women in the nation. The chairman of the commission was Eleanor Roosevelt, who was succeeded on her death by Esther Peterson, assistant secretary of labor. In a report to the President in October 1963, the commission documented attitudes and practices in government, education, and employment by which women were discriminated against and proposed corrective legislation. It took the conventional stance that a woman's primary role is domestic but asserted that needful or creative and capable women should have a greater opportunity for personal advancement in education, employment, and politics.[10] Thousands of women participated in the preparation not only of this report but of the reports issued in the ensuing years by the numerous state commissions on women that were activated.

In 1963, at about the same time that the President's commission was preparing its report, Betty Friedan's *The Feminine Mystique* was published. The book became a best-seller and was reported by many women to have changed the direction of their lives. Friedan's analysis suggested that women since World War II had been trapped by an attitude or mystique, fostered by business and its public relations departments, mass media, and functionalist social scientists, that woman's definition was to be a housewife-mother, that a woman was not being truly feminine unless she accepted as her singular identity the role of sex object and its extension as family nurturer. Friedan suggested that the solution for overcoming this mystique was in women's employment outside the home.

In the spring of 1964, *Daedalus* magazine published a special, provocative issue on women. It contained Eric Ericson's controversial "Inner and Outer Space: Reflections on Womanhood," a study of women in the labor force by Esther Peterson, and Alice Rossi's "Equality Between the Sexes: An Immodest Proposal," which has also been reported by women to have influenced new decisions about themselves.

Also in 1964, the United States Congress finally added the word "sex" to Title VII of the Civil Rights Bill, thereby prohibiting discrimination in employment on the basis of "race, color, religion, national origins or sex." This move had actually been conceived and proposed by Rep. Howard W. Smith of Virginia as an obstruction to the entire bill, and it was met with peals of laughter when first recorded in the House and was derided in the press. Supporters of women's rights were divided about its wisdom, Rep. Edith Green opposing it, for example, and Rep. Martha Griffiths supporting it. Such organizations as the American Association of University Women felt that it obstructed the issue of civil rights. But when President Lyndon B. Johnson quietly sent word that he supported the bill's passage with the sex amendment, it was passed. The Equal Employment Opportunity Commission was charged with hearing complaints from women about employment discrimination along with complaints from other minority groups.[11]

The year of organizational beginnings for the new feminism was 1966. In the spring of that year the Labor Department held a conference in Washington for representatives of the various state commissions on the status of women. Initially hopeful that something would be done by the government in response to the reports of these commissions, the women and men who participated in the conference were ultimately disappointed; and some of them decided that nothing would be accomplished until a strong organization for women's rights was formed completely separate from government, to take action in specific areas of discrimination against women.[12] To that end, on October 29, 1966, in Washington, D.C., thirty-two persons from twelve states and the capital organized the National Organization for Women (NOW) under the presidency of Betty Friedan.[13] Its Statement of Purpose reads in part:

We, men and women who hereby constitute ourselves as the National Organization for Women, believe that the time has come for a new movement toward true equality for all women in America, and toward a fully equal partnership of the sexes, as part of the world-wide revolution of human rights now taking place within and beyond our national borders.

The purpose of NOW is to take action to bring women into full participation in the mainstream of American society now, exercising all the privileges thereof in truly equal partnership with men . . . NOW is dedicated to the proposition that women, first and foremost, are human beings, who, like all other people in our society, must have the chance to develop their fullest human potential.[14]

By 1973 NOW had more than five thousand members in fifty chapters in over half the states of the country. It has a connectional bureaucratic structure, with officers and boards of directors in leadership positions at the chapter and national levels, a sliding scale of dues, and regional and national conferences. NOW works locally and nationally on court cases and legislative lobbying around questions of discrimination against women in hiring and promotion or on matters of reproduction and child care, such as opposition to abortion laws and advocacy of birth control clinics and of day care centers for children. Its rhetoric can be interpreted to mean that 51 percent of the positions of leadership in government, industry, and the professions should be held by women, since more than 51 percent of the population of the United States is female. It is generally seen as a reformist group, and its members are generally middle-class and middle-aged.

At the same time that NOW was being organized, feminist activity was beginning among younger, more radical women. Numerous young women who became involved in the civil rights movement and in New Left politics in the early years of the 1960s found themselves, even in this context of movements for radical social change, expected to play conventional subordinate roles of typing, making coffee, being available sexually for the movement's men, and keeping quiet in decision-making meetings. Ruby Doris Smith Robinson, a founding member of the Student Nonviolent Coordinating Committee (SNCC), wrote a serious paper titled "The Position of Women in SNCC," which was laughed down in an October 1964 SNCC meeting and prompted Stokeley Carmichael's contemptuous remark, "The only position for women in SNCC is prone."[15]

In 1965 and 1966 women at New Left Conferences began to present papers and open conversations about the place of women in society, and some of them began to meet separately in women's caucuses.[16] An independent women's movement was suggested by Heather Dean in an article in *Random*, published in Canada:

> Women should undergo this process of self-examination with each other, but away from men . . . women must fortify themselves against the punishment of the male chauvinist and the paternalism of the male liberal. Once women have shared the process of self-discovery and the experience of independent decision-making, they are ready for the real struggle . . . This is not a struggle against men . . . Women cannot be free until men are free . . . The solutions for women lie in solving far-ranging social problems. But this involves nothing short of revolutionary restructuring of the most basic institutions in society.[17]

The symbolic beginning of the women's liberation movement was the adoption of a Women's Manifesto by the Women's Liberation Workshop at a national conference of the Students for a Democratic Society (SDS) in the summer of 1967. In this statement the women compared their status with that of peoples of the Third World, in that women held a colonial status in relation to men. They claimed that women must fight for their own individuality, and that such a fight would strengthen the revolutionary movement. They called upon the SDS to work for communal child-care centers staffed by women and men, for the right of women to choose when to have children through the availability of birth control information and devices and of medical abortion, and for the requirement that every person in a household assume an equal share in the maintenance of the home. They made the following two demands on the movement: "We demand that our brothers recognize that they must deal with their own problems of male chauvinism in their personal, social and political relationships," and "We call upon women to demand full participation in all aspects of movement work, from licking stamps to assuming leadership positions."[18] Among the New Left-related women's groups that emerged in response to this call during the period were Boston's Bread and Roses and the Berkeley Women's Liberation Group.[19]

Also in 1967 the first women's liberation group not directly derivative from New Left politics was formed in Chicago with Joreen Freeman, Naomi Weisstein, and Heather Booth as founding members. Called the Women's Radical Action Project (WRAP), it concentrated on consciousness-raising, interaction among women through which they could become sensitive to their common situation and by which they could convert their energies into political action.[20]

The first women's liberation newsletter, called *Voice of the Women's Liberation Movement* and edited by Joreen Freeman, was published at the 1967 National Convention of the New Politics in Chicago. At this same convention Shulamith Firestone and Pamela Allen met and decided to start a women's liberation group in New York, which became the New York Radical Women. It later divided into several groups, one of which, called Redstockings, became a "radical feminist" body, emphasizing the singularity of the issue of women's freedom, as opposed to groups that it called "politico" or "feminist radical," which continued in the general movement of radical politics, regarding feminism as only one of the several revolutionary goals.[21] The Redstockings Manifesto is one of the purest expressions of the radical feminist point of view. It says in part:

> I. After centuries of individual and preliminary political struggle, women are uniting to achieve their final liberation from male supremacy. Redstockings is dedicated to building this unity and winning our freedom.
>
> II. Women are an oppressed class. Our oppression is total, affecting every facet of our lives. We are exploited as sex objects, breeders, domestic servants, and cheap labor. We are considered inferior beings, whose only purpose is to enhance men's lives. Our humanity is denied. Our prescribed behavior is enforced by the threat of physical violence.

Because we have lived so intimately with our oppressors in isolation from each other, we have been kept from seeing our personal suffering as a political condition . . .

III. We identify the agents of our oppression as men. Male supremacy is the oldest, most basic form of domination . . .

IV. Attempts have been made to shift the burden of responsibility from men to institutions or to women themselves. We condemn these arguments as evasions. Institutions alone do not oppress; they are merely tools of the oppressor . . . We also reject the idea that women consent to or are to blame for their own oppression. . .

V. We regard our personal experience, and our feelings about that experience, as the basis for an analysis of our common situation. . .

VI. We identify with all women. We define our best interest as that of the poorest, most brutally exploited women.[22]

Another radical feminist group in New York that had a widespread influence was the Feminists. Originally known as the October Seventeenth Movement, the group began in 1968 when a faction within the New York Chapter of NOW, including its president Ti-Grace Atkinson, objected to the bylaws and hierarchical structure of NOW. They separated from NOW and developed a "leaderless" system of drawing lots for tasks in their group and of distributing disks to ensure equal participation in group discussion. This system is a rigorous discipline of group consciousness-raising and women's political action. The Feminists regard sexual intercourse as an oppressive institution, and they limit their membership to no more than one-third women who are married or live with men. Ti-Grace Atkinson, whom the public views as their leader, will interact with a man only on public platforms, declaring herself to have no private relationships with men.[23]

At first as a result of radical political activity and then from a direct awareness of women's liberation activity, groups began to form all over the country, loosely organized, sometimes completely independent of other groups, and sometimes getting direct information from other groups but gathering independently. Of the hundreds of groups formed in 1967 and 1968, the Seattle Radical Women might be seen as "typical," if there is any such group. Following is a statement about themselves from a letter to a group forming in Minneapolis:

> Seattle Radical Women is an organization dedicated to exposing, resisting and eliminating discrimination against women in jobs and professions, education, legal status, social conditions, political life, and family/sexual roles. We believe that the issue of women's emancipation in this society is a first priority political, legal and economic question, and that its fundamental solution will come only with a radical change in the political, legal and economic structure of society.
>
> We are an organization different than most women's in that a basic cadre of our organization came from the radical social-ist movement. Our membership consists of working women, students and housewives of all races. Our ages range from 17 to 67. We are a principled and structured organization geared to education and action.[24]

These groups, the original groups to use the designation "women's liberation" or "female liberation," had become a sizable force in the new feminism by the early 1970s. They have no network of organizational structure and claim to have no acknowledged leadership, but are visible by the number of lecturers available from their midst, as well as the protest efforts on public platforms, in the mass media, and on the streets that they have sponsored against what they consider male chauvinist institutions. Their targets include the Miss America contest, male-only bars and restaurants, sex-segreg-ated newspaper want ads, sexist movies and lectures, restrictive clothing, employers who discriminate against women and laws that oppress women. In the early seventies they estimated their numbers variously from 10,000 to 500,000.[25] The most visible groups publish newsletters or journals, with such titles as *Bread and Roses* (from Bread and Roses, Cambridge, Mass.), *Off the Pedestal* (Bay Area Women's Liberation, California), *No More Fun and Games* (Female Liberation—Cell 16, Somerville, Mass.), *Ain't I a Woman?* (Iowa City), *Everywoman* (Los Angeles), *Up from Under* (New York), *Female Liberation Newsletter* (Minneapolis-St. Paul), *Women's Liberation*

(Kansas City), and *Women: A Journal of Liberation* (Baltimore), which comes close to being a national publication.[26]

Another major national organization, the Women's Equity Action League (WEAL), was founded in 1969 in Cleveland from which it spread. .: is made up largely of professional women, although it does have male members. Its major effort is in legal change and employment discrimination, and professional services from it are available throughout the country to women attacking legal or legislative discrimination. It has been particularly active in uncovering and attacking discrimination against women in colleges and universities, using Title VII of the Equal Employment Opportunities Law as the lever. WEAL has a structure of trustees and advisory boards on the national and local levels.[27]

By late 1970 there were feminist groups from NOW to Female Liberation to Older Women's Liberation (OWL) in every major city in the country and many smaller cities, with up to two hundred groups estimated in both New York and Los Angeles.[28] Starting with a national women's liberation conference at Thanksgiving 1968 in Chicago, numerous national women's conferences "women's liberation days," and women's marches took place in different cities.[29] Professional women's caucuses were established among women in the media, the American Political Science Association, the Anthropological Association, the Modern Language Association, the American Historical Association, and the American Association for the Advancement of Science.[30]

On July 10, 1971, the National Women's Political Caucus (NWPC) was formed in Washington, D.C. Including on their National Policy Council such influential women as Bella Abzug, Shana Alexander, Liz Carpenter, Shirley Chisholm, Myrlie Evers, Betty Friedan, Fannie Lou Hamer, Jill Ruckelshaus and Gloria Steinem, the NWPC set out "to awaken, organize, and assert the vast political power represented by women.[31] They quickly organized women into state and local caucuses all over the country and began a program of education and political involvement that had direct effect in running more women for elective office in 1972 and 1974, winning greater representation for women at national party conventions in 1972, and increasing awareness of the place of women in the mainstream of American politics.

In 1972, the Equal Rights Amendment finally passed the Congress and went to the states for ratification. Having been bottled up in committee or diluted by riders attached for floor debate for nearly fifty years, the Amendment passed the House and Senate by a lopsided majority in 1972 on the crest of the new feminism.

In the universities, women students and faculty members have organized action groups; and some universities have responded by setting up task forces on women in the university to investigate and sometimes change policies, such as admissions quotas, lower pay and lower status for women, and nepotism rules. Cases of discrimination against women in higher education have been taken to the Department of Health, Education, and Welfare; and some universities have found their federal funds withheld until they have met HEW's guidelines for "affirmative action" on the hiring of women and minorities. More than 50 women's studies programs have been launched in institutions of higher education, and more than 1200 different courses on women are being offered in American colleges and universities.[32]

Established publishing houses have joined the free presses in offering works on feminism. Ruth Herschberger's *Adam's Rib,* a lively but unsung feminist work of 1948, was reissued in paperback in 1970 by Harper and Row. Ashley Montagu's 1952 anthropological study, *The Natural Superiority of Women,* was published in paperback in 1970 by Macmillan. Hardback titles like Kate Millett's *Sexual Politics,* Shulamith Firestone's *The Dialectic of Sex,* Elizabeth Janeway's *Man's World, Woman's Place,* and Germaine Greer's *The Female Eunuch* went quickly into paperback; and they were supplemented by almost countless anthologies of new feminist writings and collections of historical and current feminist pieces. A new textbook market opened up for feminist books, met by such offerings as Elaine Showalter's *Women's Liberation and Literature,* Roberta Salper's *Female Liberation,* and Wendy Martin's *The American Sisterhood.* At least two feminist presses were founded, KNOW and The Feminist Press, making available new titles as well as reprints.

A new feminist force is surging.

The Movement Ideologies

William L. O'Neill concludes, in his book *Everyone Was Brave: The Rise and Fall of Feminism in America,* that the historical feminist movement failed in America because the early feminists defined their problem too narrowly. The real issue was the role of woman in American society, yet the feminists for some seventy years, from 1848 to 1920, focused more and more closely on the issue of woman suffrage. Thus, when women won the right to vote with the Nineteenth Amendment, their millennial euphoria prevented them from seeing that they had won a battle, not the war, and the movement died.[33]

Out of the ashes of that failure, almost two generations later, a new feminist movement is rising, which may be redefining its problem enough in O'Neill's terms to ensure success. The movement is large and has many factions, and of course could destroy itself by its fragmentation; but underneath the variant rhetoric of the many advocates and groups, its definition of the issue remains the same, namely, the general social role of women in American society is unequal to that of men. Groups and individuals from contrasting "camps" of feminists have indicated their agreement on the fundamental issue in the new feminist movement.

Betty Friedan, for example, writes that "the feminine mystique" is "Occupation: Housewife." She continues: "The new mystique makes the housewife-mothers, who never had a chance to be anything else, the model for all women . . . Beneath the sophisticated trappings, it simply makes concrete, finite domestic aspects of feminine existence—as it was by women whose lives were confined by necessity, to cooking, cleaning, washing, bearing children—into a religion, a pattern by which all women must now live or deny their femininity." A position paper from the Women's Caucus of the New University Conference reads: "The division of labor between male and female, food-getting versus housekeeping and childcare, is nearly universal and had appeared in all cultures and all ages . . .

The reality is that in the United States the traditional division of labor is an anachronism."[34]

Marlene Dixon explains: "Women struggle against their fear of being inferior . . . they seek ways of life that will truly permit them to be 'before all else a human being.' "[35]

Alice Rossi says: "We need to reassert the claim to sex equality and to search for means by which it can be achieved. By sex equality I mean a socially androgynous conception of the roles of men and women, in which they are equal and similar in such spheres as intellectual, artistic, political and occupational interests and participation, complementary only in those spheres dictated by physiological differences between the sexes."[36]

These writers all indicate that they are challenging the identity which society has assigned to women, the role women are for the most part expected to play. Betty Friedan uses the language of a vocational model; the New University Conference paper adopts a Marxian analysis; Marlene Dixon quotes Ibsen's Nora from *A Doll's House*; and Alice Rossi uses social scientific analysis; but all of them suggest they are making their case on the basis of an understanding that the fundamental role of woman must change.

Whether the call for women's liberation arises from strident outrage, argumentative conviction, or demonstrated reason—and all of these tones are present among today's feminists—the call is for a social revolution that will reorder American values at their foundation and reshape patterns of human life at the point of their conception. The women's movement is a radical movement in the most basic sense, whether one views radicality as starting with new premises or as giving new direction to old orders. There is no guarantee that the current women's revolution will eventually succeed, but its present nature contains the ideological breadth and existential commitment of enough persons significantly to shift the focus of American life.

The term "women's liberation" is popularly used synonymously with the new feminism. In addition, "women's liberation" has come to be used by many speakers when lashing out against what it stands for, even by persons who believe in its concepts but want to disavow association with its negative image. The specific term is said to have been coined by either the SDS or the women's groups that began to meet separately from New Left political bodies in 1966.[37] The women's liberation movement of young, radically political women has a distinct identity as one part of the contemporary feminist movement, which had begun several years before it emerged. However, the term quickly shifted to refer to feminism in general in both popular speech and the mass media. The straightforward meaning of the expression "women's liberation" in fact gets at the central ideology of the movement better than the term "new feminism." "Feminism" is typically defined as a position of advocating women's rights, while "women's liberation" implies advocacy of the full freedom of women. While various rights for women are still being sought by the new feminists, the goal that is shared by all advocates, despite factional differences, is full freedom. Nevertheless, for the purposes of clarity in this study, the term "women's liberation" shall be reserved for identifying the specific branch of the contemporary women's movement with which it was first associated. At no point will "women's liberation" be used as a term of opprobrium.

Repeatedly in discussions of the new feminism the analogy is made between the experience of black people and of women, between racism and sexism, and between the women's movement and the black movement. The analogy occurs fresh to women every time they begin to think in feminist terms, but it is one that has been made for the last century and a half. Just as the feminism of the 1830s grew out of abolitionism, the feminism of the 1960s was influenced by the black civil rights struggle. The parallel is profound at many points between the Negro as slave and the woman as her man's chattel, between twentieth-century black people and women being perceived and treated as inferiors.

Sarah Grimké, first an abolition leader and then a feminist, was one of the first to draw the parallel. Signing her letters "Thine in the bonds of womanhood," she wrote in 1837 of the laws setting the legal relationship between husband and wife:

> The various laws which I have transcribed, leave women very little more liberty, or power, in some respects, than the slave. "A slave," says the civil code of Louisiana, "is one who is in the power of a master, to whom he belongs. He can possess nothing, nor acquire anything, but what must belong to his master." I do not wish by any means to intimate that the condition of free women can be compared to that of slaves in suffering, or in degradation: still, I believe the laws which deprive married women of their rights and privileges, have a tendency to lessen them in their own estimation as moral and responsible beings, and that their being made by civil law inferior to their husbands, has a debasing and mischievous effect upon them, teaching them practically the fatal lesson to look unto man for protection and indulgence.[38]

Grimké was particularly concerned about the bonds of female slaves: "There is another class of women in this country, to whom I cannot refer, without feelings of the deepest shame and sorrow. I allude to our female slaves. Our southern cities are whelmed beneath a tide of pollution; the virtue of female slaves is wholly at the mercy of irresponsible tyrants, and women are bought and sold in our slave markets, to gratify the brutal lust of those who bear the name of Christians."[39]

In 1845, Margaret Fuller made the analogy between blacks and women in theological terms: "As the friend of the Negro assumes that one man cannot by right hold another in bondage, so should the friend of Woman assume that Man cannot by right lay even well-meant restrictions on Woman. If the Negro be a soul, if the woman be a soul, appareled in flesh, to one Master only are they accountable. There is but one law for souls and if there is to be an interpreter of it, he must come not as man or son of man, but as son of God."[40]

The comparison that had struck nineteenth century feminists recurred in the thought of the new feminists of the 1960s. Just as black people had been freed from slavery but were still held in social, economic, and psychological subjugation, so women, who had gained certain rights to education, property, employment, and suffrage, were still confined by social and legal prescriptions of inferiority. Among the myriad statements by contemporary feminists of the black analogy is one by Marlene Dixon:

> The very stereotypes that express the society's belief in the biological inferiority of women recall the images used to justify the oppression of blacks. The nature of women, like that of slaves, is depicted as dependent, incapable of reasoned thought, childlike in its simplicity and warmth, martyred in the role of mother, and mystical in the role of sexual partner. In its benevolent form, the inferior position of women results in paternalism; in its malevolent form, a domestic tyranny which can be unbelievably brutal.[41]

Moving the black analogy to its political dimension, Kate Millett argues: "In America, recent events have forced us to acknowledge at last that the relationship between the races is indeed a political one which involves the general control of one collectivity, defined by birth, over another collectivity, also defined by birth. Groups who rule by birthright are fast disappearing, yet there remains one ancient and universal scheme for the domination of one birth group by another—the scheme that prevails in the area of sex."[42]

Not only can the condition of women be compared to that of the black population, but the contemporary feminist movement can be viewed as having phases paralleling the stages of the black movement in recent history. In the early 1960s the civil rights movement was optimistic, integrationist, and equalitarian. By mid-decade a new black militancy, a call for black power, the slogan "Black is beautiful," and a movement toward black separatism became focal. By the end of the decade a pluralism of modes of black consciousness was apparent, with the movement directing itself in several different channels toward black equality. Similarly, the feminist movement in 1963-1967 began with an equalitarian perspective, in an integrationist mode, asking for women to receive a share in men's world. After 1967 the movement rapidly reached a point of female militancy, found advocates of female separatism, developed a confrontation strategy, and adopted the slogan "Sisterhood is powerful." By 1973, women of various persuasions could unite for achievement of specific goals, and a diversity of women's movement opinions flourished. For both blacks and women, the middle stage of both separation and confrontation has been necessary to achieve group solidarity. Self-determination must sometimes be realized through conflict, sometimes through cooperation.

As there are different tactics for the completion of women's emancipation, so there are varying ideas that shape the understanding and direction of contemporary feminism. Underlying the consensus on the general goals of the new feminism are at least three informing ideologies, which I shall call the feminist, the women's liberationist, and the androgynous paradigms.[43] Their roots go back to the American women rebels of Colonial days, to the historical feminist movement that lasted from the 1830s to 1920, and to the lonely feminist voices that went unheard in the counterfeminist period from 1920 through the 1950s. They are at once a part of a historical process and a new movement.

The feminist paradigm evolved from the central quest of the historical feminists to achieve the values, rights, privileges, and opportunities that men had established as good and which women (and their male feminist supporters) therefore adopted as good for women. These values included property rights, the right to sue for divorce and to have custody of children, educational and professional opportunities, the right to employment, and the right to vote in a democratic government. The model was male in conception and example, and women wanted a share in this male model. Thus, the feminist ideology has a masculine-equalitarian or women-equal-to-men orientation.

The feminist ideology dominated the women's rights movement up through the realization of woman suffrage in 1920 (although the seeds of the other two ideologies were even then present). It was the established doctrine, which was not questioned as essentially workable for the realization of women's equality. It is still the operating frame of reference for some of the contemporary feminists and is one of the concepts that informs their thought and action. Typical of this group are Betty Friedan (*The Feminine Mystique*); Caroline Bird (*Born Female*); Helen Gurley Brown (*Sex and the Single Girl* and the magazine *Cosmopolitan* that she edits); and the voluntary association NOW.

Since what Margaret Mead calls "feather barriers" and what the New Left sisters call "male chauvinism" have so far prevented the success of full equality for women under the masculine-equalitarian idea, two new concepts have arisen to challenge its efficacy: the women's liberationist and the androgynous. They now exist alongside the feminist view as models for realizing the goals of the women's movement.

The women's liberationist paradigm is a prowoman anti-masculinist model. Such feminists assert that the values for women's freedom should be arrived at by women. Theirs is a women-over-against-men or women-separate-from-men stance. These women—and the feminists informed by this model are all women—are sometimes quite angry with men and assert that women should separate from men, either permanently or temporarily, to establish female identity and to support each other psychically as women. This is the old masculinist concept turned upside down, with the assertion that values should be determined by women rather than men and that society, or at least their part of it, should be run by women. The separation from men might be more symbolic than personal, but it signifies an opposition to a masculinist or male-created social order and a determination to replace it with a female-created scheme of things. Spokeswomen of this group are Kate Millett (*Sexual Politics*), Ti-Grace Atkinson and the New York Feminists, Betsy Warrior, Dana Densmore, and Abby Aldrich Rockefeller of Cell 16 in the Boston area, all advocating female self-determination over and against men.

The androgynous paradigm represents a women-and-men-equal-to-each other view. It takes the position that values should be arrived at, decisions made, and society ordered on the basis of women and men together. It holds that tasks, values, and behavior traditionally assigned to one sex or the other should be shared by them both, except for behavior dictated by purely physiological differences. This is a cultural understanding of society's common behavior expectations being rooted in that society's fundamental beliefs, values, and myths. It has no single organizational base, but writers articulating this view include Elizabeth Janeway (*Man's World, Woman's Place*), Alice Rossi ("Equality Between the Sexes: An Immodest Proposal"), Carolyn Heilbrun (*Toward a Recognition of Androgyny*), Cynthia Ozick ("The Demise of the Dancing Dog"), and Germaine Greer (*The Female Eunuch*).

There are, of course, feminists, feminist writings, and feminist actions that do not neatly fit this paradigmatic structure, but in general this is the ordering framework in which the new feminism can be analyzed. Some of the differences among the factions are rhetorical. Other differences relate to focus and emphasis. Still others have to do with the philosophical understanding of human nature and the possibilities for male-female relationships and male-female roles in society. It is on the last point that they diverge most significantly. The contrasts among the three paradigms can be shown schematically (see table).

All three viewpoints are grounded in historical American feminism, though the dominant framework from the past is the feminist paradigm. To understand the historical context of the new feminism, it is appropriate to look first at the women's movement out of the American past.

The Historical Women's Rights Movement

In the colonial and the early national periods of American history, there were no feminists, but there was some female rebellion. In the colonies and on the frontier, women's lives were filled with domestic production—growing, preparing, and preserving food, making clothing, caring for the ill and the newborn, meeting the hardships of the wilderness. Social roles were along sexual lines with women in charge of household activity and men in charge of public and outdoor action. Status was not rigid when the demand for subsistence required of both women and men constant effort to keep alive and healthy; and it was not uncommon in colonial towns for women to run shops along with their men or for widows to continue family businesses after their husbands' deaths. It was usual on the frontier for women to chop wood, drive wagons, and kill hogs alongside their men. They did not have time to think about women's rights when everyday life required total involvement.

However, legally women were totally dependent on men.

*examine
this/her
together*

Comparison of the Ideologies of the Women's Movement

Characteristic	Feminist ideology	Women's liberation-ist ideology	Androgynous ideology
Ordering principle	Women-equal-to-men	Women-over-against-men or separate-from-men	Women-and-men-equal-to-each-other
Source of standard	Established by men, adopted by women	Arrived at by women	Arrived at by men and women together
Analysis of problem	Women subordinate or secondary to men	Women as sex objects, property, laborers	Loss of legitimacy of traditional male/female roles
Identification of enemy	Socioeconomic attitudes and institutions	Men, other women, capitalism, the family	Cultural value orientations, institutional structures
Techniques for change	Court cases, electoral process, information dissemination, voluntary groups	Consciousness-raising, separation from men for female psychic support, awareness and exercise of woman power	Educational process, voluntary groups, information dissemination
Primary focus for change	Political	Social	Cultural
Strategy	Pressure	Conflict	Conversion
Goals	Integration (collapse of diversity into unity)	Segregation (diversity at expense of unity)	Pluralism (diversity within unity)

Under the law women's persons and their property were owned by their husbands or nearest male kin, and they were expected to defer to and obey them.[44] Calvinistic sternness in religion held many women in subjugation to the masculine rule. The first women rebels were religious. Anne Hutchinson, the most notable example, sought to interpret religious truth and to teach it according to her own light rather than by the Puritan law. Driven from Boston, she was then brought back to trial, where the primary accusation against her was that she taught other women to be "rather . . . a Husband than a Wife."[45]

isolated voices

Another Boston woman, Mary Dyer, a Quaker and defender

of Anne Hutchinson, was executed on the gallows for attempting to "publish truth" as she saw it. Another example of men's judgment of women in Colonial Massachusetts was the witch hangings. Women were not allowed to deviate from religious law, their deviancy in such cases often taking the form of opposition to the parish minister, and men were free to be their judges.[46]

Another colonial woman rebel was the poet Anne Bradstreet, who asks in the following poem, written in 1642, that she be accepted as an intelligent and imaginative person:

> I am obnoxious to each carping tongue,
> Who sayes, my hand a needle better fits,
> A Poets Pen, all scorne, I shall thus wrong;
> For such despight they cast on female wits;
> If what I doe prove well, it wo'nt advance
> They'l say its stolne, or else, it was by chance. . .

> Let Greeks be Greeks, and Women what they are,
> Men have precedency, and still excell,
> It is but vaine, unjustly to wage war,
> Men can do best, and Women know it well:
> Preheminence in each, and all is yours,
> Yet grant some small acknowledgement of ours.[47]

A manual for women, *The Whole Duty of a Woman: Or, an Infallible Guide to the Fair Sex,* gives the societal expectation for the colonial women's role: "There are but three states of Life, through which they can regularly pass, *viz.* Virginity, Marriage, and Widowhood, two of them are states of Subjection, the first to the Parent, the Second to the Husband, and the third, as it is casual, whether ever they arrive to it or no . . . a condition the most desolate and deplorable."[48] In 1647, Margaret Brent tested this assumption in the Maryland assembly by asking to cast two votes in that body, one as Lord Baltimore's attorney, another as a landholder. She was granted one vote as attorney—reminding us that women functioned as attorneys, in medical practice as midwives, and as teachers in the colonies before these practices became professionalized by male standards of education and examination.[49]

The conditions of beginning urbanization and industrializa-

tion, the emergence of a distinctive middle class, and the availability of greater leisure for women, coupled with the
rigidification of social sexual roles in the early nineteenth century, gave rise to a movement of feminism that had been called *Movement*
for by isolated voices since the time of the American Revolution. Thomas Paine, an ideological leader of the Revolution,
was one of the first to speak publicly against women's position.
In 1775, he said of women that, "even in countries where they
may be esteemed most happy, (they are) constrained in their
desires in the disposal of their goods, robbed of freedom and
will by the laws, the slaves of opinion."[50]

Some women felt that the new Constitution ought to give
equal rights to women. Abigail Adams wrote to her husband,
John Adams, at the Constitutional Convention: "Do not put
such unlimited power into the hands of the husbands.
Remember, all men would be tyrants if they could. If particular
care is not paid to the ladies, we are determined to foment a
rebellion, and will not hold ourselves bound by any laws in
which we have no voice or representation."[51]

Many people date the beginning of the international feminist
movement,—and at each of its stages it was an international
phenomenon,—from the publication in 1792 in England of
Mary Wollstonecraft's book *A Vindication of the Rights of
Women*. She stated her thesis: "The first object of laudable
ambition is to obtain a character as a human being, regardless
of the distinction of sex . . . trifling employment has rendered
woman a trifler . . . For man and woman, truth, if I understand
the meaning of the word, must be the same."[52]

Judith Sargent Murray in America, a prominent Massachusetts matron, had published a feminist piece in 1790 in the
Massachusetts Magazine, under the name Constantia. She
declared: "Should it still be vociferated, 'Your domestic
employments are sufficient'—I would calmly ask, is it reasonable, that a candidate for immortality, for the joys of heaven,
an intelligent being, who is to spend an eternity in contem-
plating the works of Deity, should at present be so degraded, as
to be allowed no other ideas, than those which are suggested by
the mechanism of a pudding, or the sewing of a seam of a
garment?"[53]

The first well-known speaker for women's rights in America,

Frances Wright, was a wealthy Scotswoman who came to America in the 1820s and spoke for individual freedom and individual roles. She also advocated sexual freedom outside of marriage. For a long time afterward, her views on free love were a detriment to the reception of feminist views with more conventional goals of educational and legal reform.[54]

Much of the early nineteenth-century women's rights activity rose out of women's involvement in the antislavery movement. The first Female Anti-Slavery Society was formed in Boston in 1832.[55] Women were quick to make the analogy between the slaves' bondage and their own lack of rights.

Many of the women who joined the antislavery movement and then turned to women's rights were Quakers, for the history of the Quaker group shows a great toleration for women. Its founder, George Fox, early recognized the validity of women's experience in the faith, allowed them to preach, and wrote, "Women are to take up the cross and follow Christ daily as well as men . . . they have an office as well as the men, for they have a stewardship to the Lord as well as man."[56]

Two of the first antislavery public speakers who turned to women's rights were the Grimké sisters, Angelina and Sarah, who were Quaker converts. Angelina Grimké stated her case in a letter to Catharine Beecher, herself a reformer for women's education:

> The investigation of the rights of the slave has led me to a better understanding of my own. I have found the Anti-Slavery cause to be the high school of morals in our land—the school in which *human rights* are more fully investigated, better understood and taught, than in any other . . . Human beings have rights because they are moral beings . . . This regulation of duty by the mere circumstance of sex, rather than by the fundamental principle of moral being has led to all the multifarious train of evils flowing out of the anti-Christian doctrine of masculine and feminine virtues. By this doctrine, man has converted into the warrior, and clothed with sternness, and those other kindred qualities, which in common estimation belong to his character as a man; whilst woman has been taught . . . to sit as a doll . . . to be humored as a doll, or converted into a mere drudge to suit the convenience of her lord and master.[57]

When Angelina Grimké married Theodore Weld in 1838, he signed a statement giving up his legal rights to her person and property.[58] Similar statements were signed by Robert Dale Owen when he married Mary Robinson in 1832 and by Henry Blackwell when he married the leading feminist Lucy Stone in 1855.[59] Angelina Grimké and Theodore Weld also were known *hmmm* for practicing birth control by self-restraint, birth control being another issue important to the question of women's rights.[60]

More specific agitation for legal reform in matters regarding women and for education for women was also going on in the first half of the nineteenth century, without its advocates espousing full equality for women. The law regarding women was an issue of great concern to many early nineteenth-century women. Blackstone's *Commentaries* was followed by most American lawyers for the interpretation of law and was reflected in state laws. His concept of the civil death of women in marriage was especially abhorrent to feminists: "By marriage the husband and the wife are one person in law; that is, the very *X* being or legal existence of the woman is suspended during her marriage, or at least, is consolidated into that of her husband under whose wing, protection and cover, she performs everything." Ernestine Rose, one of the leaders in opposition to the oppressive laws based on this concept, which was known as *femme couverte* or "covered woman," commented: "The being of a wife is said to be merged in her husband. Has nature there merged it? Has she ceased to exist or feel pleasure and pain? When she violates the laws of her being, does he pay the penalty?"[61]

In fact, the harsher laws were seldom applied, but their existence in principle spelled injustice. Under the law, women gave up control of their property to their husbands, even down to personal items, although husbands seldom took their wives' personal goods to pay their own debts. Wealthy families guaranteed a daughter's dowry and inheritance by a marriage contract. However, in the rare case of divorce, if a contract did not exist, the husband had the right to everything, including custody of the children. The occasionally strict application of these inequitable laws gave the feminists ammunition for their campaign.[62]

After twelve years in committee, a Married Women's Property Act was passed in 1848 by the New York State Legislature, giving women full control over their real and personal property while they were married and protecting their property from their husband's debts. It seemed a radical measure, for which feminists like Ernestine Rose, Pauline Wright Davis, and Elizabeth Cady Stanton had stumped the state, but its actual momentum in the legislature had come from conservative and aristocratic men who wished to safeguard their wives' and daughters' fortunes. Except for the southern states, most states followed New York's lead on property law, and over the next few decades factory laws and laws giving the innocent party custody of the children in case of divorce were passed in most states.[63] Legal reform attracted numerous middle-class women, and even the wealthy and privileged saw the value for their vested interest in changing the law. This realization was to give impetus to the broader women's rights movement.

Urbanization and industrialization in the first half of the nineteenth century as well as the democratic fervor of the Jacksonian period also influenced reevaluation of the rights to education. Robert Dale Owen wrote in 1829, "Inequality is of the mind as well as of property. The only security for the enjoyment of equal rights is, not agrarian laws or any laws whatever, but equal, national, republican education."[64]

Horace Mann supported public education for both boys and girls. Hannah Mather Crocker published the first book advocating women's education in 1818, explaining: "There can be no doubt but there is as much difference in the powers of each individual of the male sex as there is of the female; and if they received the same mode of education, their improvement would be fully equal."[65]

The pioneer women in education were Emma Hart, who set up a school for girls in her home in New York State; Emma Willard, who founded Troy Seminary in Troy, New York, on the Erie Canal in 1821; and Mary Lyon, who in 1837 founded Mount Holyoke College where bright girls were taught botany, chemistry, and moral philosophy rather than domestic skills. The schools founded by these women began to produce teachers. Another leading pioneer was Catharine Beecher, who propagandized and raised money for western education on the eastern seaboard. Neither an abolitionist nor a feminist, she felt that the reasons women and Negroes should be educated were to free them from Calvinistic religion and to make them good mothers and devout servants.[66]

In 1833 Oberlin College was founded and set an example for coeducation by admitting women. The college was especially important to the feminist movement because it educated several of its leaders, such as Lucy Stone and Antoinette Brown. Still, the first Oberlin women took a simpler course than the men and were expected to serve men at table and to keep quiet in mixed classes.[67]

Between 1820 and the Civil War, two hundred finishing schools were founded for women, but widespread coeducation or education for women did not exist until well after the Civil War, in spite of the public high-school education that began to be available to girls as well as boys.[68]

The immediate origin of the first women's rights meeting was the rejection of the American women delegates to an international antislavery conference in London in 1840. Here Lucretia Mott, a Quaker religious leader and antislavery speaker, met Elizabeth Cady Stanton, honeymooning at the conference with her husband. Incensed over the rejection, the two women began to plan an organization for women's rights. Nothing was done until 1848, when perky, vivacious Stanton, bored with life in a small town in western New York and chafing under the care of five children with a husband often absent speaking for abolition, put an advertisement in the Seneca County *Courier* for a convention on women's rights. Women came in wagons from all over the county, finally making a procession into Seneca Falls. Nineteen-year-old Charlotte Woodward was among these women and was the one member of the convention who lived to see passage of the Nineteenth Amendment.

Lucretia Mott's husband presided over the meeting, for none of the women knew how. Stanton had drawn up the resolutions, her husband having left town when he heard of her plans. The group passed resolutions asking for opportunities for women in education, trade, commerce and the professions and for rights in property, free speech, and the guardianship of children.[69] The final, unthinkable issue was the vote; and after much controversy, the demand for woman suffrage was made publicly for the first time in America. The high point of the day was when Stanton read the "Declaration of Sentiments," a document modeled after the Declaration of Independence. It said in part:

> We hold these truths to be self-evident: that all men and women are created equal; that they are endowed by their Creator with certain inalienable rights . . .
>
> The history of mankind is a history of repeated injuries and usurpations on the part of man toward woman, having in direct object the establishment of an absolute tyranny over her. To prove this, let facts be submitted to a candid world.
>
> He has never permitted her to exercise her inalienable right to the elective franchise.
>
> He has compelled her to submit to laws, in the formation of which she has no voice . . . taken from her rights of property . . . framed the laws of divorce giving all power in his hands . . . monopolized nearly all profitable employments . . . denied her facilities for obtaining a thorough education . . . Now . . . we insist that they (women) have immediate admission to all the rights and privileges which belong to them as citizens of the United States.[70]

Woman suffrage came to be the dominant issue for women's freedom in the latter half of the nineteenth century, but other campaigns also occupied women's attention. The constricting mode of dress of women, the issue of women entering the professions, the laws regarding women in factories and their place in relation to wages and working conditions were all concerns that women worked for.

Harriot Hunt was a pioneering leader for dress reform. Victorian women wore heavy whalebone corsets, many petticoats, and long restraining dresses. Hunt, an early psychotherapist, urged that health reform include dress reform: "Without a healthy form in which to manifest itself, the soul may struggle for use and find all its desires crushed." Gerrit Smith, a wealthy reformer, wrote of Victorian women's dress, "So long as she remains in her clothes-prison she will be dependent and poor."[71]

Dress reform brought about the bloomer costume, consisting of loose trousers gathered at the ankles and a knee-length skirt, and named for Amelia Bloomer, a women's rights editor. The outfit was worn by many of the braver feminists—Elizabeth Stanton, Susan Anthony, Lucy Stone, and the Grimké sisters—but they were so ridiculed that they soon abandoned it. In the Fourierist utopian communities such a balloon pants costume had been worn by the women as a part of their concept of greater freedom for women.[72]

In the mid-nineteenth century some women began to enter the professions. Elizabeth Blackwell became the first woman doctor and Antoinette Brown the first woman minister. Blackwell doggedly fought at being a woman doctor and helped to found a women's medical school. Brown, after a successful struggle to become educated and ordained, gave up her ordination because of her increasing theological liberalism. Throughout her life, however, she continued to be a writer, leader, and speaker for women's rights.[73] Other women followed their examples into professional life, but the personal effort was strenuous.

Factory work at first seemed like liberation to women in the nineteenth century, but they soon learned that long hours and low wages brought detriment to health and morale. An observer wrote of the Lowell factory girls that they "wear out their health, spirits and morals without becoming one whit better off than when they commenced labour. The bills of mortality in these factory towns are not striking, we admit, for the poor girls when they can toil no longer go home to die."[74]

Women's wages were still an issue in mid-century, although some economic progress had been made. During a Kansas referendum on woman suffrage in 1867, one legislator proclaimed, "of all the infernal humbugs of this humbugging women's rights question the most absurd is that women should assume to be entitled to the same wages for the same amount of labor performed as a man."[75]

In 1845 Margaret Fuller, having become the first woman newspaper literary critic and recognized as a leading transcendentalist thinker, published her feminist book *Woman in the Nineteenth Century*. She stated her thesis:

We would have every arbitrary barrier thrown down. We would have every path laid open to Woman as freely as to Man. Were this done and a slight temporary fermentation allowed to subside, we should see crystallizations more pure and of more various beauty . . . Were thought and feeling once so far elevated that Man should esteem himself the brother and friend, but nowise the lord and tutor, of Woman—were he really bound with her in equal worship—arrangements as to function and employment would be of no consequence. What Woman needs is not as a woman to act or rule, but as a nature to grow, as an intellect to discern, as a soul to live freely and unimpeded to unfold such powers as were given her when we left our common home.[76]

Although Fuller came before the time of the organized women's rights movement, her attention to the subject and to the publication of her book are an index to the importance of the issue of women in society in her time.

In the decade of the 1850s there were several National Women's Rights Conventions under the leadership of Lucretia Mott, Elizabeth Cady Stanton, Susan B. Anthony, and Lucy Stone.[77] But the Civil War eclipsed the women's rights activities, and their leaders' time was spent on the war effort, in which they showed that they were capable of carrying out many responsibilities. Not insignificantly, many women found meaningful work in nursing, relief work, teaching, and government offices during the war.[78]

A blow was struck to their hopes when the Fifteenth Amendment specifically included the word "male" in granting Negro suffrage. The feminist leaders now saw the vote as the primary means of gaining women's equality. In 1869 two organizations were formed largely on the basis of a difference in strategy of their leaders. Susan B. Anthony and Elizabeth Cady Stanton and their followers formed the National Woman Suffrage Association, working in individual states to some extent but concentrating on introducing a woman suffrage amendment into Congress every year. Lucy Stone and her husband, Henry Blackwell, formed the American Woman Suffrage Association with a concentration on state work. The first organization began to publish a newspaper called *Liberation,* and Lucy Stone's group published *Woman's Journal.*[79]

These women arduously and carefully organized, spoke, wrote petitions, and lobbied in the state legislatures and federal Congress. Their actions yielded them much abuse such as the arrest of Susan B. Anthony by federal officials when she and other women voted in Rochester, New York.[80]

In 1869 the territory of Wyoming was the first to grant suffrage to women and the first to bring the issue before Congress in its petition for a charter for statehood. Opposition in the House and Senate brought such comments as: "It is a reform against nature"; "Let her stay in the sphere to which God and the Bible have assigned her"; "They are going to make men of women, and the correlative must take place that men become women."[81]

In 1871 and 1872, Victoria Woodhull skyrocketed into prominence in the movement. She was a feminist who believed in free love and spiritualism, and in 1871 she was able to get the issue of woman's suffrage before a congressional committee, making her momentarily a heroine in the National Woman Suffrage Association. The following year she became the first woman candidate for President, but was blocked by Susan B. Anthony from leadership in the National Woman Suffrage Association. Woodhull is most remembered for exposing the Beecher-Tilton scandal, the love affair between the noted liberal minister Henry Ward Beecher and Elizabeth Tilton, wife of the reform editor Theodore Tilton. Since Beecher had been president of the American Woman Suffrage Association, the two suffrage organizations felt reverberations from the scandal for years.[82]

Wyoming was finally brought into the Union in 1890 with the woman suffrage provision. By constitutional amendment Colorado, Idaho, and Utah adopted woman suffrage in the 1890s. Also in 1890 the two woman suffrage organizations joined to become the National American Woman Suffrage Association, and two new leaders arose, Anna Howard Shaw and Carrie Chapman Catt.[83]

The Populist movement and later the Progressive movement gave impetus to the reform. The central issue for the feminists was the vote, but the reform of factory laws regarding hours and working conditions, the rise of labor unions for women or to which women could be admitted, the settlement house

movement led by such persons as Jane Addams in which lower
and middle class women could meet and work together, the
birth control movement under the leadership of Margaret
Sanger—all these affected women's role in society considerably
and involved the energies of many women. An ideological relationship existed between the prohibitionists and the feminists,
for many felt that women's moral consciousness would lead
them to vote dry, and some women were active in prohibition
groups.

In the first two decades of the twentieth century the National
American Woman Suffrage Association worked steadily in
referenda and before the state legislatures. After 1910 it was
aided in its effort to get a federal amendment before Congress
by the Congressional Union, later the National Woman's Party,
led by Alice Paul. Paul, schooled in the radical tactics of the
British suffrage movement, brought new life to the flagging
goal of the federal amendment, and after 1911 she organized
parades and pickets for an all-out campaign. Woodrow
Wilson's party platform carried a woman suffrage provision,
but he allowed World War I to cause a postponement in its
coming before Congress.[84]

The constitutional amendment known as the "Anthony
amendment," from Susan B. Anthony's untiring effort before
the national Congress for its passage, passed the House in 1918,
but it failed by two votes to get the two-thirds majority required
in the Senate. Wilson intervened in its favor but was ineffectual
in changing votes. When it came before the Senate again in
February 1919, it failed by one vote, but after a new Congress
dominated by Republicans was installed in March, the Nineteenth Amendment finally passed and was sent to the states for
ratification. At last, when Tennessee gave the crucial vote for
ratification, the Nineteenth Amendment granting woman
suffrage became the law of the land with the signing of the
proclamation by the Tennessee governor on August 26, 1919,
making possible the female vote in November 1920.[85]

Victory was won. Women now had the full rights of men—or
so they thought. The year 1920 seemed to some the millennium.
Because the vote for women was the central symbol of equality
with men, the ratification of the Nineteenth Amendment was

the height of achievement for the feminist movement. Carrie
Chapman Catt, who had led the movement through the fight
for passage and ratification, had early in 1919 reorganized the
National American Woman Suffrage Association into the
League of Women Voters. The League was planned as a
nonpartisan political organization, but the League's members
would no longer be feminists.[86]

The women who wrote, spoke, and acted for change in
women's role in American society from the colonial period to
1920 had a masculine model or paradigm for the change they
sought. The women wanted to be like men. They wanted the
rights and opportunities men had. They did not ask for a bold
reconstruction of society. Rather, they asked that they, the dis-
possessed, be allowed to participate on an equal basis in already
established institutions and opportunities. They wanted to be
equal with men in what men had already demonstrated as
valued modes of living. They accepted as good men's values of
holding property, obtaining education, participating in professional life or factory work, and voting in a democratic political
system, and they wanted a share in these values. They defined
their oppression in relation to what men had and saw the male
controllers of society as their oppressors.

The concomitant to the masculinist model was an equalitarian model. In the earlier feminism the idea that women are
inferior to men and should be subordinate to them was
challenged and fought on several fronts, but it was fought on
men's terms on the assumption that men were right in valuing
education, work, and democracy in the particular way that they
did under the masculine model. Although the equalitarian view
did have the effect of planting the seeds of revolution, of
pointing toward radical change by stating the problem of
women's oppression and opposing it, it was almost always
limited by the unquestioned assumption that the masculinist
way of doing things was the right way. The early feminists'
achievements were piecemeal, though constructive. It was a
good thing for women to begin to become educated like men, to
become professionals, to gain the vote. But the equalitarian
mode had within it an unspoken acceptance of the masculinist
framework; it was a masculine-equalitarian unit. Herein lies its

failure to be revolutionary. If women's goal is to be like men, they tacitly accept the very premise they claim to reject—that women are inferior to men.

There were exceptions to this model. Margaret Fuller's larger vision of the development of woman's spirit, her intellect, and her talent was more comprehensive than the masculine model. She argued that women did not necessarily want to be like men but wanted to be free. Victoria Woodhull's self-assertion in business, in social theory, and in politics moved beyond a simple male model. Jane Addams and the settlement house movement, Margaret Sanger and the birth control movement, all anticipate the androgynous paradigm of creating new social roles and structures above and beyond the established male model; but they were outside the mainstream of the women's rights movement, which finally focused on suffrage in a masculine-equalitarian mode.

Feminism was dormant though never dead from the 1920s through the 1950s. Then in the early 1960s a new feminism appeared. By the 1970s, American society was in the midst of a paradigm change regarding the equality of women. The feminist paradigm is still in operation, but it is being contested by a prowoman antimasculinist idea, the women's liberationist paradigm, and by a root challenge to all gender expectations, the androgynous paradigm. Under the women's liberationist paradigm, women oppose the masculinist order and sometimes operate as separatists from men. Under the androgynous paradigm, the roles of both men and women in sociopolitical, economic, familial, and psychosexual life are conceived anew.

At this time, the three ideologies are competing for dominance in American life. There are still many women and more men who follow the masculine-equalitarian model for women's role in American life. There are more Americans than one would suspect who look back to the presuffragist period to a purely masculine superior model. However, there is evidence in the behavior and thinking of some groups and individuals that an androgynous model and a women's liberationist model are active and vital.

2

The Feminist Perspective: Women Equal to Men

The women's rights branch of contemporary feminism has been called conservative feminism. Its informing ideology is the "feminist" one of women-equal-to-men, constructed on a masculine-equalitarian model. Most male feminists participate in this kind of thinking, and it is the basis for many of the institutionalized forms of the women's movement that have attained some measure of general public respect—the National Organization for Women, the Women's Equity Action League, the National Women's Political Caucus.

Democratic government, the law and the judicial system, the nuclear family, the public school, the vocational order—all male-derived ideas and institutions—are not challenged in themselves by this kind of feminism. Rather, it asserts that women should have full and equal participation in these values and organizations alongside men and should enjoy the entire spectrum of opportunities to achieve and to be publicly validated that applies to men. To label this kind of thinking "conservative" or "women's rights" is a relative matter, for its realization in society would require the most radical reorganization of American life known since the nation began, with women assuming half of all positions as judges and members of Congress, business executives, college presidents, and truck drivers; with day care centers for children established in the Senate office building, universities, and local factories; with contra-

ceptive means and medical abortions available to all. Advocacy of the Equal Rights Amendment to the United States
Constitution, which has as its goal the eradication of all legal
distinctions between women and men, is in line with this
thought.

The feminist ideology is reformist in that it calls for social
change of an order that would shift public leadership and
occupational dominance from men primarily to women and
men equally. The social revolution that it calls for contrasts
with the one sought under the women's liberationist view in that
the latter seeks a new female consciousness, a new definition of
what is female, and a new kind of female ascendancy. The
feminist view contrasts with the androgynous ideology in that
its revolution is basically a social one, while the androgynous
one seeks a cultural change, which would involve a more
thoroughgoing examination of underlying attitudes and values
and an investigation of the validity of current institutions and
practices for the potential overthrow of both. The lines between
the three theories are not precise, and some degree of attention
to the validity for women of special attitudes and values is
implicit in the feminist assertion of female equality to men in
office and vocation, but the diverging focus among the three
attitudes is clear. The focus for masculine-equalitarian thinkers
is on full and equal participation of women in the existing structures of society.

The feminist ideology provided the framework for much of
the historical women's rights effort, particularly during the fifty
years before 1920 when feminism narrowed to the question of
woman suffrage, but also dating back to the series of women's
rights conventions that began with Seneca Falls in 1848. The
most familiar names from the history of the women's movement are the antecedents of the feminist branch: Susan B.
Anthony, Lucy Stone, Elizabeth Cady Stanton, Carrie Chapman Catt, and Anna Howard Shaw.

Social Analysis

The publication of Betty Friedan's *The Feminine Mystique* in
1963 was a signal of the resurgence of American feminism. Her
sensitive and provocative analysis of the plight of the American

woman rang true for thousands of women and sparked the
flames of considerable feminist reflection and activity. Friedan
documents a counterfeminist, reactionary image of women
that had come to dominate Americans' understanding of wom-
en's identity and role since World War II. The core of her
research was interviews with thousands of women, who reported a vague, amorphous discontent, a distress that she calls
"the problem that has no name." Having all the external signs
of feminine achievement—successful husbands, children,
attractive homes—the women Friedan interviewed nevertheless
felt lost and unfulfilled. Their problem, Friedan determines,
was what was symbolized by writing on the census form "Occupation: housewife," which she calls "the feminine mystique." The mystique is a new incarnation of the ancient belief that women are mysteriously and definitively different
from men and can be fully feminine only in the uniquely female
order of bearing and nurturing children and having sexual
relations with and nurturing those children's father. Since
World War II, this return to the housewife image as a comprehensive definition for American women had taken on a tran-
scending and somewhat mystical fortification in the American
consciousness. Friedan explains:

> The feminine mystique says that the highest value and the
> only commitment for women is the fulfillment of their own
> femininity. It says that the great mistake of Western culture,
> through most of its history, has been the undervaluation of
> this femininity. It says this femininity is so mysterious and
> intuitive and close to the creation and origin of life that man-
> made science may never be able to understand it. But
> however special and different, it is in no way inferior to the
> nature of man; it may even in certain respects be superior.
> The mistake, says the mystique, the root of women's troubles
> in the past is that women envied men, women tried to be like
> men, instead of accepting their own nature, which can find
> fulfillment only in sexual passivity, male domination, and
> nurturing maternal love. . .
>   Fulfillment as a woman had only one definition for
> American women after 1949—the housewife-mother. As
> swiftly as in a dream, the image of the American woman as a

changing, growing individual in a changing world was forgotten in the rush for the security of togetherness. Her limitless world shrunk to the cozy walls of home.' *P 37-38*

Friedan documents this syndrome with considerable social evidence of the promulgation from all sides in the 1940s and 1950s of the view that the proper sphere of woman is the home, that completeness for woman's life comes exclusively through homemaking. In the powerful mass media of television and publishing, the dominant image of women in programming and advertising was as housewife and sex object. Consumer researchers discovered that the stay-at-home wife buys more things less carefully than the career woman, and they promoted the housewife image not only to sell goods immediately but to sell the image itself in order to maintain the housewife market for more goods. Men editors of women's magazines and what Friedan calls "Uncle Tom housewife writers" published only fiction in which women gave up career for family or nonfiction which merely developed the market for the advertisers' products. These were published at the expense of material that would stretch the mind and challenge the imagination. Social scientists bought the definitions of women as primarily sexual and nurturing, following Freud's assertion that "penis envy" is definitive for women and Helene Deutsch's dichotomy of men as aggressive and women as passive. They followed the functionalists in sociology and anthropology, typified by Talcott Parsons, who said, "the woman's fundamental status is that of her husband's wife, the mother of his children."[2]

The fallacy of such functionalists, Betty Friedan claims, is in accepting society's definition of woman. Friedan bemoans the use of Margaret Mead's work in this context as a kind of sanction for a narrow-minded, natural childbirth-breastfeeding cult, which reduces woman to a definition by biology. Yet Mead's own life example is that of a woman who has excelled professionally and broken the housewife model.[3]

Friedan claims that the children of America's housewives are smothered by too much attention and suggests that momism has become a serious psychological problem in America. She further claims that the American educational system contributes to the mystique by subtly guiding girl children away from subjects and occupational goals that are challenging and by suggesting to girls that their destiny is in housewifery and motherhood.[4]

In this powerful cooperating network of forces, Friedan sees the advancement and extension of the mystique. It has resulted in the infantilization of American women, their enclosure within the four walls of home, doing work that can be accomplished by an eight-year-old child. Being told by the mass media, the women's magazines, the business community, the functionalist social scientists, the psychiatric professionals, and the educational system that her destiny is in the home, the American woman has bought the mystique, only to find that she has no strong central core of identity, that she suffers from "the problem that has no name."

The answer that Betty Friedan provides for this problem is in meaningful work outside the home. She maintains that women must begin to make life plans of their own, that their needed human identity can be found in commitment to a vocation. This commitment must be made by individual women who search out for themselves the work in the public sphere that has most meaning to them and through which they can make a public contribution, but such activity also must be supported by public attitudes and in particular at all levels of educational planning. Because work for which one is paid confers the primary status in our society as well as providing opportunities to grow in relationships and in abilities, it should be the central means by which women find a full new identity for themselves. Friedan asks:

> Who knows what women can be when they are finally free to become themselves? Who knows what women's intelligence will contribute when it can be nourished without denying love? Who knows of the possibilities of love when men and women share not only children, home, and garden, not only the fulfillment of their biological roles, but the responsibilities and passions of the work that creates the human future and the full human knowledge of who they are? It has barely begun, the search of women for themselves. But the time is at hand when the voices of the feminine mystique can no longer drown out the inner voice that is driving women on to become complete.[5]

Friedan regards the larger social framework that limits both society's expectation of women and women's expectation of themselves as too narrow and stultifying for a free humanity, as too confined even for what many women have been doing all along. The solution she proposes, work away from home, is the long-standing means by which men have been able to test and evaluate who they are and thereby achieve identity. What Friedan is really saying is that women should follow the male model. She thinks that women should be equal to men in the same way that men are equal to each other in American society. The means for valuing humanity is on the basis of what work they do, and women should have an equal opportunity to create for themselves the possibility of achieving public identity and respect on the basis of vocation. Like her sisters of the past in the suffragist movement who wanted the vote as men had it, Friedan asks for the contemporary American woman a vocation comparable to the man's. Her book thus signaled the resurgence or coming again of feminism in its most familiar form, dating from 1848 to 1920. Hers is a restatement of the male-equivalent idea that had operated for Elizabeth Blackwell and Antoinette Brown, Lucy Stone and Susan B. Anthony, in which the values of vote and vocation, both male-derived, are values for women, too.

Nowhere in *The Feminine Mystique* does Friedan deal with the question of what happens to the masculine role if the feminine role is massively altered, nor does she deal significantly with the question of variations in the patterns of family life if the central source of female identity is vocation rather than home, nor does she discuss the implications for the economy if all housewives should suddenly seek outside employment. Rather, she provides a powerful and socially indicting statement about the definition of woman in the minds of the majority of Americans just past the middle of the twentieth century. After a brief emergence of the "new woman" in the 1920s and 1930s, with her new right to vote, her new possibilities for a career outside the home, and most of all, her open search for her own sexuality, Americans returned to a conception of woman that in most of its facets was nineteenth century.[6] Friedan's terms for this regression are middle class, as

was most of nineteenth century feminism. Even her research
method had a parallel in the nineteenth century. In 1846
Catharine Beecher was struck by the observation that women
were repeatedly subject to vague illnesses. She conducted a poll,
writing numerous letters to her acquaintances in various cities
and asking each of them to report on the health of ten women,
rating them on a scale from "perfectly healthy" through levels
of "feeble," "delicate," and "sickly." Her replies from over
two hundred towns indicated that only two towns could report a
majority of healthy women. Beecher's response to this information was to launch a campaign for health and physical
education, but it is likely that her poll provided evidence for a
psychological and social discontent as at least part of the source
of such widespread female ill health.[7]

Friedan's delineation of the feminine mystique can be linked
to the dominant mid-nineteenth century assumption about
women, which Barbara Welter calls the "cult of true womanhood." Welter discovered the repeated occurrence of the
undefined phrase "True Womanhood" in a plethora of
nineteenth century sermons, tracts, reports on women's education, magazines for women, fiction, and essays, giving adequate
evidence that the term defined itself for the nineteenth century
reader. Her reading of the abundant materials made clear what
the phrase meant: "The attributes of True Womanhood, by
which a woman judged herself and was judged by her husband,
her neighbors and society could be divided into four cardinal
virtues—piety, purity, submissiveness and domesticity. Put
them all together and they spelled mother, daughter, sister,
wife—woman. Without them, no matter whether there was
fame, achievement or wealth, all was ashes. With them she was
promised happiness and power."[8]

Friedan's analysis of the woman problem in 1963, and the
solution she offers in terms of women finding fulfillment
through work, provide the contemporary basis for the feminist
paradigm. In Friedan's actions since coming to public prominence, particularly through the National Organization for
Women, and in her later writings she has continued to assert
that women should have the same rights and opportunities
enjoyed by men. However, there are at times suggestions that

her thinking is moving in the direction of the androgynous paradigm. In an essay on feminist ideology in the 1970 anthology *Voices of the New Feminism,* she continues to abhor the definition of women wholly as sex objects and as mothers, although she affirms that sexual activity and motherhood can be meaningful when they are entered into by free choice in the context of a "full human creativity."[9]

Friedan calls for women to unite as a political force to seek power for women in government, in order to have a voice in all public issues in proportion to their 51 percent majority in the population. She objects to tokenism as worse than nothing and calls for the revolution to apply to everybody, demanding such points as that educational institutions provide child care facilities. All these statements are in the masculine-equalitarian vein. But she continues:

> Man . . . is not the enemy. Men will only be truly liberated, to love women and to be fully themselves, when women are liberated to be full people. Until that happens, men are going to bear the burden and the guilt of the destiny they have forced upon women, the suppressed resentment of that passive stage—the sterility of love, when love is not between two fully active, fully participant, fully joyous people, but has in it the element of exploitation. And men will also not be fully free to be all they can as long as they must live up to an image of masculinity that denies to a man all the tenderness and sensitivity that might be considered feminine. Men have in them enormous capacities that they have to repress and fear in themselves, in living up to this obsolete and brutal man-eating, lion-killing, Ernest Hemingway image of masculinity—the image of all-powerful masculine superiority.[10]

In this statement Friedan is approaching the androgynous ideal of women and men being equal to each other. However, her major work is written squarely from a masculine-equalitarian perspective.

Bird

In *Born Female*, published in 1968, Caroline Bird deals further with women in vocational life. She shares Friedan's emphasis on work as the symbol of fulfillment in women's life, describing as "sexist" the attitude of relegating women to a rigid predetermined sex role. She considers current sexist attitudes that separate men and women in employment: "One is the idea that women should work inside and men outside. Another earmarks service work for women and profit-making for men. Other rules reserve work with machinery, work carrying prestige, and the top job to men. Most sex boundaries can be explained on the basis of one or another of these three rules."[11]

These subordinating rules are put into practice by a group whom Caroline Bird calls the "new masculinists," men and women who still feel that women should serve men, either in the home or at work, and that man should hold the superior positions. She contrasts these people with others who participate in "the androgynous life," although for her androgyny is defined only in terms of work. She pinpoints four social factors that make possible new assumptions about jobs. One is the vital statistics of birth, marriage, and death, in which birth control and younger marriages have given women many years to work beyond the childbearing years. The second factor "that is working to make the lives of women more like those of men is *education*." She demonstrates statistically that the more years a woman spends in school, the more likely she is to work. The third factor "making women's lives more like those of men is the *experience of employment itself*." The fourth factor is the desegregation of work, that is, the rise of many new inside jobs, such as computer programming, which carry status and yet have not been labeled as exclusively male or female.[12]

Caroline Bird is optimistic that dual vocations in families will break down the masculinist concept of feminine subservience. Still, she solves the conflict in terms of the feminist ideology. She does not acknowledge that the masculine role, too, must change in order for an androgynous ideal of male-female relations to be realized. She uses the term "androgynous," but in the same breath with "equal *to* men." She allows work to be primary in defining what is valuable about human life. One's work can be fulfilling, but it can also be tedious, in office or factory as well as home. Work is thus a shaky basis for defining human life, male or female, although it is the basis that masculine-dominated American society has given us in the past.

Masculine-Equalitarian Organizations

Several highly visible and powerful feminist organizations have become active since the mid-1960s, working from a basis of the women-equal-to-men or masculine-equalitarian theory.

NOW

The three most prominent of these organizations are the National Organization for Women, founded in 1966 under the presidency of Betty Friedan; the Women's Equity Action League, founded in 1968 under the leadership of Dr. Elizabeth Boyer; and the National Women's Political Caucus, begun in 1971 with Rep. Bella Abzug, Rep. Shirley Chisholm, Gloria Steinem, and Betty Friedan offering leadership. Several other long-lived women's groups, such as the National Federation of Business and Professional Women's Clubs, the Women's Department of the United Auto Workers, the Young Women's Christian Association, and the League of Women Voters, have shifted their public statements and action in the direction of overtly feminist positions of a masculine-equalitarian sort.[13]

NOW

Since its founding, the National Organization for Women (NOW) has been active at the local and national level on a number of fronts of women's rights, serving as a standard-bearer for a variety of feminist causes and often literally scaring government and community leadership into response. The organization has worked for equal employment for women, serving as a watchdog for the Equal Employment Opportunity Commission in its enforcement of Title VII of the 1964 Civil Rights Act, taking cases to the commission from local chapters, and filing complaints with the Department of Health, Education, and Welfare (HEW) over discrimination against women in employment. NOW has attacked sex-segregated job advertising. It has persisted in working for passage and ratification of the Equal Rights Amendment to the Constitution. It has opposed sex discriminatory laws, such as state protective labor laws. It has demanded maternity rights for women who work, called for revision of divorce and alimony proceedings that discriminate against both men and women, and advocated revision of tax laws that currently do not permit working parents to deduct home and child care expenses from their income tax. NOW has called for repeal of all antiabortion laws and was the first group to define the abortion issue in civil libertarian terms of "the right of a woman to control her own body." It has called for the wide availability of child care facilities, to be used at the desire of the parents in the community, and has occasionally established child care facilities of its own. It has conducted studies of and a campaign against the image of

women in the mass media, making available to women its mass
media monitoring kit, and taking a case to the Federal Communication Commission against WABC-TV in New York.
NOW has advocated a greater level of women's participation in
industrial training programs and leadership positions in federal
poverty programs. It has sought equal participation of women
and men in religious life, for which it set up an ecumenical task
force that does research and provides materials for religious
groups. To celebrate August 26, the anniversary of women
gaining the right to vote, NOW organized a "Women's March
for Equality" in various cities in 1970, 1971, and 1972, which
included parades, meetings, and a plea to contribute that day's
pay to women's causes.[14]

The NOW Statement of Purpose, adopted at its organizing
conference in 1966, indicates specifically how women are discriminated against in education, industry, politics, government,
and the professions. It pledges NOW to engage in an active
course of attack on such discrimination and states NOW's
vision in masculine-equalitarian terms:

> The purpose of NOW is to take action to bring women into
> full participation in the mainstream of American society
> now, exercising all the privileges and responsibilities thereof
> in *truly equal partnership with men* . . .
>   WE BELIEVE THAT women will do most to create a new
> image of women by acting now, and by speaking out in
> behalf of their own equality, freedom, and human
> dignity—not in pleas for special privilege, nor in enmity
> toward men, who are also victims of the current,
> half-equality between the sexes—but in active, self-respecting
> partnership with men. By so doing, women will develop con-
> fidence in their life, their choices, their future and their
> society.[15]

The NOW "Bill of Rights" for women pledges seven goals:

    I. Equal Rights Constitutional Amendment
    II. Enforce Law Banning Sex Discrimination in Employ-
ment
    III. Maternity Leave Rights in Employment and in Social
Security Benefits

IV. Tax Deduction for Home and Child Care Expenses for Working Parents

V. Child Care Day Centers

VI. Equal Job Training and Allowance Opportunities for Women in Poverty

VII. The Right of Women to Control Their Reproductive Lives.[16]

The Bill of Rights further guarantees: "The right of women in poverty to secure job training, housing, and family allowance *on equal terms with men,* but without prejudice to a parent's right to remain at home to care for his or her children; revision of welfare legislation and poverty programs which deny women dignity, privacy and self-respect."[17]

NOW occasionally refers to the current role expectations as being limiting for men, describes an ideal family structure in which both parents would share child care and domestic chores, and implies that men should be free from socially imposed role norms, as in its statement asserting the "parent's right to remain at home to care for his or her children." These implications fall under the androgynous concept, but they are not representative of the great majority of NOW's statements and actions. Rather, NOW works out of a fundamental conceptualization that is masculine-equalitarian, as articulated in its intent to secure for women a "truly equal partnership with men."

NOW has been tremendously effective in bringing credibility to the women's movement and in focusing on crucial issues. It started out at the forefront of the movement in 1966, and has continued to develop legal and legislative confrontations that have effected significant changes in women's lot in American society. It has been criticized from the Left as being establishmentarian and has been called "the NAACP of the women's movement," but the solid, respectable attention it has earned and the gains it has made have often formed a base for more radical feminists to build upon. NOW's ideological stance declares that what is open to men in society should also be open to women.

The Women's Equity Action League (WEAL) has a membership composed largely of highly competent and

WEAL

respected professional women—lawyers, educational adminis-
trators, professors, counselors, judges, and legislators. Its drive
for membership has been among women who already hold some
degree of public power. It has focused attention on three areas
of sex discrimination: employment, education, and de facto tax
inequalities.[18] Its 1971 National Committee Reports show
achievements in such matters as forcing federal contract compliance on equal employment for women in higher education
and commerce, ending discriminatory help-wanted advertising,
combating discrimination in medical education and medical
practice, and taking legal action on behalf of women who had
experienced discrimination in employment.

WEAL is best known for filing about 350 complaints with
HEW against institutions of higher education, showing discrimination against women in hiring and promotion, which
resulted in cutting off federal funds for some university projects
at such places as the University of Michigan and Harvard until
"affirmative action plans" had been developed for sex equality
within the universities. WEAL has also publicized the fact that
commercial firms having federal contracts are liable under the
law for sex discrimination. In 1971, WEAL took action with the
Treasury Department to gain compliance with federal equal
opportunity guidelines in twenty-seven Dallas banks that were
depositories of federal funds, resulting in a Treasury Department investigation and the promotion of 35-40 women to bank
officialdom. On October 5, 1970, WEAL took class action
against all medical schools on the basis of discrimination
against women in admissions. It distributed three thousand
posters to colleges and universities advising premedical women
students how to proceed if they met discrimination in admissions. WEAL has established a Legal Defense and Education
Fund and has provided legal services to a number of women, in
such cases as a disabled female war veteran who was refused
gynecological services under the Veterans' Administration,
women who were fired by a construction company on the basis
that the company was not complying with state protective
legislation, a teacher who could not get a dependency allowance
for her husband whom she was putting through school, and two
teachers who were required by their school board to take
maternity leaves against their will.[19]

WEAL's membership brochure emphasizes the need to press for employment equality:

> As with almost any basic issue, this real dignity for women has economic implications. Women have historically been paid less than men for equal effort and the more desirable career areas have always been preempted by males. However, if women are not expected to accept full responsibilities for supporting themselves and, often, their dependents, they must be allowed to prepare themselves and to compete equally in the job market, and to reap equal benefits from their efforts, without hindrance, and without onus for doing so.[20]

WEAL has been particularly effective in attacking legal and educational discrimination against women.

NWPC The National Women's Political Caucus (NWPC) was begun as a vigorous, multipartisan political organization to support women for public office, elective and appointive, at all levels, to lobby for women's issues in legislative sessions, and to foster a higher level of women's participation in all areas of political life. The founding conference of July 10-11, 1971, in Washington, D. C., which included three hundred women from diverse backgrounds, proposed a plan for organizing women at the grass roots level and for running candidates for public office who were feminist and antiracist. An explanatory statement reads: "We believe that women have a deeper and more tenacious interest in certain kinds of programs that have vital national significance: child care, non-violence and peace preservation, and measures to protect the specific rights of women such as repeal of abortion laws, dissemination of birth control information, guaranteed annual income ($6500), and equal employment and education opportunities."[21] The conference endorsed diversity by agreeing to policy-making by consensus through reports from its radical caucus, black caucus, and prime-of-life caucus (women twenty-three to thirty-two years old). A National Policy Council was elected, comprised of prominent women with established public reputations, such as Bella Abzug, Shana Alexander, Liz Carpenter, Shirley Chisholm, Betty Friedan, Fannie Lou Hamer, LaDonna Harris, Wilma Scott Heide, and Gloria Steinem.

Within a year, NWPC was able to organize local and state women's political caucuses in every state in the Union, to make women's representation an issue in precinct and primary contests across the country for delegations to the national party conventions, to help to organize campaigns for numerous women candidates for local and state office, and to provide feminist assessments in a number of races regarding the sensitivity of officeholders and candidates to women's concerns. Most significantly, it was largely responsible for raising the percentages of women delegates to the Democratic and Republican national conventions from their 1968 levels of 13 and 17 percent, respectively, to 39 and 30 percent in 1972.[22] At both 1972 conventions, NWPC was prominently present in organizing and communicating with women delegates, in challenging credentials, and in getting a women's plank into the platforms; and at the Democratic convention it supported Shirley Chisholm's presidential candidacy and ran Frances Farenthold for Vice President.[23]

NWPC defines its priorities as the areas of civil rights, human rights, economic rights, and a national commitment to women. Foremost in the civil rights area is its commitment to ratification of the Equal Rights Amendment, coupled with securing amendments to existing civil rights legislation so as to abolish all discrimination based on sex.

In the human rights area NWPC asks for implementation of the recommendations of the Presidential Commission on Population Growth and the American Future, which would lead to repeal of all laws that interfere with a woman's choice to decide her own reproductive and sexual life, as well as passage of child care legislation, health care legislation that includes maternity, abortion, and birth control benefits for any woman, legislation to end hunger and malnutrition, housing legislation to end discrimination against women and against families headed by women, and reform of criminal justice procedures affecting women.

The NWPC position on economic rights has included elimination of tax inequities against women, amendment of the Social Security Act to provide equal retirement benefits to working women, widows, and their children, extension of the Internal Revenue Code to include tax deduction for child care and disabled dependent care as a reasonable business expense, extension of disability benefits to temporary disabilities related to childbearing and abortion, and extension of minimum wage, overtime, and unemployment benefits to all workers. The call for a national commitment to women includes a call for the appointment of women to all positions of national responsibility, such as Cabinet posts, agency heads, and Supreme Court justices, on an equal basis with men; inclusion of women in all government studies and commissions; passage of a Women's Equality Act and a Women's Education Act in 1973; and passage of legislation making available federal grants on a matching basis for state Commissions on the Status of Women.[24]

Like NOW and WEAL—in fact it duplicates some of their membership—NWPC is a high-level masculine-equalitarian organization. It seeks the inclusion of women in the existing male-dominated political process. NWPC is solely political, however, while NOW and WEAL include political action but also make judicial appeals, and NOW, the most broadly based of all, works for a general social program as well.

In a sense, these masculine-equalitarian organizations are continuing the work of the National American Woman Suffrage Association, their forebear in feminist ideology. The women's rights movement in America from the 1830s to the Civil War had in it elements of a number of issues, such as property rights, rights to education and employment, rights to divorce and child custody, as well as rights to the franchise—all of them representing women-equal-to-men concepts, or the feminist view. After the Civil War and passage of the Fifteenth Amendment without the inclusion of woman suffrage, the National Woman Suffrage Association and the American Woman Suffrage Association were formed, and for most feminists the single issue became the vote. The two associations merged in 1890, and thereafter the new National American Woman Suffrage Association (NAWSA) steadily lobbied and campaigned for prosuffrage candidates in the federal Congress and the states. After 1913 NAWSA was helped in its cause by Alice Paul's more radical Congressional Union, later to become the National Woman's Party. The new group threw fresh energy into the effort for passage of the federal amendment, and after 1917 it adopted such militant tactics as picketing the White House, burning copies of President Wilson's speeches in public ceremonies at the Lafayette Monument, chaining themselves to the White House fence, and going on hunger strikes after being arrested. Meanwhile, NAWSA continued its campaign through legally constituted channels, until in 1920 the Nineteenth Amendment granting women's suffrage was passed and ratified.[25]

It was the belief of the leaders of NAWSA—Lucy Stone, Susan B. Anthony, Elizabeth Cady Stanton in the early days; Anna Howard Shaw and Carrie Chapman Catt in the first two decades of the twentieth century—that the granting of the suffrage would effect the final, full realization of equality for women. This conviction was poignantly illustrated in a letter from Susan B. Anthony to Elizabeth Cady Stanton in 1902:

> We little believed when we began this contest, optimistic with the hope and buoyancy of youth, that half a century later we would be compelled to leave the finish of the battle to another generation of women. But our hearts are filled with joy to know that they will enter upon this task equipped with a college education, business experience, the right to speak in public—all of which were denied to women fifty years ago. They have practically but one point to gain—the suffrage: we had all.[26]

Contemporary feminists are all too aware that Susan B. Anthony was wrong, that women are still not first-class citizens half a century after passage of the "Anthony Amendment." Groups like NOW, WEAL, and NWPC have extended and amplified the issue areas that were the concerns of the nineteenth century feminists, and they have taken up the battle where NAWSA stopped. Their platform embraces the informing ideology of Susan B. Anthony's movement: that women should be equal to men, should have the same rights, privileges, and opportunities as men. They are continuing the feminist cause whose roots were in the nineteenth century struggle for equal rights for women in America.

The Equal Rights Amendment

The Equal Rights Amendment to the United States Constitution passed the Senate on March 22, 1972, by a vote of 84 to 8. It had passed the House of Representatives on August 10, 1970, by a vote of 350 to 15, and again on October 12, 1971, by a vote of 354 to 23. In 1972, it was sent to the states for ratification. The proposed Twenty-Seventh amendment reads:

> Equality of rights under the law shall not be denied or abridged by the United States or by any state on account of sex.
> The Congress shall have the power to enforce, by appropriate legislation, the provisions of this article.
> This amendment shall take effect two years after the date of ratification.[27]

This amendment has been introduced into Congress every year since 1923, for many of those years almost solely owing to the efforts of Alice Paul's National Woman's Party. Unlike the National American Woman Suffrage Association, which upon passage of the Nineteenth Amendment, under the leadership of Carrie Chapman Catt, turned itself into the nonpartisan and nonfeminist League of Women Voters, the National Woman's Party saw the need for a more extensive legal alleviation of discrimination against women and devoted itself exclusively to the passage of a comprehensive equal rights amendment to the Constitution. In the summer of 1972, an elderly Alice Paul began closing the party offices on Constitution Avenue, her life's work and her party's accomplished by the combined forces of changing times and new groups of younger, more vociferous feminists—just as she and her party in the decade before 1920 had provided the radical thrust for the more moderate women's rights movement in order to win passage of the woman's suffrage amendment.

During the 1920s, controversy over the Equal Rights Amendment became a chief force in the dissolution of feminism. The National Women's Party first proposed the amendment in 1923, which at that time read: "Men and women shall have equal rights throughout the United States and every place subject to its jurisdiction."[28] This proposal started a major battle among women's advocates with the National Woman's Party carrying the banner of full emancipation for women, which they thought the Equal Rights Amendment would bring. On the other side were what William L. O'Neill has called social reformer groups—such as the League of Women Voters, the National Consumers' League, and the Women's Trade Union League—who felt that the suffrage amendment had already brought equality for women and that eradication of legal and social sexual distinctions between women and men would be harmful to women. The dispute centered on the existing industrial protective legislation for women. The social reformers felt that the hard-won laws setting wages, hours, and working conditions for women should be maintained for women's welfare. They argued that the professional, career-oriented National Woman's Party members were thinking in narrow and rigid terms of only the personal professional fulfillment of women and were blinding themselves to the horrors of factory conditions that the protective laws had alleviated for thousands of industrial working women collectively. The social reformers also subscribed to a notion that women were imbued with a special nature because of motherhood and the need it created to be sheltered by men, and they often felt that women should not compete for jobs held by men. Prestigious legal support for this position was provided by Felix Frankfurter and Louis Brandeis. The argument was also defined as the Woman's Party holding to an abstract, idealistic principle, and the reformist groups working for practical, concrete gains for women.

The controversy exploded in a Labor Department Women's Bureau conference on the industrial problems of women in 1926, at which the social reformers found a partisan in the bureau's chief, Mary Anderson. Anderson allowed a debate to be held on the merits of the Equal Rights Amendment and appointed an investigative committee on protective legislation, but she permitted the social reformers to prevent the investigation from being carried out. Thereafter the persistent effort to place the Equal Rights Amendment before Congress was the often lonely and unpublished mission of the National Woman's Party.[29]

In its fifty-year history before Congress, the Equal Rights Amendment has had essentially the same intent, although the wording was changed in the 1940s. Between 1923 and 1938, hearings were held before subcommittees of the judiciary committees of the House and Senate, and the amendment was three times reported to the full Committee of the House. In 1940, it was included for the first time in the platform of a major party, the Republican Party. By 1943, it had been submitted five more times to the full judiciary committees of the House and Senate. It did not reach the floor of the full House until the Ninety-First Congress in 1970, although it was reported favorably many times by the Judiciary Committee. Major opposition to the amendment over the years was based on the fear that state and federal protective legislation would be put in jeopardy. Even after such legislation was waived in heavy industry for the sake of the war effort during World War II, with no detrimental effect on women, this argument continued to be made.[30]

The Senate responded more favorably to the amendment over the years. It held extensive hearings before its Judiciary Committee in 1945, 1948, and 1956. Its first floor debate on the amendment took place in 1946, when the amendment failed, 38 yeses to 35 noes, falling short of the required two-thirds majority needed. In 1950 and 1953, the amendment passed the Senate with the so-called "Hayden rider," the qualification that "The provisions of this article shall not be construed to impair any rights, benefits, or exemptions now or hereafter conferred by law upon persons of the female sex."[31]

In 1960, the Senate again approved the Hayden rider, but sent the bill back to committee. The amendment continued to come up in the Senate in the 1960s but kept failing, and no public hearings were held.[32] By 1970, there was a concerted lobbying and letter-writing effort on the part of feminist groups favoring the amendment; and on February 17, 1970, Wilma Scott Heide, NOW's chairman of the board, and twenty other women disrupted a hearing before the Senate Subcommittee on Constitutional Amendments on the amendment to enfranchise eighteen-year-olds, demanding a hearing on the Equal Rights Amendment. The result was a hearing in May 1970, chaired by Senator Birch Bayh, who is himself a feminist.[33]

Shortly thereafter in the House, which had never held a floor debate on the Equal Rights Amendment, Rep. Martha Griffiths, a long-time feminist, took the surprise action of using the discharge petition, a rarely employed parliamentary procedure, to force the amendment out of the Judiciary Committee onto the House floor for a vote on August 10. After a debate of only one hour, the amendment passed the House by a wide margin.[34]

In the Senate, the full Judiciary Committee held hearings in September 1970; and the Senate leadership put the House-passed resolution on the amendment directly on the Senate calendar for discussion in October 1970. After amending the resolution to impose a seven-year limit on the ratification process and to make the amendment effective in two years rather than one year after ratification, the Senate failed to take further action on the amendment in that session. On November 22, 1971, the House again voted in favor of the amendment; and on March 14, 1972, the Judiciary Committee of the Senate reported the amendment favorably to the Senate floor.[35] After a futile and lonely attempt to block the legislation by Sen. Sam J. Ervin, who had opposed it for years and who tried to amend the bill for the Equal Rights Amendment to retain most of the sexual distinctions in existing law, the Senate passed the bill for the Equal Rights Amendment with only eight dissenting votes.

Supporters of the amendment ranged from ultraconservative Republican women who would not on any count call themselves feminists to radical feminists who challenge most social institutions, such as the family, and consider sexual relationships to be political phenomena. Opponents were a similarly unlikely coalition of conservative male politicians, labor unions, and feminist radicals from New Left politics.[36] Groups registering support of the amendment included the American Association of University Women; the American Civil Liberties Union; professional women's groups in medicine, dentistry, nursing, accounting, mass media, law, and microbiology; religious groups, including the American Jewish Congress, Church Women United, the Council for Christian Social Action of the United Church of Christ, and the St. Joan's Alliance of Catholic Women; unions and workers' groups, such as the League of American Working Women, the International Brotherhood of Painters and Allied Trades, and the International Brotherhood of Teamsters. Others favoring the amendment included the National Association of Colored Women, the Ladies Auxiliary of Veterans of Foreign Wars, the General Federation of

Women's Clubs, the National Education Association, the
National Welfare Rights Organization, the National Woman's
Party, Common Cause, and NOW. Prominent expert opinion
in constitutional law was divided, with Paul Freund of the Harvard Law School providing arguments to support Sen. Ervin's
opposition to the amendment, while Thomas Emerson of the
Yale Law School and Leo Kanowitz of the University of New
Mexico Law School, author of *Women and the Law,* provided
testimony in support of the amendment.[37]

Proponents of the Equal Rights Amendment feel that it is
necessary because equal treatment of women under the law has
not been granted through court application of the Fifth and
Fourteenth Amendments. As late as 1971, in *Reed* v. *Reed,* the
Supreme Court left the burden of proof of sex discrimination in
law on the individual woman plaintiff, a burden of proof that is
no longer necessary in cases of racial discrimination. The areas
of state and federal law in which proponents of the amendment
feel that women are discriminated against include laws establishing age of majority; laws establishing domicile, which bind a
woman to her husband's legal residence; and laws regarding
marriage, guardianship, property ownership, and business
ownership, which place women in a dependent relationship to
men. Also discriminatory are the criminal statutes that pre-
scribe harsher penalties for women committing the same crimes
as men and the legal codes regarding adultery and prostitution.
Laws regarding occupational limits, the so-called "protective
laws," have effectively discriminated against women in not
allowing them to enter occupations that entail overtime work or
certain kinds of weight-lifting. An opportunity in state-sup-
ported higher education has sometimes been denied to women
by college or university regulations favoring men. Finally,
women have not been equal to men with respect to the military
draft.[38]

A summary of the desirable effects of the Equal Rights
Amendment is offered in the Report of the 1970 President's
Task Force on Women's Rights and Responsibilities:

It would guarantee women and girls admission to publicly
supported educational institutions under the same standards

as men and boys, but it would also require women to assume equal responsibility for alimony and support of children . . .

It would require that women not be given automatic preference for custody of children in divorce suits. The welfare of the child would become the primary criterion in determining custody.

It would require Federal, State, and local governments to grant women equal opportunity in employment.

It would render invalid any current State laws providing longer prison sentences for women than for men for the same offense.

It would impose on women obligation for military service. They would not be required to serve in functions for which they are not fitted, any more than men are so required.

Once the equal rights amendment is ratified, the burden of proving the reasonableness of disparate treatment on the basis of sex would shift to the United States or the State. Presently the burden is on the aggrieved individuals to show unreasonableness.[39]

The effect of the application of the Equal Rights Amendment is potentially the most far-reaching legal change for women in American history, and it is likely to bring about social change. In a real sense, it holds the possibility of effectuating the feminist ideal, which first received organizational expression when wagonloads of women rolled in to the Seneca Falls convention in 1848 and Elizabeth Cady Stanton stated their grievances to society. The ratification and application of the Equal Rights Amendment should eradicate legal distinctions between men and women, which will mean in most cases that women are equal-to-men, that women have the same rights, privileges, and obligations as men. As Rep. Martha Griffiths said to quell the furor over the possibility of women being drafted for military service: "The draft is equal. That is the thing that is equal. But once you are in the Army you are put where the Army tells you where you are going to go."[40]

In two areas where some people feel that women have been given favored treatment—child custody and alimony decisions, and industrial protective regulations—men would benefit from the leveling process of the amendment. Leo Kanowitz has said that protective legislation should protect people, not just women, so that laws regarding weight-lifting, rest periods, building facilities, and time limitations on work could potentially benefit all workers, just as the elimination of protective laws could work to the detriment of all workers.

The Equal Rights Amendment is masculine-equalitarian because it takes the male standard of existing law and says that women should have the same rights and possibilities which the legal system allows to males. In order to participate in this male standard, women will be required to give up some areas of special privilege, designed for them in the past by men with a view to keeping women on a pedestal, but which from the first were a means of consigning women to a dependent and inferior status.

Women and the Labor Force

Cold, dry statistical tables and charts can arouse the anger of feminists on the subject of female employment. Tables from the Department of Labor's *Handbook on Women Workers,* compiled by the Women's Bureau, show that the 1967 median income for year-round, full-time white male workers was $7,164; for nonwhite male workers, $4,528; for white women workers, $4,152; for nonwhite women workers, $2,949. Charts of median income indicated by educational attainment show that women with eight years of education averaged $1,404 per year, men $4,518; women with four years of high school averaged $2,673, men $6,924; women with four years of college averaged $4,164, men $9,728; and women with five or more years of college averaged $6,114, men $10,041. The ten top occupations of women were secretary, sales woman in retail trade, private household worker, elementary school teacher, bookkeeper, waitress, professional nurse, sewer or stitcher in manufacturing, typist, and cashier.[41] One can see from these facts that the average woman worker earns little more than half the income of the average male worker; that advanced education is of small benefit to the earning power of women as compared to men, since the woman with five years or more of college averaged less income than the man with only a high school education; and that the concentration of women workers is in service-type occupations, whether of the white collar variety such as office or sales work, the blue collar kind such as domestic or industrial labor, or the professional kind such as elementary school teaching and nursing. The provision of such information made the *Handbook on Women Workers* a kind of sacred scripture for the women's movement.

Esther Peterson, who was assistant secretary of labor at the time, reported in 1964 that the 1960 census showed there were some women in all 479 occupational categories listed in the census report, but she warned that this did not mean that all occupations were readily open to women:

> There is still considerable prejudice on the part of employers, educators and women themselves as to what is "men's work" and "women's work." The very fact that most newspapers divide their classified ads into "Help Wanted—Men" and "Help Wanted—Women" attests to this fact. When this view is held by school counselors and teachers, there is little likelihood that young women will be alerted to the new fields for which they might have aptitudes.
> This attitude extends to many apprenticeship programs in the skilled occupations. In 1954 a count of female names listed among registered apprentices in seven states indicated that fewer than 1 per cent of that group were women . . . Automation, of course, is making it possible for more women to do more jobs by eliminating heavy lifting, dangerous working conditions, and other difficulties. The problem is to change the habits of thought which do not even consider women for jobs in particular industries or plants simply because women have never been employed there.[42]

The issues that have been pinpointed by contemporary feminists regarding women and employment include: the designation of certain kinds of jobs as "women's work"; the discrepancy between incomes earned by men and by women doing the same work; the blocking of women from being hired to certain jobs by employers and employment agencies and from being promoted within their firms and institutions; the discriminatory treatment of women on the job; the lower pay that usually accompanies the jobs considered "women's jobs"; the preva-

lent attitudes about why women work; the special category of
domestic employment; the unique situation of the black woman
worker; and the need for child care facilities for women workers.[43]

Much organizing has been done by NOW and WEAL, as well
as within specific employing institutions by women employees
and by women seeking employment, to challenge discrimination
against women in employment through the courts and before
the Equal Employment Opportunity Commission (EEOC).
One example of success is the fact that, since the time when
Esther Peterson first noted the practice, many metropolitan
newspapers have stopped running sex-segregated "help
wanted" ads. This has been the result of pressure exerted by
local NOW chapters on newspapers in the form of protest confrontations in some cities, charges to the EEOC in other cities,
and court suits in still others.[44]

At the ideological level, feminists have isolated a configuration of "myths" about women and work that continue to
operate in people's minds and to effect discrimination against
women in employment. Marijean Suelzle, a sociologist, identifies eight of these myths and refutes each one. The first is:
"Women naturally don't want careers, they just want jobs."
Suelzle explodes this myth by asserting that generalizations cannot be made about women as a class any more than about ethnic
groups as a class. Further, she points to areas of cultural conditioning in education, mass media, and family life that promote
the image of women as noncareer-oriented. The facts of
women's employment today refute this image: "Today almost
half of all women 18 to 64 years of age in the population are
workers (49 percent) . . . female participation in the labor force
today drops off at age 25 but rises again at age 35 to a second
peak of 54 percent at ages 45 to 54 . . . Today almost half the
women at age 35 can expect to work 24 to 31 more years. More
than one-half of today's young women will work full-time for
25 more years. Today 37 percent of all workers are women."[45]

The second myth is: "If women do pursue a career they tend
to be more interested in personal development than in a career
as a way of life." Statistics on working women from the
Women's Bureau refute this claim. One-tenth of all women

remain single, and these single women work an average of 45 years, two years longer than the 43-year average men work. Another one-tenth of all married women have no children and work an average of 35 years. Many married women with children tend to work, drop out when the children are young, then resume work when the children are in school. Such women, reentering the labor force around age thirty-five, average another 24 years of work. Apart from these facts, attitudes about motherhood inhibit the employment of many mothers of preschool children. These attitudes are made concrete by employment policies that do not allow maternity leave without penalties and by the grossly inadequate availability of child care facilities.

The third myth is: "There will be a higher absenteeism and turnover rate amongst women than among men, due to the restrictions imposed by children on working mothers." Suelzle reports that according to the Women's Bureau, labor turnover rates are "more influenced by the skill level of the job, the age of the worker, the worker's record of job stability and the worker's length of service with the employer than by the sex of the worker." Further, a study showed that women actually averaged fewer days absent from work than men—5.3 days absent for women, 5.4 for men over a one-year period.[46]

The fourth myth is: "Women are only working for pin money, for extras." Suelzle again uses Women's Bureau statistics to refute this. One-tenth of all families in America are headed by a woman, and almost one-third of these families live in poverty. Often in families where both husband and wife work, the wife's income makes the difference for economic survival.

The fifth myth is: "Women control most of the power and wealth in American society." Suelzle points out that this argument is based on stock ownership and consumer activity. Once again the Women's Bureau figures counter the argument. In 1967, only 18 percent of the total shares of stocks reported by corporations were owned individually by women, while 20 percent were owned individually by men, 58 percent by institutions. Further, the male make-up of the boards of directors of virtually all public corporations indicates that the control of corporate wealth is securely in male hands. As for consumer purchasing power, it is true that housewives are the major purchasers of small consumer items for their families; but decisions about major purchases such as house or car are rarely made by the wife alone.

The sixth myth is: "It will be too disruptive to an efficient work orientation if women and men are permitted to mingle on the job." Suelzle replies that the invoking of a sexual problem at work is usually made when there is a threat of men working with or under the supervision of women, and its source is usually a prejudice among men who have never had women co-workers or supervisors. She explains: "Myths concerning sexuality on the job are mostly invoked when there is a danger of a crossing-over of female and male status and pay differentials on the job. Although the principle of 'equal pay for equal work' is widely accepted and sometimes even legally enforced, great care is taken to ensure that women and men are not given the same job titles and corresponding opportunities for advancement."[47]

The seventh myth is: "Women are more 'human-oriented,' less mechanical, and they are better at tedious, boring or repetitive tasks than men are." This myth bars women from scientific and technical education, from industrial trainee programs, and from labor union participation. Yet women who have been given the chance have been able to perform with competence in a wide range of technical occupations in times of crisis, such as war, and are today being trained in small numbers in every conceivable kind of job. "What doesn't change," according to Suelzle, "is that whatever men do is regarded as more important, and gets more rewards, than what women do. The boundaries are defined by status, not aptitude, for even in traditionally female fields the persons in the highest positions of authority are most likely to be men."[48]

The eighth myth is: "Women need to be 'protected' because of their smaller size." Protective laws should protect people, retorts Suelzle, and qualifications for jobs requiring physical strain should be determined medically, not sexually.[49]

This entire set of myths creates a vicious circle, continuing the stereotyping of women and promoting discrimination against women in work. Attacks on this prevailing ideology about women and work have been combined with practical efforts by women to gain employment, to better the conditions of work where women are employed, and to seek advancement for women.

The issue of equal employment for women is a women's rights issue. The effort to get women jobs as miners or eyeglass lens grinders, as FBI investigators or shop managers, and to establish the rule that women must have equivalent titles and equivalent pay to men for the jobs they do, is posited on the assumption that the work men do and the pay they receive for it, the currently operative male model, is a system in which women want a share. The standards for employment and distribution of income have been established by men, and the feminists are saying that women ought to be equal to men in the economic system as it now exists. Men compete with each other for jobs not on the basis of need, but on the basis of ability of the exertion of various kinds of power; yet a double standard prevails for women, with their need being imposed as a consideration by employers. Fatherhood has not been a factor in the employment of men; yet motherhood is a prime consideration in the hiring of a woman. Training programs for men have assumed that men will make a career of the work they enter; but women are often kept out of training programs on the assumption that they will not have a career; and women are asked to guarantee ahead of time that they are career-oriented, a guarantee never asked from a male trainee. Feminists are saying on the issue of work that women should have the same expectations held for them, the same opportunities available to them, and the same assumptions about individual talent and capability made for them, as are true for men.

The related issue of child care comes under the feminist paradigm when it is directly related to work. The demand for child care facilities comes from all sorts of feminists, but this is a masculine-equalitarian demand when it is tied specifically to employment. The concern of the masculine-equalitarians is that women be freed from the traditional child care responsibility of the mother for the purpose of holding a job, that government, industry, or other public institutions make child care available, either free or for payment, so that she has a safe, comfortable, perhaps even creative place to leave her children, in order that she can work. This still assumes that the primary responsibility for the care or arrangement for children is the mother's. Child care is advocated under both the women's liberationist and the androgynous paradigms, but for different reasons. The women's liberationist sometimes advocated day care centers on the basis that child care is the responsibility of society rather than of the mother or parents, arguing that the child needs to live its life in a context broader than the nuclear family. The androgynous thinker asks for day care facilities on the basis that both parents are responsible for the child, that work of both parents should intersect with the life of the child, and that the child should have a life of its own in its own public sphere.

Female Sexuality

Deliberate theorizing about female sexuality has not been much of a part of the effort of feminists of the masculine-equalitarian type. Much more central has been the pragmatic attempt to change law and social practice to make women equal to men in the public sphere. However, the theory of sexuality that logically follows the feminist concept is a rejection of the sexual double standard under which males are free to have premarital and extramarital sexual affairs, but women are expected to confine their sexual expression to marriage. A writer who articulated this view to a wide audience is Helen Gurley Brown, editor of *Cosmopolitan* and author of *Sex and the Single Girl*. Not considered a feminist by many activists in the movement, Brown nevertheless has consistently made this particular feminist point in the pages of *Cosmopolitan*. A major symbol of this attitude was her publication of the picture of a male nude as a centerfold in the March 1972 issue, in direct parallel to the female nude pictures that regularly appear as the centerfold of *Playboy*.

Sex and the Single Girl, a best seller in 1962, was hailed as a piece of feminist literature. Yet it is hard to take Brown seriously as a descendant of Mary Wollstonecraft, Lucy Stone, or even Margaret Sanger, although she does claim quite forthrightly that women, single or married, should not live without sex. *Sex and the Single Girl* is a kind of *I Hate To Cook Book* of helpful hints for the single woman (her "girl" is presumably an adult woman). Most of the book offers pieces of advice on how to bolster one's ego with men, how to keep slim and attractive on health foods, how to use cosmetics advantageously, and generally how to be alive and vital *for* men. The "revolutionary" chapter is on how to have an affair; and the supposedly radical claim is that single women should enjoy sex often, with different men and without guilt.[50]

This book scarcely deserves mention as a feminist piece beyond the fact that it attacks the sexual double standard that has been a part of female subjugation: men can have sex freely, women are expected to be chaste outside of marriage. Brown is a masculine-equalitarian thinker, as far as she goes. Her single women are decorating themselves and making themselves available for men by men's standards, according to a purely sexual definition of themselves.

Dana Densmore, a prowoman antimasculinist feminist, in an outraged article on the book, asks Helen Gurley Brown:

> What is your own sexual self-image? How much narcissism and masochism are in it? And how much does your sexual self-image condition your whole self image?
>
> In the heady joy of the sexual encounter are you reveling in masochism euphemistically calling your surrender "womanly"?
>
> Why should you like being dominated by a man? What is there to recommend a man who makes decisions without consulting you, who expects you to conform to his ideas about how women should act?[51]

While both viewpoints on sexuality are within the women's movement, they conflict vigorously.

Women and Religion

Since the rise of the new feminism, there has been considerable feminist activity within organized Christianity, but little or no overtly religious Jewish feminism. The feminist Christians function largely within the institutional framework of churches

in America, and they are reacting in part to their own and to
non-Christian accusations that the source of much of the oppression of women is in the Judeo-Christian tradition. Christian
feminism manifests itself in several forms. Groups gather in
local settings, in women's caucuses of major ongoing national
religious bodies, and in specially organized feminist units, both
for consciousness-raising and for calling the churches to reassess the understanding and role of women in religion. In some
cases, as in Church Women United, the National Council of
Churches' national and local organization, and the women's
divisions of national church boards, including those of the
Episcopal Church, the United Methodist Church, and the
Lutheran churches, redefinitions have been made of their self-
understanding as women's groups, moving them out of a
church auxiliary concept. In Protestant seminaries and church-
related colleges, women's caucuses have been formed and
women's studies programs have been demanded and sometimes
begun. Leader of these programs is the women's project of the
Boston Theological Institute, made up of the seven seminaries
in the Boston area. Most of the major religious publishing
houses have published one or more feminist books, such as
Augsburg's *After Eve* by Alan Graebner, Abingdon's *The New
Eve* by Kathleen Neill Nyberg, and Beacon's anthology *Voices
of the New Feminism* edited by Mary Lou Thompson. A new
militancy among some Catholic nuns led to the organization of
the National Coalition of American Nuns; and feminist Catholic theological writers have emerged, such as Sidney Cornelia
Callahan, Rosemary Radford Ruether, and most notably, Mary
Daly.

   The three main foci of the Christian feminists have been the
theological and doctrinal interpretation of women, the ordination of women to the ministry, and the status and role of
women in the churches. On the point of theological assumption,
the ideas opposed by the theological feminists are:

   —that God is male
   —that woman's subordination to man is divinely ordained
   —that woman by nature is either ''evil'' or ''pure'' as
symbolically incarnated in Eve and Mary
   —that ''God's plan'' for women was revealed through St.
Paul.[52]

The feminists see the ordination of women as centrally important both practically and symbolically, for it is the ordained clergy that interprets scripture and tradition, determines church policy, and furnishes leadership in the parish and the church hierarchies. Currently, the Roman Catholic Church does not ordain women; and although thirty of the thirty-three major Protestant and Orthodox denominations do allow ordination, women ministers account for only a fraction of a percent of the total clergy. If more women were ordained, it would symbolically acknowledge that women are equal to men in leadership, policy-making, and interpretation of the faith; and it would at the practical level elevate women to the role where authority in the church lies.[53]

The third focus of the Christian feminists, on the general status and role of women in churches, has led to objections both to how women are professionally employed by the churches and to the modes of participation available to women among the faithful in the parish and the church hierarchies. In national and area church boards and agencies, the percentages of women holding executive positions are equivalently lower, and the discrepancies between salaries paid to female and male professionals are equivalently greater, than for their secular counterparts. The paid local church work most available to women includes positions such as education director, music director, or church secretary—areas of employment stereotypically feminine and often offering little opportunity for advancement.[54] The lay woman church volunteer is most often assigned to children's work, the flower committee, or the hospitality committee, while church councils and executive boards from the parish to the national level are dominated by men. These are the distinctions and stereotypes with which the religious feminists are taking issue.

This religious feminism falls largely under the feminist heading. For the most part, the theological rethinking has thus far concerned itself with identification of the doctrinal and historical underpinnings of religious discrimination against women, which is a necessary task for a starting point, and the model used for how standard humanity ought to be considered and treated is the model of man. A new theological model for humanity has only begun to be asserted by religious feminists. Its possibilities are suggested at times by Mary Daly, a Boston

College theologian, Peggy Way, a nationally prominent
United Church of Christ minister and feminist, and the writers
of the working papers of the 1970 National Conference on the
Role of Women in Theological Education. Such a new theological model might move in the direction of the androgynous
paradigm. The manner and rhetoric used to confront the practical issues of ordination of women and participation of women
in religious institutions is almost entirely masculine-equalitarian. The fact of ordination as the route to leadership in the
church is the historical male religious model, and a call for participation in a full range of existing masculine-originated institutional structures is essentially the basis for equality that these
women demand. An interesting exception was the decision in
1969 of the Woman's Division of the United Methodist Board
of Missions, a rich and powerful unit of that denomination, to
be self-consciously separatist rather than to merge with its
"parent" board in the general church. This group of moderate,
often tradition-oriented women made a feminist commitment
and decision that falls under the women's liberationist heading.

One example of the religious feminist literature is *The
Church and the Second Sex* by Mary Daly, published in 1968.
Daly takes seriously the attacks on the Roman Catholic Church
made by the French atheistic existentialist Simone de Beauvoir
in *The Second Sex*. The five points of de Beauvoir's attack as
Daly reports them are: the Christian religion has served as a
device for the oppression of women, church doctrine conveys
the notion that women are naturally inferior, Christian antifeminism is rooted in a notion of antisexuality, woman's exclusion from the church hierarchy implies her exclusion from
any kind of authority, and women find a sense of transcendence
through religion.[55]

Daly, a devout Roman Catholic theologian, sees de Beauvoir's attack as the opening of a dialogue through which the
Christian can realize both the truth about the church's position
on women and the hopefulness about the possibilities for
women within Christianity. She roots her case for Christian
feminism in the record of contradictions within Christian history. The biblical writers were cultural products of ancient
times, when the lot of women was indeed subservient, and bib-

lical exegetes through the ages have used the role of Eve as temptress in the Fall to assign women to a place of moral and intellectual inferiority in the universe. Daly points out that even the biblical record in Genesis provides a contradiction. While the earlier creation story found in Genesis 2, known to biblical scholars as the J document, has been emphasized with its account of Eve's creation from Adam's rib, the later creation story, the P document in Genesis 1, has a very different stress:

> The later creation story gives no hint that woman was brought into being as an afterthought. On the contrary, it stresses an original sexual duality and describes God's act of giving dominion to both. The plural is used, indicating their common authority to rule: "And God said, Let us make mankind in our image and likeness, and let them have dominion . . ." (Gen. I:26). The following verse says: "God created man in his image. In the image of God he created him. Male and female he created them" (Gen. I:27). This is understood by exegetes to mean that the image of God is in the human person, whether man or woman.[56]

Likewise, the New Testament provides contradictory evidence on the understanding of women. The Pauline texts are most often invoked to show the subordination of women, including the well-known passage from Ephesians (5:22-24): "Wives, be subject to your husbands, as to the Lord. For the husband is the head of the wife as Christ is the head of the Church, his body, and is himself its Saviour. As the Church is subject to Christ, so let wives also be subject in everything to their husbands." But even in Paul's writings, the basis for the dominant-subordinate hierarchy is broken (Gal. 3:27-28):[57] "For as many of you as were baptized into Christ have put on Christ. There is neither Jew nor Greek, there is neither slave nor free, there is neither male nor female; for you are all one in Christ Jesus."[57]

Daly notes further that biblical antifeminism does not occur in the words and actions of Jesus but that Jesus frequently departed from the custom of his times in treating women as respected persons.[58] In analyzing subsequent ecclesiastical and theological history, Daly sees the most important contradiction

as between the church's and the theologians' definition of
women as inferior and the ultimate message of Christianity that
all human beings have "equal dignity and rights."[59]

Daly is hopeful that "winds of change" in the church since
Vatican II and the vitalization of the ecumenical movement will
bring about a new understanding of women. She cites Pope
John's statement in the encyclical, *Pacem in Terris*: "Since
women are becoming ever more conscious of their human dignity, they will not tolerate being treated as mere material instru-
ments, but demand rights befitting a human person both in
domestic and in public life." There is a new equalitarian spirit
in Catholic journalism, among Catholic priests and bishops
who press for the right of women to serve in the Mass, among
Catholic priests and couples who take a public stand in favor of
using artificial contraception to limit family size and thereby
free women from unwanted maternity, and particularly among
nuns who demand to hold authority in their own order and who
are rapidly developing new forms of understanding Christian
obedience and practice in their religious vocations.[60] What must
come next, according to Daly, is the ordination of women to the
priesthood, a new role of authority for the nun, and coeducation at all levels in religious education.

Daly proposes that one set of theological ideas about women
be exorcised and a constructive new set of viewpoints be
adopted. The old concepts to be rid of are: the idea of the
Eternal Feminine, the notion of God's plan for women, and the
conception of Mary as the model. The Eternal Feminine is a
view of a static nature of all women:

> The characteristics of the Eternal Woman are opposed to
> those of a developing, authentic person, who will be unique,
> self-critical, self-creating, active and searching. By contrast
> to these authentic personal qualities, the Eternal Woman is
> said to have a vocation to surrender and hiddenness; hence
> the symbol of the veil. Self-less, she achieves not individual
> realization but merely generic fulfilment in motherhood,
> physical or spiritual (the wife is always a "mother to her
> husband" as well as to her children). She is said to be timeless
> and conservative by nature. She is shrouded in "mystery,"
> because she is not recognized as a genuine human person . . .

It is, of course, the "symbol" of woman that these authors are talking about, but the symbol turns out to be normative for the individual . . . The androcentric society which engenders this type of speculation tends to see men, but not women, in personalist rather than in static, symbolic categories.[61]

"God's plan" for women to be subject to men's authority and to be circumscribed by nature for motherhood is propagated by those who would invoke divine sanction for the system that locks women into patterns of subordination. Its use is typified by the priest who wrote: "Lest we forget, let it be repeated here once more: Woman's true sphere is within the family circle. He who would substitute anything else, frustrates here true nature, disrupts the providential plan of God and creates serious problems for society at large, which becomes filled with neurotic, unhappy, useless and very often, and worst of all, disruptive women."[62] The view of Mary as model challenges all women to see the virgin purity of Mary, the centrality of her motherhood, and her worship of her male child as their own model for their lives.[63]

New avenues for theology, Daly suggests, include an affirmation of the evolutionary process of ideology, specifically making possible new and changing definitions of women in the modern world. Important in theology is the very definition of God, for most of theology attributes a male personality to God, in spite of affirmations that God is a transcendent reality beyond gender. Finally, the understanding of an open revelation must supersede a static world view, making clear that openness to present experience is as valid a route to theological understanding as is reference to the past for both experience and conceptualizations.[64]

Ecclesiastically, Daly's proposals are masculine-equalitarian. She makes her analysis of the church's history and her recommendations for change in church thought and lines of authority to the end of giving women the same considerations and chances that men have. However, in discussing the possibilities for theological reflection on the nature of God and the nature of revelation, she opens the door to a kind of scholarship and piety that could be androgynous. A few years later, in her 1973 book *Beyond God the Father,* Daly moves even closer to the androgynous position.

The anthology *Women's Liberation and the Church: The New Demand for Freedom in the Life of the Christian Church,* which contains essays by Protestant and Catholic feminist writers, further documents themes of contemporary feminism in a religious perspective. Its thesis is that liberation, the freeing of the spirit, is the core of the Christian gospel from New Testament times; and that a paradox of the faith is that women have not become full participants in the free humanity within the church which the church proclaims.[65] Davida Foy Crabtree notes the influence of church tradition on the contemporary viewpoint that woman is "an aesthetically-minded, child-centered individual who has no talent for or interest in ordained ministry, administration, or policy-making positions." She calls on the church to abandon those conceptualizations of woman as sex object, manifested in Eve, and as holy mother, manifested in Mary, and to return to "the fundamental ground of the Gospel" that would "set free those life-giving values which are chained to woman's pedestal."[66] Using a Marxian analysis, Rosemary Radford Ruether criticizes the church on the same point of having lost its own roots as a source of liberation:

> Christian culture took over and absorbed the classical view of man and its myth of salvation, and so molded its social institutions accordingly that it now finds itself the foe of the new culture-bearers of its own original tradition. This is nowhere more true than in the social structure and culture of that group which is most closely associated with the church: the clergy. They appear as almost the last bastion of the "old Humanity" where anti-feminine, anti-bodily patriarchalism still reigns. This means that the church can only recover its own original gospel of the New Creation of the resurrected body by dying to a culture and social structure with which it has most deeply identified itself.[67]

Sidney Cornelia Callahan describes the personal quest of a devout Catholic woman to be both mother and career woman, affirming this as an active possibility for women, while at the *her her has diff. views*

same time holding to a traditional Catholic opposition to artificial contraception and abortion. Several of the writers encourage women to go to seminary and to become ordained
ministers. Peggy Way provides a theological grounding for her
ministry as a woman, arguing that neither Scriptures, church
history, nor denominational sanction are the authority for her
ministry, but that she is authorized in Christ and by the persons
to whom she ministers.[68]

The anthology contains rich appendices of ecclesiastical
documents about women from denominational groups and
theological conferences. One report surveys the low level of
women's representation in official deliberations of the National
Council of Churches and calls on the council for full participation by women. Another documents the small number of
women employed as denominational executives and the discrepancy between salaries of men and women. Still another
shows sex-role stereotyping in nursery church school literature.
One collates studies of ministers' wives in a number of
countries, showing from William Douglas' study in the United
States that ministers' wives cannot be automatically stereotyped.

Although religious feminism is essentially masculine-equalitarian in its attention to breaking a feminine stereotype and to
gaining for women an equal participation with men in church
structures, it contains an element of the androgynous position.
Examples are Peggy Way's quest for a new kind of authority
for the female minister, and Mary Daly's suggestion that a new
theological formulation of a doctrine of humanity and a doctrine of God must be made.

Feminist Fiction

Alix Kates Shulman is well known in feminist circles for her
much-publicized marriage contract with her husband in which
the couple divides equally housekeeping and child care responsibility, a contract that provides a model of possibility for
family life in the androgynous paradigm. She is a member of
Redstockings, a radical feminist group in New York. Since her
first publication in 1969 of a piece of fiction in *Aphra*, the
feminist literary journal, she has published a biography of

Emma Goldman, edited an edition of Emma Goldman's works, and published three children's books. Her 1972 novel, *Memoirs of an Ex-Prom Queen,* is explicitly a women's liberation piece of fiction.

The novel is a documentary of the female life of the heroine, Sasha Davis, from puberty past age thirty. On the night that Sasha is crowned queen of the prom, she "goes all the way" with her steady boyfriend, Joey, the athletic hero who has been "dry humping" her for months. As a teenager, she discovers her "joy button" and practices pleasure with herself in the darkness of her bedroom before her parents come up to bed. At the same time, she has an insatiable quest for knowledge and a private drive to "be somebody" and silently determines to be a lawyer, not telling the sisters in the sorority whose singular ambition is to make it with a boy. She learns early that she is beautiful, and from her parents and her sorority sisters she is made aware that this is the sole asset a woman has, though it is a divisive asset among women. In high school she goes away to a college weekend and has sexual relationships with a college man in the attic of his fraternity house, only to discover in subsequent weeks that he is in love with another girl. She runs away from home to take a job as a resort waitress, where she is nearly forced to have an affair with one of the chefs to keep her job, and where she becomes friends with an aged millionaire who years later in New York invites her to his home, gives her an etching, and tries to seduce her. In college she falls in love with philosophy, only to entice the philosophy professor into an extended affair in her off-campus apartment. The affair ends when the professor's wife appears in the apartment and confronts Sasha with a brittle, calculated outline of how the professor's several affairs with students can affect his professional future and his children.

In graduate school at Columbia, Sasha is appalled to find that the female graduate student has no status with her male colleagues. She very deliberately and analytically contracts a marriage with an illustrious graduate student in another department. They agree to take turns going to graduate school, but when he gets a prestigious fellowship, she drops out of school permanently and works at clerical jobs to support them.

During a fellowship year for him in Germany, she leaves him and travels alone over Europe, having a series of affairs with men she picks up along the way, and contracting venereal disease from one lover in Spain. By this time, she is keeping a coded list of her affairs and has begun to feel that her beauty is fading, that she is looking old, the terrible fate of the woman in her twenties. She is obsessed with the impending doom of age thirty, when she believes any possibility of her own vitality will be ended. Upon returning to New York, she begins an affair that is for the first time based on intense romantic love. She divorces her husband, becomes pregnant, and has an illegal abortion, after which she marries, this time for love and in anticipation of children. The marriage is a glorious romance until the children come, at which time she throws herself into motherhood with a total commitment to what must be the most splendid babies who were ever born; but the marriage becomes strained and empty as she no longer has time for leisurely lovemaking or exciting companionship because of the children. At the end of the novel, she has her long romantic hair cut back to the short style she wore as prom queen; her husband perceives this as a rejection of him; and she turns away from him to telephone her divorced college friend, who has struggled and made a life of her own for herself and her child.[69]

The thesis of this novel is clear: women are trapped by the cultural expectation that above all they be beautiful sex objects. The companion piece to the novel could well be Philip Roth's *Portnoy's Complaint,* which catalogues the sexual activities of Portnoy in his emergence from boyhood to manhood. Alix Shulman does precisely the same thing for the girl in *Memoirs of an Ex-Prom Queen.* Neither Alexander Portnoy nor Sasha Davis achieves a satisfactory adult identity, for the primary interest in both books is frankly sexual activity. Both books are in fact high class pornography.

Memoirs of an Ex-Prom Queen is written from the feminist perspective in the same fashion as is *The Feminine Mystique.* It presents the problem of women's identity in terms with which no feminist would argue. Its literary mode is in the mainstream of contemporary American fiction, of such male writers as Norman Mailer and Philip Roth, with the description of sexual exploits as the central narrative device. Therefore, Alix Shulman is writing about women as men write about men. She is giving men a taste of their own medicine on women's behalf. In the process, however, her achievement is to make women equal to men, to deal with women's sexuality on the same terms as male writers have dealt with male sexuality.

sum

The feminist ideology holds that women should be equal to men. It starts with a belief that women have been stereotyped as centrally sexual and relational, while men have been allowed to be autonomous individuals. The stereotype of women has tied them to the home for their primary identity, while men have realized their identity in public performance, especially in the choice and development of a vocation. Proponents of feminist ideology want to achieve for women the same kinds of choices and opportunities that men have had, particularly in participation in politics, which leads to decision-making for the society, and in vocation, which leads to contribution to the society and to fulfillment for the individual.

Historically, the feminist ideology informed the nineteenth-century women's rights movement, which in the twentieth century led to the achievement of woman suffrage. In the more recent rise of the new feminism, this ideology shaped the beginning of a new feminist consciousness, typified by Betty Friedan's attack on the "feminine mystique," which became the social understanding of a whole new generation of feminists. It is the ideology that brought together disparate advocates to seek the passage of a comprehensive Equal Rights Amendment aimed at abolishing all legal distinctions between men and women. It is a model that says men and women are of the same humanity, hence the treatment of them should be the same.

3

The Women's Liberationist Perspective: Women Over Against Men

The women's liberationist paradigm is a model of women over against men or women separate from men. On the one hand, it celebrates women and affirms whatever women feel and think and do. This is its prowoman dimension. On the other hand, it is antimasculinist, against things male-derived and sometimes against males themselves. Its primary focus for change is social. Its strategy is conflict. The source of its standard for a new social order is in women themselves.

The women's liberationist position has several levels of expression. One is an overt female separatist viewpoint, which calls for women to isolate themselves from men in order to come to terms with what it means to be female and at times to assert female dominance in the society. For some, this separatism is seen as temporary, to gain a strength of female identity and a sense of female solidarity, "sisterhood," which will be a basis of power when women later interact with men individually and collectively. For others, separatism simply means "women only" meetings for consciousness-raising and for developing political strategies without allowing male participation in the decisions about what their feminism is or how it will be expressed. At the other extreme of the women's liberationist position is vehement man-hating with the personal rejection of men.

Another expression of women's liberation makes a social analysis of women in terms of class structure. This is usually done from a socialist perspective; and while it does not always embody a man-hating attitude, it is antimasculinist in that it pits women against men in a class struggle wherein women as a group are perceived as equivalent to an oppressed class in the historical context of the dominant male class controlling property under capitalism. One faction, the feminist radicals, defines women as caught up with other oppressed groups in the economic class structure, while another significant segment, the radical feminists, maintains that women are a separate sexual class; but both groups see men as the originators of the class structure.

Women's liberationism encompasses recently felt and explosive female rage. The majority of its most explicit exponents are younger women in their twenties who made up the core of the original women's liberation movement, which began in 1967 and 1968 as a distinct part of the broad movement of contemporary feminism. Yet today its beliefs are part of the total ideology of thousands of new-found feminists in America.

It is likely that this rage, this attack on things male, and this aspiration for the unity of women in sisterhood were felt by early feminists in the nineteenth and early twentieth centuries, but the Victorian age was not a time when such bold rejection of men, their creations and ideas, could be dared. Victoria Woodhull threatened women's secession from male life to gain political equality in her "Great Secession" speech at the convention of the National Woman Suffrage Association in 1871; and Susan B. Anthony, that forger of so much egalitarian thought and effort, was at times put out by the amount of time given by her cosuffragists to husbands and their desires. In an attack on marriage laws, in 1860 she sounded very much like today's women's liberationists when they make the same attack.

> Marriage has ever been a one-sided matter, resting most unequally upon the sexes. By it, man gains all—woman loses all; tyrant law and lust reign supreme with him—meek submission and ready obedience alone befit her. Woman has never been consulted . . . By law, public sentiment and religion, from the times of Moses down to the present day, woman has never been thought of other than as a piece of property, to be disposed of at the will and pleasure of man

. . . she has no voice whatever in saying what shall be the basis of the relation. She must accept marriage as man proffers it, or not at all.[1]

Sexual Politics

Kate Millett provided one ideological framework for the women's movement with the 1970 publication of her book *Sexual Politics*. She asserts that women are a collectivity equivalent to a social class in Western society, that patriarchy has been the class ordering principle that designates men as the master class and women as the subordinate class. Her term "sexual politics" indicates the real power men hold over women, a phallic ascendency deemed in the social order to be synonymous with superiority. Because sexual intercourse in Western culture is regarded as male mastery of female receptivity, coitus becomes a "charged microcosm"[2] of the beliefs and values of the culture. Politics, for Millett, is the way in which power relationships are structured; and she sees sexual politics as the historical and present exercise of power by men as a group over women as a group. Declaring that there is a political significance in the divisions of society into classes, castes, races, and sexes, she says that women, like races, are a collectivity by birth. Male political dominance is laid down by the cultural ordinance of patriarchy:

> A disinterested examination of our system of sexual relationship must point out that the situation between sexes now, and throughout history, is a case of that phenomenon Max Weber defined as *herrschaft*, a relationship of dominance and subordinance. What goes largely unexamined . . . is the birthright priority whereby males rule females. Through this system a most ingenious form of "interior colonization" has been achieved. It is one which tends moreover to be sturdier than any form of segregation, and more rigorous than any class stratification, more uniform, certainly more enduring. However muted its present appearance may be, sexual dominion obtains nevertheless as perhaps the most pervasive ideology of our culture and provides its most fundamental concept of power.
>
> This is because our society, like all other historical civilizations, is a patriarchy. The fact is evident at once if one recalls

that the military, industry, technology, universities, science, political office, and finance—in short, every avenue of power within the society, including the coercive force of the police, is entirely in male hands. As the essence of politics is power, such realization cannot fail to carry impact.[3]

Millett calls her theory of sexual politics "notes toward a theory of patriarchy." Developing the core of her theory, she provides ideological, biological, sociological, class, economic, educational, anthropological, and psychological evidence for patriarchy as being the governing archetype in Western society, the model and practice for ordering society by which women are rendered subordinate, segregated, and powerless. At the ideological level, patriarchy assigns sexual distinctions in the socialization process to temperament, status, and role. Males, assuming higher status, are encouraged to develop temperament—"aggression, intelligence, force, and efficacy"—which sustains mastery for them. Women's role tends to arrest them at the level of biological experience. Under patriarchy the argument is maintained that men's heavier muscle structure makes them stronger than women and therefore superior. To extend this notion, men are encouraged more than women to maintain their physical bodies through diet and exercise. Yet, Millett argues, individual physical prowess counts for little in societies where technology, weaponry, and intelligence are the basis for exercising political power; and it is the class of people at the bottom of the social scale who presently have to perform the more rigorous physical work, whatever their personal strength. The structure of power is far more a class division than a biological one.[4]

Millett discredits the lack of distinction between sexual and gender characteristics in our culture. Sexual attributes are biological and given, while gender determination is social: "Psychosexual personality is . . . postnatal and learned . . . Because of our social circumstances, male and female are really two cultures and their life experiences are utterly different—and this is crucial. Implicit in all the gender identity development which takes place through childhood is the sum total of the parents', the peers', and the culture's notions of what is appropriate to each gender by way of temperament, character, interests, status, worth, gesture, and expression.[5]

Sociologically, Millett sees the family, together with the legal and religious sanctions of the family, as not only the microcosm of the patriarchy that is society, but also the primary social unit that fosters and carries out patriarchy. That the father is head of the family is the principle assumed in both the family name and kinship lines, in the legal codes for census, property, and taxation, and in the religious assumptions of male preeminence. In spite of the modifications of law regarding women's rights, under patriarchy marriage and kinship remain in the feudal tradition as a kind of property right for the man: "patriarchy decrees that the status of both child and mother is primarily or ultimately dependent upon the male. And since it is not only his social status, but even his economic power upon which his dependents generally rely, the position of the masculine figure within the family—as without—is materially, as well as ideologically, extremely strong."[6]

Regarding class, Millett thinks that men belong to a "caste of virility."[7] In the middle and upper classes, men have more real power derived from social status, while in the lower class, mere women work at production so that status based on production has to be shared with women. Thus, sexual status becomes the dominant claim to authority among men of the lower class. Yet across class lines the "caste of virility" makes men ascendant and powerful even over educated and socially prominent women. The "machismo" of the lower class man gives him power even over the upper class woman, whose status is after all derived from that of her husband and father.

Woman's work under patriarchy is predominantly effort for which she is not paid, and in the instances where she is employed, she is paid much less than men. In a capitalist society, where status is based largely on income, this is a very significant factor. It means that just as woman's social position is derivative from her relationship with males, so is her economic standing. Similarly in education, in a society that is based on industry and technology, women are instructed to use the machines (refrigerators, automobiles) that men build, but not to construct or repair them.

Under patriarchy, force is in the hands of males; and females are socialized to remain passive in the face of it. Millett believes that the use of violence and coercion under legal sanction and in social interaction is in direct relation to male sexual self-understanding. Rape is understood as an affront by one man against another, with the assailant attacking the other man's woman. Feelings of cruelty, evil, and mastery are associated with sex—the man "taking" the woman sexually. Sexual humor in pornography and more recently in the literature of high culture makes this clear.[8]

Millett groups all ideas about myth and religion under the heading of anthropology. In this category, she focuses on the myth of feminine evil from primitive and religious sources. Menstruation makes the woman taboo. The female's genitals are some kind of wound or defect. Pandora opening her box (her vulva) drives man to his death. Eve is the primordial temptress, the source for sin and evil in the world. Such is patriarchy's justification for subordinating women: they are mythically responsible, through their sexuality, for bringing sin into the world.[9]

Psychologically, women are made more sex objects than persons:

> When in any group of persons, the ego is subjected to such invidious versions of itself through social beliefs, ideology, and tradition, the effect is bound to be pernicious. This coupled with the persistent though frequently subtle denigration women encounter daily through personal contacts, the impressions gathered from the images and media about them, and the discrimination in matters of behavior, employment, and education which they endure, should make it no very special cause for surprise that women develop group characteristics common to those who suffer minority status and a marginal existence.[10]

Millett develops her theory of sexual politics in the context of literature and intellectual history. She shows that the novels of D. H. Lawrence, Henry Miller, and Norman Mailer reveal the cultural belief that the power of sexual mastery of men over women is the central symbol of political dominance and subordination. By contrast, the literary works of Jean Genet question this belief by showing the powerlessness of the male homosexual, the queen, who deliberately but artificially takes on the role of woman. As Genet says in *The Balcony,* the recreation of manipulation, role-playing, mutilation, and violence will continue in an endless cycle if woman does not cease to play whore and mascot to man's role as general, bishop, and king.

Millett thinks with Engels that a central point of the sexual revolution must be to forsake the monogamous family:

> There is one more cardinal point in Engels' theory of sexual revolution . . . 'With the transformation of the means of production into collective property, the monogamous family will cease to be the economic unit of society. *The care and education of children becomes a public matter'* . . . There is something logical and even inevitable in this recommendation, for so long as every female simply by virtue of her anatomy, is obliged, even forced to be the sole or primary caretaker of childhood, she is prevented from being a free human being. The care of children, even from the period when their cognitive powers first emerge, is infinitely better left to the best trained practitioners of both sexes who have chosen it as a vocation . . . The radical outcome of Engels' analysis is that the family, as that term is presently understood, must go.[11]

Millett offers a hopeful postscript on the possibility of nonviolent revolution led by a coalition of blacks, youth, women, and the poor who have recently become aware of their oppression and can unite to reject the power of the caste of violence and virility. Such a revolution would discard sex, race, and economic class as bases for power.

Millett's analysis of patriarchy falls under the women's liberationist rubric. She sees women as over against men as a group in society. Power and authority are held by men, and women are the subjects of that authority. Women have to unite as women to throw off the power of sexual politics.

Important to her theory are her labels for what sociologists call "social stratification," yet unfortunately she is not precise in her use of the language of caste and class. Karl Marx gave Western society the impetus for making a sociological analysis

on the basis of social class, and his definition of class rested on
the social group's relation to economic production. Later sociologists have modified the Marxian definition of class to include political and social levels of honor as well as economic
status. Caste is a status group into which one is born and from
which there is no escape by education or skill or political or
economic advancement; it is usually sanctioned theologically or
ideologically.[12] In *Sexual Politics,* Millett clearly designates
women as a status group apart from men. She avoids calling
them a "class," saying that women's position is more invidious
than class distinction, although at many points in her analysis
she is talking about "women as a class" in a Marxian sense. In
other places, however, she speaks of men as the "caste of virility," which would make women the lower caste. She also speaks
of women as being born into their social position, which would
suggest caste. Perhaps she needs another word, maybe the one
Juliett Mitchell used for a similar concept, women's "estate."

The Dialectic of Sex
Shulamith Firestone is one of the most profound theorists to
come out of the Women's Liberation Movement. In *The Dialectic of Sex,* also published in 1970, she offers an analysis of
society and the ideas that shape it which is the most comprehensive yet done with a feminist intention, and her program for a
feminist revolution is all-encompassing.

Firestone begins with Marx and Engels, saying that the shape
of a feminist revolution must be socialist, but she argues that
conventional dialectical materialism does not go far enough.
What now must be obliterated is the class distinction based on
sex itself. Marx and Engels failed to perceive that the most per-
verse of class systems is based not on production but on reproduction, the classes of male and female rooted in biology and
legitimated throughout history. Now for the first time in history
we are advanced enough technologically to abolish that original
biologically determined class system which has always been with
us. Just as the seizure of means of production would eliminate
economic classes, the gaining of control over means of reproduction would eradicate sexual classes.[13]

Like Marx and Engels, Freud did not go far enough, accord-

*one of the
reasons
the G's
movement
is often
supportive of
even abortion*

ing to Firestone. He provided a valuable understanding of human motivation and human relationships, particularly in his recognition of the Oedipus complex and the Electra complex, but he did not adequately understand the source of these childhood identifications with the mother. Firestone claims that the Oedipus complex, the young boy's wish to take the mother sexually and to kill the father, can be appreciated only in terms of power. In the patriarchal nuclear family, it is the mother who cares for the young boy and is close to him emotionally, and he is primarily attached to her. As he grows older, he begins to be told to "act like a man," and he realizes the difference between the world of the man and his mother. His mother is oppressed by the man, powerless, and his identification with his mother is a recognition of his own, the child's, oppression or powerlessness with her. In the same way, the girl child is first homosexual or identified with the mother, then moves to a seductiveness of the father, the Electra phase. Firestone explains this too as a realization of power. The girl child knows that power is with the man and moves to attempt to participate in that power.[14]

Firestone writes that racism is sexism extended. The black and white polarity is an extension of the nuclear family in the family of man, with the white man as father, the white woman as dependent wife and mother, the blacks as children who are considered property.[15]

Under the present patriarchy, children are segregated and oppressed as a separate category of people. Their humanity is not recognized in the stratification of family and education. They too should be able to express themselves sexually and to make decisions that shape their lives and form society. Childhood as it now exists is captivity without power.

Love and romance have been used to designate women's inferiority. Never have we come to terms as a culture with the full potential of love. Instead, women have been taught to be preoccupied with love, which has operated as a force to keep women dealing in mystical and idealizing terms with what is actually men's power to control women as an inferior class.[16]

The tyranny of our cultural history has divided achievement into male and female modes. Men have become masters of science and technology, the technological mode, while the feminine has been expressed in the aesthetic mode. Yet the male has dictated what is appropriate in the aesthetic mode. For example, in the history of painting, it has developed that pictures of the female nude body are considered highly aesthetic and "the nude" as a high art form has become synonymous with the female body, while the occasional painting of the male nude is the exception. The technological mode is ascendant in our culture, and women by training and acculturation are excluded from it. But it is a warped mode, soulless. For culture to be complete, a merging of the aesthetic and the technological modes will be necessary. An antecedent of this possibility is the art of the film, where science and its products are made to work for beauty.[17]

Firestone's program for achieving the feminist revolution includes abandoning the nuclear family, reproducing artificially, and developing what she calls cybernated socialism for the social order. Reforms in the family are unworkable for effecting a true feminist revolution and for finally destroying the historical biological class system. Rather, complete new forms of corporate life must be shaped to liberate women and children from their oppression. A pluralism of plans for people's living arrangements should be designed. She proposes three: single professions, living together, and households. Single professions are already familiar—the choice of individuals to live alone and singularly pursue a profession. The second, living together, is also already known, that is, the commitment of a couple of different or like sex to live together for sexual relations and companionship without need of a legal or socially sanctioned contract. The third, households, would be a new kind of contractual arrangement by which a group of people, perhaps ten, of all ages and both sexes, would agree to live together and share their lives for a specific period of time, after which they would make a new contract with each other, a new group, or a mixture of old and new people. Children as well as adults could contract in and out of households. This would be the unit into which babies would be brought, but as soon as children wanted to decide with whom to live, they could do so.[18]

In the new society, reproduction would be artificial. Firestone believes that birth control is imperative on today's planet. She also believes that pregnancy and childbirth are barbaric and are a major source of the demeaning of women. It is possible, she argues, to produce children artificially; and this should be the means of getting children under the new cybernated socialism. If persons in households wanted to have babies naturally for the experience, they could do so; but all adults in households would have responsibility for all the immature members, so that relationships based on biology would no longer have any meaning.

Full and creative use of cybernation would minimize the need for work and give all persons more time to play, freeing people to do what they wanted. This means that education could take place much faster, with adults and children participating in learning together and discovering what they needed to know. Household chores and public chores could be reduced enormously by the work of machines. Firestone does not, however, indicate who will tend and repair the machines. She draws a utopian conclusion that the feminist revolution could be the key to a new "ecological balance" in which the economy, the family, "work," and "play" would be redefined for a new humanity for all.[19]

To the extent that Firestone's analysis of the causes, variety, and extent of sexism in society is made in class terms, her position is clearly in the women's liberationist paradigm. However, her analysis of women's life as in the aesthetic mode and men's life as in the technological mode, and her hope for the future merger of the two, anticipates the androgynous position.

Although Firestone is a brilliant and discerning theorist of the new feminism, to whom attention should be paid, her program for the future leaves much to be desired. In her enthusiasm for turning over work and childbearing to machine technology, she risks turning humans into machines. And in her opposition to the nuclear family, she fails to provide a stabilizing public norm for the identity of her pluralism of families.

Critique

The Class Analysis

Fundamental to the feminism of the women's liberationist view is a social analysis of women in class terms. There is no precise agreement on what the class status of women means among the women's liberationists, and there are at least two ways of defining what the class of women is. Further, the terms "class" and "caste" are used much more frequently than they are defined in discussion and writing about the separateness of women and men.

The basic difference between the two kinds of class analysis in women's liberation reflects the two branches of radicalism in the movement, feminist radicalism and radical feminism. Essentially, the feminist radicals see women's oppression as equivalent to the class oppression of poor and colored and Third World peoples and expect women to be liberated when the capitalistic economic system, with its exploitation of women as workers in the factory and home, is overthrown. The radical feminists, in contrast, see the sexual dichotomy as being the fundamental class structure that keeps women down, despite the other class structures. Kate Millett's *Sexual Politics* and Shulamith Firestone's *The Dialectic of Sex* are both written from the radical feminist perspective. There exist some other fairly pure expressions of these two feminist class analyses, as well as a wide variety of mixtures of these views.

A germinative essay for feminist radicalism was "Bread and Roses" by Kathy McAfee and Myrna Wood, published in 1969. In this article, the writers justify a priority for women's liberation in radical politics, in the then existing New Left. They do not define women as a separate class, but point out that women are peculiarly victimized in the economic class structure, by a number of factors:

(1) Male Chauvinism—the attitude that women are the passive and inferior servants of society and of men—set women apart from the rest of the working class . . .

(2) Women are further exploited in their roles as housewives and mothers, through which they reduce the costs (social and economic) of maintaining the labor force . . .

(3) Working class women and other women as well are exploited as consumers . . .

(4) All women, too, are oppressed and exploited sexually . . . A woman of any class is expected to sell herself—not just her body but her entire life, her talents, interests, and dreams—to a man. She is expected to give up friendships, ambitions, pleasures, and moments of time to herself in order to serve his career or his family. In return, she receives not only her livelihood but her identity, her very right to existence,

for unless she is the wife of someone or the mother of some-one, a woman is nothing.[20]

McAfee and Wood advocate a union of women's liberation with a worker's revolution, adding: "The importance of a working class women's liberation movement goes beyond the need for unity. A liberation movement of the 'slaves of the slave' tends to raise broader issues of people's oppression in all its forms."[21]

Writing of "Double Jeopardy: To Be Black and Female," Frances Beale is neither precisely Marxist nor precisely radical feminist, but she does indicate that she sees black women as being especially subjugated by the class system: "the Black woman in America can justly be described as a 'slave of a slave.' "[22] She understands that black men have been oppressed and brutalized too, but black women are not to be blamed for that oppression. Rather, "The capitalist system found it expedient to enslave and oppress them and proceeded to do so without consultation or the signing of any agreements with Black women."[23]

Black women have been economically exploited, Beale charges, as well as misused for research under the name of "birth control." Black women live under the same exploitative economic system that white women live under, so they have much in common. However, black women cannot be a part of a movement that sees the struggle as simply against male chauvinism: "Any white group that does not have an anti-imperialist and anti-racist ideology has absolutely nothing in common with the Black Woman's struggle."[24]

Historical socialist theory is expanded significantly in Juliet Mitchell's "Women: The Longest Revolution." She finds in the treatment of women's role in the thought of Marx, Fourier, Engels, and Bebel a normative ideal of the emancipation of women, but this concept is merely "an adjunct to socialist theory, not structurally integrated into it." In her own class analysis of women, Mitchell compares the dependence of women on men to the worker's dependence on the capitalist. In other words, "within the world of men their [women's] position is comparable to that of an oppressed minority."[25]

This class analysis is prowoman and antimasculinist, fitting the women's liberationist concept. Mitchell's own solution, however, is masculine-equalitarian, falling under the feminist paradigm. She thinks traditional socialism has been in error in calling for the abolition of the bourgeois family. Instead, women must become more fully involved in production:

> The exclusion of women from production—social human activity—and their confinement to a monolithic condensation of functions—in a unity—the family—which is precisely unified in the natural part of each function, is the root cause of the contemporary social definition of women as *natural* beings. Hence the main thrust of any emancipation movement must still concentrate on the economic element—the entry of women fully into public industry . . . Economically, the most elementary demand is not the right to work or receive equal pay for work—the two traditional reformist demands—but the right to equal work itself.[26]

Defense of a classical socialist approach drawn from Marx and Engels continues to be made in the new name of women's liberation. Evelyn Reed, taking issue with Ti-Grace Atkinson's position that women are a class and Roxanne Dunbar's position that women are a caste, seeks to interpret Marxism as a sufficient basis for the liberation of women: "What Marxists say is that we live under an international *class* system. And they further state that it will require not a caste war, but a *class struggle*—of all the oppressed, male and female alike—to consummate women's liberation along with the liberation of all the oppressed masses." Reed believes in orthodox Marxist terms that women's oppression originated in the development of a class society based on private property, the family, and the state. Prior to the development of capitalism, women and men were equal in sisterhood and brotherhood.[27]

Similarly in a book edited by Linda Jenness of the Socialist Workers Party, *Feminism and Socialism,* the conventional Marxist argument is made that it is the class system itself, created by capitalism, that oppresses women. In that book Betsy Stone writes:

> We believe that these problems stem from the capitalist

system, not the "Masculine Mystique." It is true that there are many ways in which sexist ideas are used to uphold the various evils of this system. But the problems go much deeper than the question of male chauvinist ideology. The reason we are oppressed as women, the reason we are discriminated against on the job, the reason we don't have free child care, is not because of the psychological traits of males, but because equal pay and free child care go against the interests of a capitalist, profit-oriented system. If we want to win our full liberation, we are going to have to oppose the political parties that perpetuate that system, and expose them for what they are—rotten, undemocratic, and unrepresentative of the needs of the American people.[28]

The feminist radicals, then, those feminists whose preference is to think about and work for women's liberation in the context of a spectrum of needs for liberation, view women as analogous to a class or as caught in the economic class system. This view is informed by classical socialism.

The radical feminists, who also often use social theory as a starting point, depart from the feminist radicals at the point of class analysis as well as on the point of the primacy of feminism. In one way or another, they suggest that women per se are a class.

The Redstockings Manifesto, a condensation of much radical feminist ideology, states: "Women are an oppressed class. Our oppression is total, affecting every facet of our lives. We are exploited as sex objects, breeders, domestic servants and cheap labor. We are considered inferior beings, whose only purpose is to enhance men's lives. Our humanity is denied. Our prescribed behavior is enforced by the threat of physical violence."[29]

An essay that was influential in shaping the idea of women as a class is Roxanne Dunbar's "Female Liberation As the Basis for Social Revolution." Dunbar was a founding member of Boston Female Liberation—Cell 16. She pushes the Marxist class analysis back to a more fundamental division by sex, in much the same way that Shulamith Firestone did: "The origin of caste (therefore class) was the subjugation of the female sex. The struggle against the basis of oppression is at a higher stage of revolution than the archaic strategy of the present radical analysis.''[30] Dunbar elaborates on the caste and class analysis in a paper written with Vernon Grizzard, "Caste and Class: The Key to Understanding Female Oppression":

> Why is it important to say that females constitute a lower caste? . . . A caste system establishes a definite place into which certain members of a society have no choice but to fit . . . . The clearest historical analogy of the caste status of females is African slavery in the ante-bellum South . . . Two patterns of dominance/subservience emerged in the ante-bellum Southern caste system, which are analogous to patterns of male-female relation in industrial societies. One pattern is the paternalistic one; the other is the exploitative pattern . . . Though the paternalistic pattern may seem less oppressive or exploitative for females, it is in actuality more insidious. The housewife remains tied by emotional bonds to a man, cut off from the more public world of work, and able to experience the outside world only through the man.[31]

The class designation of women also appears in local women's liberation statements about how women perceive themselves. Cataloguing the various kinds of resistances to consciousness-raising in women, Irene Peslikis of the New York Women's Liberation lists one resistance as "Thinking that male supremacy is only a psychological privilege with 'ego' benefits as opposed to a class privilege with sexual and economic benefits.''[32]

The class analysis was made from the beginning of the women's liberation movement. One of the papers written in 1968 that argued forcefuly for a separate women's movement and which was widely distributed was "Toward a Female Liberation Movement," by Judith Brown and Beverly Jones. The writers, originally members of the Gainesville, Florida, chapter of Students for a Democratic Society, sometimes speak of women as a class, sometimes as a caste. In dealing with marriage and motherhood, the older woman, Beverly Jones, states: "The relationship between a man and a woman is no more or less personal a relationship than is the relationship between a woman and her maid, a master and his slave, a teacher and his student. Of course, there are personal individual qualities to a particular relationship in any of these categories but they are so overshadowed by the class nature of the relationship, by the volume of class response as to be almost insignificant.'' And Judith Brown writes, ''We have emphasized the plight of the married woman in her relationship with a power-oriented representative of the master caste.'' She concludes, ''We have not conned ourselves into political paralysis as an excuse for inaction—we are a subjugated caste.''[33]

The most deliberate discussion of women as a class appears in the working papers of a New York group, The Feminists, originally called the October Seventeenth Movement, which was a radical break-off from the New York NOW. Through holding an ideology of leaderless organization, the group is strongly influenced by its founder, Ti-Grace Atkinson, who writes: ''the raison d'etre of all groups formed around the problem of women is that women are a class . . . some groups have been driven back from the position of *all* women to some proposed 'special' class such as 'poor' women and eventually concentrated more on economic class than sexual class. But if we're interested in women and how *qua* women are oppressed, this class must include *all* women.'' [34] Another paper from the Feminists states:

> Males originated class and have fostered terrible inequities in society through the oppression of one group by another; their justifications of these inequalities began when they first declassed women out of humanity. Thus, ''humanity'' or ''society'' in effect refers only to those individuals making up the male class—all men . . . The class of men is self-defining and well organized vis à vis its counterclass—the class of women.
> The class of women is a class defined by the class of men. Both classes together constitute all those individuals called human beings; since, in addition, this political division is the basic one in all societies, it is the *primary class system.*[35]

The groups of radical feminists who deliberately analyze women as a caste or class apparently mean the same thing by the terms. Women as a group, they assert, have been separated out in humanity and oppressed, and they must recognize that their separateness is fundamental. The ones who call the separateness "caste" see it as a state stigmatized by being born female. The ones who call it "class" see it as a social, political, and economic exploitation created by men and based entirely on sex.

Man as the Enemy

A central question for the feminist revolution is, "who is the enemy?" According to the women's liberationist view, the answer to the question is "Men." In some cases, this identification of men as the enemy means men collectively as a class. In others, it means men as people, any and all male human beings. For many, it calls for revolutionary social and psychological reorganization. For many more, it engenders vituperative outrage and venomous anger vented on anyone who is man. For still others, it is both.[36]

In the context of describing women as a class and making a primary affirmation of all women, the Redstockings Manifesto characterizes men as the enemy:

> We identify the agents of our oppression as men. Male supremacy is the oldest, most basic form of domination. All other forms of exploitation and oppression (racism, capitalism, imperialism, etc.) are extensions of male supremacy: men dominate women, a few men dominate the rest. All power structures throughout history have been male-dominated and male-oriented. Men have controlled all political, economic and cultural institutions and backed up this control with physical force. They have used their power to keep women in an inferior position. *All men* receive economic, sexual, and psychological benefits from male supremacy. *All men* have oppressed women.[37]

This kind of thinking implies an opposition to men, a polarity of women and men against each other. Conflict with men is indicated, and rejection of men is the logical conclusion. All feminists who make this kind of argument do not in fact personally reject men. Members of Redstockings are themselves a case in point, many of them continuing to have meaningful interaction with men. However, sexual polarity and conflict between the sexes are implied in this thinking.

In the essay "Toward a Female Liberation Movement," Beverly Jones and Judith Brown speak to this point. They appreciate the term "male chauvinism," contributed by the Women's Caucus of the Students for a Democratic Society, which indicates a social condition; but they call for a recognition of women's oppressor in terms that are personal: "In the life of each woman, the most immediate oppressor, however unwilling he may be in theory to play that role, is 'the man.' While 'male chauvinism' isn't sacred, if we're searching for a better name for the enemy, let's not de-escalate."[38]

Likewise, in a hard-hitting and poetic rejection of the male political Left, "Goodbye to All That," Robin Morgan says:

> White males are most responsible for the destruction of human life and environment on the planet today. Yet who is controlling the supposed revolution to change all that? White males (yes, yes, even with their pasty fingers back in black and brown pies again) . . . It seems obvious that a legitimate revolution must be led by, *made* by those who have been most oppressed: black, brown, and white *women*—with men relating to that the best they can. A genuine Left doesn't consider anyone's suffering irrelevant or titillating; nor does it function as a microcosm of capitalist economy, with men competing for power and status at the top, and women doing all the work at the bottom (and functioning as objectified prizes or "coin" as well). Goodbye to all that.[39]

For Morgan, the emphasis is more prowoman than antimale, but it is clear to her that men must be opposed for women to be liberated. The same understanding is true for Marlene Dixon, who advises: "Woman must learn the meaning of rage, the violence that liberates the human spirit. The rhetoric of invective is an equally essential stage, for in discovering and venting their rage against the enemy—and the enemy in everyday life is men—women also experience the justice of their own violence." And writing like so many of the feminists about her personal struggle for identity in relation to her childhood family, her work, and her husband, Sally Kempton in "Cutting

Loose" calls man the enemy who has found his best ally in his victim: "Woman's Liberation is finally only personal. It is hard to fight an enemy who has outposts in your head."[40]

The men-rejecting argument is drawn to its extreme conclusion in two documents widely read in the women's movement: Valerie Solanis' *The SCUM Manifesto* and Betsy Warrior's "Man As an Obsolete Life Form." In both of these essays, the writers tell the world how to be rid of men, since men are the creators of the society in which we live, a society that offers utterly nothing to women.

Valerie Solanis, an artist, is best known to the public as the woman who shot Andy Warhol. Her *SCUM Manifesto* is excerpted in many anthologies and regularly appears on feminist-circulated bibliographies. The manifesto outlines her own individual program of objectives, chief of which is to eliminate men: "Life in this society being, at best, an utter bore and no aspect of society being at all relevant to women, there remains to civic-minded, responsible, thrill-seeking females only to overthrow the government, eliminate the money system, institute complete automation, and destroy the male sex."[41]

According to Solanis, since it is now possible to reproduce people without the aid of men or women, and since men are merely incomplete females, all fetuses beginning life in female form, men are useless to human female life. Furthermore, men spend their lives trying to complete their female selves, through projecting onto women their male traits of "vanity, frivolity, triviality, weakness," and taking upon themselves the characteristics of strength, courage, and vitality that are female—in the process doing an enormous job of public relations on women and men and making of the world a "shit-pile."[42] She catalogues the conditions in the world for which men are responsible, including war, niceness, politeness, and dignity, suppression of individuality; animalism (domesticity and motherhood) and functionalism; authority and government; philosophy, religion, and morality based on sex; prejudice; great art and culture; and boredom.

To rectify the situation, Solanis proposes to establish a Society for Cutting Up Men (SCUM). Women members of the society would take over complete control of the labor force, the money system, the government, and the airwaves. They would "unwork" at jobs, give the public free use of the transportation system, and destroy "cars, store windows, 'Great Art.' " They would break up all mixed (male and female) couples and would kill all men not in the Men's Auxiliary of SCUM.[43]

SCUM would not drop out of society, but would encourage men to do so, and would operate in a criminal rather than a civil disobedience mode. After the elimination of money, the need to kill men would end, for men would lose their power over women. Women would then revamp the educational system and the cities for an entirely female society. They would advise the remaining men either to kill themselves or to sit back and watch.[44]

Somewhat more temperate than Solanis in her explanation of why men should be killed is Betsy Warrior, a member of Boston's Female Liberation Group—Cell 16, who in "Man As an Obsolete Life Form" makes the case for human male extermination on ecological grounds. She believes that man's violence and war-making attributes are about to destroy the earth, and women should realize that man is an anachronism and destroy him before he destroys the rest of humankind (women). Like Solanis, Warrior contends that babies can be produced from test tubes, so that women's primary need for men at the moment is to provide sperm banks. Otherwise, like the dinosaur, man is no longer suited to or needed in the balance of nature. Population control is necessary, because plagues and famines have been conquered by science, and men's tendencies to aggression and war make them unfit for contemporary life. For those women who still need to be reminded of men, an alternative to their extinction might be male preserves or zoos where they could be observed from time to time.[45]

The Prowoman Direction

In tandem with the antimale attitude and often superseding it in focus is the prowoman course of thought. Some of the feminists who think it is necessary to name men as the enemy emphasize that it is important to be *for* women, and that mutual support and affirmation of women by women is paramount to the success of the movement.

Robin Morgan's essay "Goodbye to All That," written to

celebrate women's takeover of the radical underground newspaper *Rat,* and declaring radical feminism's separation from
the male political Left as well as her own independence from
men, concludes with a wild and bitter affirmation of women:

> Women are Something Else. This time, we're going to kick
> out all the jams, and the boys will just have to hustle to keep
> up, or else drop out and openly join the power structure of
> which they are already the illegitimate sons . . . Women are
> the real Left. We are rising powerful in our unclean bodies;
> bright glowing mad in our inferior brains; wild blood we who
> hemorrhage every twenty-eight days; laughing at our own
> beauty we who have lost our sense of humor; mourning for
> all each precious one of us might have been in this one living
> time-place had she not been born a woman; stuffing fingers
> into our mouths to stop the screams of fear and hate and pity
> for men we have loved and love still; tears in our eyes and
> bitterness in our mouths for children we couldn't have, or
> couldn't *not* have, or didn't want, or didn't want *yet,* or
> wanted and had in this place and this time of horror. We are
> rising with a fury older and potentially greater than any force
> in history, and this time we will be free or no one will survive.
> *Power to all the people or to none.* All the way down, this
> time.[46]

Likewise, after identifying men as the enemy, Marlene Dixon
says women must believe in themselves. She thinks the greatest
drawback to the women's liberation movement is women's
"belief in their own inferiority."[47] She offers an affirmation of
women:

> The heart of the movement, as in all freedom movements,
> rests in women's knowledge, whether articulated or still only
> an illness without a name, that they are not inferior—nor
> chicks, nor bunnies, nor quail, nor cows, nor bitches, nor ass,
> nor meat . . . Women know that male supremacy is a lie.
> They know that they are not animals or sexual objects or
> commodities. They know their lives are mutilated, because
> they see within themselves a promise of creativity and per-
> sonal integration. Feeling the contradiction between the es-
> sentially creative and self-actualizing human being within

her, and the cruel and degrading less-than-human role she is compelled to play, a woman begins to perceive the falseness of what her society has forced her to be. And once she perceives this, she knows she must fight.[48]

Both Robin Morgan and Marlene Dixon express the prowoman argument within a context of establishing man as the enemy. Other prowoman writers prefer to fix the locus of enmity more precisely within women. Susan Brownmiller writes of "the enemy within" in an article by that title, in which she places the blame for women's incapacity on their own suspicion and distrust of each other and themselves. She describes the personal memories from childhood of young girls who say they would not go to a woman doctor, or who aspire to no creative and independent career goals of their own. She describes the jealousy and hostility that she and her fellow female researchers on a magazine felt against the one woman who had reached the status of writer, and the hostility she herself experienced from female researchers when she became a television network writer. She says that women themselves fear a loss of femininity when they achieve recognition by aggressive effort and in a competitive arena. Yet femininity, she believes, is indestructible. Some women overcome feelings of inferiority within themselves but unwittingly continue to regard other women in a negative light, which prevents their uniting to improve their condition: "Many women who reject the 'woman is inferior' psychology for themselves apply it unsparingly to others of the same sex. An ambitious woman frequently thinks of herself as the only hen in the barnyard, to reverse a common metaphor. *She* is the exception, she believes. Women must recognize that they must make common cause with *all* women. When women get around to really liking—and respecting—other women, why then, we will have begun."[49]

Brownmiller's argument has many parallels from nineteenth-century American feminism. Making a speech before a woman suffrage convention in 1893, Alice Stone Blackwell remarked,

It is often said that the chief obstacle to equal suffrage is the indifference and opposition of women, and that whenever

the majority ask for the ballot they will get it . . . When Lucy
Stone tried to secure for married women the right to their
own property, they asked with scorn, "Do you think I would
give myself where I would not give my property?" When
Elizabeth Blackwell began to study medicine, the women at
her boarding house refused to speak to her . . . It is a matter
of history with what ridicule and opposition Mary Lyon's
first efforts for the education of women were received, not
only by the mass of men, but by the mass of women as well.[50]

The contemporary argument that men are the enemy is being
shifted, however, by some of the radical feminists to the notion
that institutions are the enemy. Writing in *A Journal of Female
Liberation,* Dana Densmore throws out the challenge, "Who
Says Men Are the Enemy?" Making a much more direct attack
on men than Morgan or Dixon makes, she nevertheless stresses
that sexism and male supremacy are the enemy, not men. Men
do threaten, ridicule, smear, and repress women in an attempt
to maintain their superiority; but women can respond to these
attacks by walking out on their men. Oppression can only take
place, she believes, by the consent of the oppressed; and women
consent to be oppressed, to be victimized by men out of their
own belief in their inferiority. Men do not need to be done away
with. Rather, women need to confront them, walk out on them,
march.[51]

The group that appears to be the clearest representative of the
prowoman approach is Redstockings. They have come to be
known in the movement for what they deliberately call the
"pro-woman line." One of their members interprets this to
mean that women should "take the woman's side in *everything.*
A woman is never to blame for her own submission. None of us
need to change ourselves, we need to change men."[52] Their
Redstockings Manifesto reads:

We identify with all women. We define our best interest as
that of the poorest, most brutally exploited woman.
We repudiate all economic, racial, educational or status privileges that divide us from other women. We are determined to
recognize and eliminate any prejudices we may hold against
other women . . .

In fighting for our liberation we will always take the side of women against their oppressors. We will not ask what is "revolutionary" or "reformist," only what is good for women.[53]

Two significant expressions of the prowoman approach that have added considerable strength to the women's liberation movement are the concept of sisterhood and the method of consciousness-raising. Just as in the black power movement the slogan "Black is beautiful" gives courage and pride to its users, so the motto "Sisterhood is powerful" encapsules for the women's movement the new excitement over belief in themselves and in each other that women are experiencing. The phrase shows up on lapel buttons and posters, meets instant recognition in meetings and publications, and has become a symbolic rallying point for experienced as well as fledgling feminists. It is sometimes rendered graphically and nonverbally by means of the biological symbol for female with an equal sign or a clenched fist in the center. The equal sign symbol is masculine-equalitarian, indicating political pressure for equality with men, while the clenched fist symbol is prowoman, signifying social conflict for women's liberation, but both designs stand for the verbal message "Sisterhood is powerful." The slogan first appeared in a leaflet written by Kathie Amatniek of the New York Radical Women and distributed at the Jeannette Rankin Brigade, an antiwar demonstration made up of a coalition of women's peace groups which took place at the opening of Congress in January 1968.[54]

The slogan "Sisterhood is powerful" has both personal and collective meaning. Women individually or in groups have again and again had flashes of insight that their experience of being a woman is not their sole, lonely province but the common lot and bond of women, the potential unifying force for solidarity and support among half of humankind. Historically, with the impetus of the Women's liberation movement, thousands of women—many of them organized into groups called Women's Liberation or simply in meetings set up by and for women, and many more not formally collected into groups—began to reassess what being a woman means in rela-

tion to other women. This led them to take themselves seriously, perhaps for the first time, and to take other women seriously
as persons and as allies, "sisters." Sisterhood means female
solidarity, respect for women as women, support for all women
by women.[55]

Sisterhood is part ideal and part reality in contemporary feminism. For some feminists, it is genuinely experienced as a new
and fresh way of living. It is also postulated as what ought to
be. As a symbol, it has had the creative effect of raising the
estimation of women's value in women's eyes.

Sisterhood is realized as an affirmation and a commitment.
It begins when it dawns on a woman that women are not inferior to men. This insight applies to herself and to other women.
The women's liberationists say that women really believe they
are inferior from a lifetime of conditioning to be daddy's girl,
the cheerleader rather than the athlete, the secretary rather than
the executive. Women's lack of self-respect, drawn from living
secondary and derivative lives, fosters a lack of respect for
women in general. Women do not see other women as worth
attention, since they do not see themselves as deserving respect.
The first step to sisterhood is self-affirmation.[56]

Second, sisterhood must be based on an understanding that
all women are in it together. All women are sisters. It is
common for bright, articulate, and successful women to think
they have made it on their own, that they are exceptions, not
"like" other women. Most women of prominence will admit to
being or having been "man-identified women." Yet, say the
movement women, these women who curry the favor of the
male establishment ultimately have more in common with
women than with the agents of their prominence and
oppression, men. The division that separates women as a group
is something all women can understand, and this understanding
can unify them. No significant divisions among women need
exist—prostitute or bunny or wife, black or Chicano or white,
old or young, married or single, educated or dropout, reformist
or revolutionary.[57]

Finally, sisterhood establishes a unity over against men. If
not men personally, at least the stereotypes and the world of

power that they hold make men the source of the need for the sisterhood of womankind.

Closely related to the concept of sisterhood is the political method of consciousness-raising. Female consciousness-raising is a politics of experience akin to the national liberation movement's village self-awareness campaigns and the black movement's "telling it like it is." According to the consciousness-raising technique, members of a small group of women share their own experiences on any subject that has to do with being a woman, each member having a turn to tell about what has happened to her regarding abortion, housework, sexual relations, child care, marriage, shopping, making office coffee, curtailing ambitions, getting educated, or whatever. Early women's liberationists invariably called it "rapping on oppression." The term "consciousness-raising" has come to have wide currency as the name for whatever process by which many and disparate women become aware of their own condition of belittlement in common with womankind, whether they call it their plight or discrimination or oppression.

The desired and sometimes realized effect of consciousness-raising is sisterhood and cohesive political action. This kind of political action is new. It is personal and interactive rather than structural.

Consciousness-raising began as a deliberate method at the start of the women's liberation movement in Chicago and New York in 1968. During the first meetings of the New York Radical Women, the members sought a way to talk to each other in specifically radical feminist terms. Carol Hanisch and Kathie Amatniek had become impressed during their year in Mississippi with the Student Nonviolent Coordinating Committee by the way in which black people spoke up in testimonials about what had been done to them by "the Man." They also reminded themselves of Mao's slogan, "Speak pain to recall pain." The plan of "going around the room" gave quiet as well as articulate members a chance to share feelings and experiences that showed their common oppression by men as they focused on questions such as, "If you've thought of having a baby do you want a girl or a boy?" "What happens to your relationship when your man earns more money than you, and what happens when *you* earn more money than him?''[58]

Redstockings, in conjunction with its "prowoman line," formulated the first full guidelines for consciousness-raising. The document, called "Protective Rules for Consciousness-raising" and written in 1968, was read at the beginning of each session. The rules stipulate that each sister must testify on the question at hand, that others must not break off any sister's testimony until it is complete, and that judgments on a sister's testimony are not allowed. Sisters must give compelling reasons for urging points of view. Generalizations are to be drawn after testimonies are complete, placing the question in its political context, and position papers are to be written about the group's conclusions.[59]

Consciousness-raising in more or less the form developed by Redstockings swept the movement in the next two years and for many women's liberation groups became either their basis for forming or one part of their effort. The small, loosely organized unit became the basic unit of the movement, and the focus for the small group was usually consciousness-raising.[60] For example, a notice in a March 1970 issue of the *Female Liberation Newsletter,* a journal and newssheet that served as an umbrella for several Twin Cities feminist groups, reads: "Consciousness-raising is still the most vital part of our activity, reaching new women, developing mutual trust, coming to genuine understanding of the problems that confront us in our down-to-earth, day-to-day lives." *Life* magazine reported in 1971 that the Non-Violent Feminists of Milwaukee, as a typical grass-roots women's liberation group, "deserve credit for refining the humble rap to a high art form. Scarcely the evening goes by . . . without a scheduled rap on abortion, contraception, employment discrimination, law or 'Herstory' (the hitherto suppressed history of women).''[61] The Women's Liberation Collective of Palo Alto, California, announced in its "Women's Revolutionary Manifesto":

> Let us join together in groups (fifteen or less) to discuss all aspects of womanhood. To understand the nature and extent of our oppression, we must discuss everything from diapers to orgasms, from political economy to the woman's page,

from the desire to have children to the desire to be married to the desire to own a home. We must analyze everything we talk about. We must encourage women from various classes and minorities to meet in groups and talk about our real problems on an honest basis.[62]

And questions for consciousness-raising prepared in 1970 by the High School Women's Liberation Coalition in New York City include:

> Can you play basketball, soccer, football?
> Did you ever pretend to be dumb?
> Are your brothers asked to help clean house?
> How many famous women do you know about (not counting Presidents' wives or movie stars)?
> In extracurricular coed organizations, do girls make decisions? Or do they take minutes?
> Are girls with boyfriends winners? What did they win?
> Do you believe boys get sexually aroused fast, at a younger age, and more often than girls?
> Who told you *that*?[63]

Consciousness-raising is, then, a highly personal and political tool, by which women make themselves and one another more acutely aware of their mutual sharing in the women problem. It is not a therapy but a revolutionary method. It takes place among women, with men excluded from the interaction. The process and any action it might direct is against men, for men are the agents of the oppression that consciousness-raising seeks to clarify and repudiate. In the testimonial "About My Consciousness-Raising," Barbara Susan summarizes the theory of consciousness-raising,

> Consciousness raising is a way of forming a political analysis on information we can trust is true. The information is our experience. It is difficult to understand how our oppression is political (organized) unless we first remove it from the area of personal problems. Unless we talk to each other about our so called personal problems and see how many of our problems are shared by other people we won't be able to see how these problems are rooted in politics . . . We also see male suprem-

acy as a political system inasmuch as all men are in col-
lusion in forcing women into inferior and unproductive positions . . . It is our hope that consciousness raising in groups of
women who are not the same will help us to understand each
other and help us all in building a movement which answers
to the needs of more than just the most privileged woman.
Our analysis is an expanding one, it changes as more and
more women enter the movement and contribute their knowledge and experience thereby widening and correcting our
understanding of oppression.[64]

Female Sexuality and the Vaginal Orgasm

A number of contemporary feminists are saying that
marriage as we now know it must go. A few are recommending
celibacy for some or all women.[65] Some are advocating all-
female communes.[66] At least one, Ti-Grace Atkinson, is for
forsaking what she calls "the institution of sexual intercourse."
By far the most significant demand is that female sexuality be
redefined on women's terms as women understand it. The essay
around which the movement's argument on female sexuality
solidified is Anne Koedt's "The Myth of the Vaginal Orgasm."
Koedt's paper, prepared for the first national women's liberation conference in 1968, quickly became a major ideological
treatise for the movement.[67] It has been repeatedly reprinted
and anthologized, has served as the topic of discussion for
countless women's groups, and has added a new idiom to popular speech, "the myth of the vaginal orgasm."

Koedt argues that men have defined what is "normal" and
pleasurable for women sexually, as they have defined what is
abnormal; but their definitions are false, because they do not
correspond with the reality of female biology: "Whenever
female orgasm is discussed, a false distinction is made between
the vaginal and the clitoral orgasm. Frigidity has generally been
defined by men as the failure of women to have vaginal orgams.
Actually, the vagina is not a highly sensitive area and is not
physiologically constructed to achieve orgasm. The clitoris is the
sensitive area and is the female equivalent of the penis."[68]

Koedt calls Freud the father of the vaginal orgasm, since he
held that both clitoral orgasm and vaginal orgasm are exper-

ienced by women, the clitoral orgasm is the experience of the sexually immature, the adolescent, and that a woman having intercourse with a man comes to have vaginal orgasm as the full and mature orgastic event. Koedt states that this Freudian belief, generally held, is propagated by men for their own benefit, since the man most readily comes to orgasm with the penis inside the vagina. Men foist this belief onto women with the further belief that a women is frigid if she does not have vaginal orgasm. Yet the evidence of women's own experience, if they could only believe it, is otherwise: "Men knew that the clitoris was and is the essential organ for masturbation, whether in children or adult women. So obviously women made it clear where *they* thought their sexuality was located. Men also seem suspiciously aware of the clitoral powers during 'foreplay' when they want to arouse women and produce the necessary lubrication for penetration."[69]

The clitoris, then, is the female sexual organ. Unlike the vagina, it has very sensitive tissue and becomes erect on stimulation. Its only function is sexual. It is "a small equivalent of the penis, except for the fact that the urethra does not go through it as in the man's penis." The vagina is most centrally related to the reproductive function, is not especially sensitive inside, and is even of minor importance as an erotic area. Thus, vaginal orgasm is a falsehood.[70]

Koedt lists reasons that men perpetuate the myth of the vaginal orgasm. They prefer penetration for their own sexual pleasure. They see women as invisible and do not take into account women's total humanity. The penis is the epitome of masculinity, and men fear being sexually expendable if sexual penetration is not the essential factor in women's sexual attainment. Men want to control women, and they fear lesbianism as providing not only a sexual partnership but also a full and complete companionship between women.[71]

Critics of Koedt in particular and of women's liberation in general have been quick to charge that her kind of thinking is a defense for female homosexuality, that the movement is "just a bunch of lesbians." Although the argument that the locus of female sexual excitation is the clitoris does help to legitimate the female-to-female sexual experience, it is by no means restricted to that purpose. It legitimates the search for a wider range of heterosexual activities as well.

Koedt's celebration of the clitoris was made in much the same way in 1948 in Ruth Herschberger's then underrated book, *Adam's Rib*. She said with a real sense of humor:

> In the symphony of love, the lost chord is a small organ lying somewhat north of the vagina . . . The clitoris, hidden by a hoodlike fold of the labia, is so tiny and insignificant in size that various thinkers have referred to it, darkly, as the missing penis . . . However, this is no more reasonable than to assume that the difference between men and women is "the missing clitoris"—in men . . . The Clitoris, then, is not supposed to be as sensitive as the vagina, certainly not more sensitive. It shouldn't be, but it is . . . The experience of the clitoris is highly localized, staccato, demanding, and intense. The experience of the vagina, however intense it may be, is relatively more responsive, kinesthetic, and diffuse.[72]

Herschberger offers an acute linguistic analysis of why the clitoris has been discriminated against in pronunciation. Nobody knows how to say it, and any pronunciation goes, even in medical schools. The soft *i* is persistent, but *Cleet or-iss* or *Clite or-iss* would be preferable. She offers the theory that subconscious male scholarship has equated it with light words, like *flit* and *bit,* rather than emphatic words, like *flight* and *bite.* Normally, its Greek root would be transmitted with the strong vowel, *kleit-*, while the equivalent Latin for the male organ would be the weak vowel, *pen-*. She wonders what would have happened if the word Freud had had to deal with was *pennis envy.*[73]

Lesbianism

In 1970, the issue of lesbianism surfaced in the women's movement. At the second Congress to Unite Women, in New York, a group of lesbians pushed for the recognition of lesbians as a part of the women's movement, for the women to see all women as sisters regardless of their sexual preference. A Gay Liberation Movement of both homosexual men and homosexual women had begun. In the same year, Kate Millett and other prominent feminists publicly announced themselves as bisexual, stating at a press conference: "Women's liberation and homosexual liberation are both struggling towards a common goal: A society free from defining and categorizing people by virtue of gender and/or sexual preference. 'Lesbian' is a label used as a psychic weapon to keep women locked into their male-defined 'feminine role.' The essence of that role is that a woman is defined in terms of her relationship to men."[74]

Controversy ensued within the movement, many heterosexual women fearing that to endorse lesbianism could hurt the cause of women's liberation by channeling all the attention onto homosexuality. Lesbian women were bitter, calling themselves the last minority within the minority. As Gene Damon, editor of the radical lesbian journal *The Ladder,* wrote: "Certainly many of us are ardent feminists. Equally certainly many of the women's rights groups shun and fear Lesbians because of the 'brand' they fear they will receive. It comes as no surprise whatever to the Lesbian civil-rights worker to find that she is, among some of these brave women's groups, once again, *persona non grata.*"[75]

Since 1970, some valuable insights have been gained by the women's movement from homosexual women; and homosexual women have grown increasingly willing to "come out," organizing and publishing themselves as lesbians. Lesbians perhaps more than any others have forced the issue of the meaning of sisterhood. They have shown how utterly basic is women's sexual identity to their own and society's understanding of them, by confronting "straight" women with their feelings of threat when it is implied that they might sexually love another woman.

Lesbian women point out that they themselves encounter all the discrimination that other women experience, plus the threat of law and social practice which make their sexual expression criminal, their most meaningful relationships socially reprehensible, and their sexual identity a reason for loss of employment. In homophile conferences of both men and women, lesbians say that they are expected to play the predictable feminine role of secretary of the group and maker of the coffee.[76]

Radical lesbianism has become an authentic wing of the women's movement. Increasingly, in the name of feminism, lesbians are feeling the freedom publicly to declare themselves homosexuals. Many have organized into radical lesbian groups, and lesbian publishing ventures have begun. The Daughters of Bilitis, publishers since 1956 of *The Ladder,* have been joined in their once lonely cause by more than seventy-five groups of women in all parts of the country organized around their feminist homosexuality. In 1972 a lesbian commune in Washington, D.C., The Furies, along with some male homosexuals, took over the name and mailing list of the magazine *motive,* whose demise as a fine religious and cultural journal had been hastened by a controversy over its issue on women in 1969. The women published one final issue entirely on lesbianism, with the graphics, poetry, photography, and essays all by and about lesbians, paralleling an issue on male homosexuality by the men. Two new lesbian feminist newspapers are available, *The Furies* from Washington and *Ain't I a Woman* from Iowa City. Gay women's conferences and workshops occur.[77]

One might assume that, because of their sexual orientation, lesbians must be prowoman and antimasculinist from the start, but to do so would miss the point. The preferences of lesbians for social and political intercourse are as varied as heterosexual people's. They love and hate men in general in quotients comparable to other women. Many lesbians have no particularly feminist consciousness. However, organized radical lesbians have made a contribution to women's liberationism both by pressing for an awareness of comprehensive sisterhood and by setting up women-only groups for the pursuit of specifically women's freedom.

Abortion

Abortion was a principal issue in contemporary feminism up to the Supreme Court decision in 1973. The issue itself was dealt with ideologically in several different ways, but the essential form that the feminist argument for abortion took was the right of women to control their own bodies.

Appeals for abortion reform and the organization of groups to change or repeal antiabortion laws were begun outside the sweep of feminism; but from 1968 to 1973 the issue catapulted into a major feminist focus. The National Association for Repeal of Abortion Laws coordinated lobbying efforts for the legislative repeal of existing state laws. The National Women's Abortion Action Coalition became a significant single-issue radical feminist organization. The establishment by women of abortion counseling services was combined with legislative lobbying and court cases both to seek to appeal existing law and to make women aware of the right to abortion. For example, an Abortion Defense Fund was set up in Chicago for seven women known as the "Abortion 7," who had been arrested on charges of committing abortions.[78] Three hundred women challenged the Rhode Island abortion laws in federal district court on grounds that "the state's anti-abortion laws: 1) violate the spirit of the 19th amendment, which provides for women's full participation in public affairs, 2) deny poor women equal protection of the laws, since rich women can go to New York for abortions, 3) violate women's right to privacy in marital and sexual matters and to be free from involuntary servitude in caring for unwanted children and 4) constitute cruel and unusual punishment."[79]

Most frequently, the demand for abortion, its availability and legalization, was made in terms of the right of women to control their own bodies. A leaflet from the Minnesota Women's Abortion Action Coalition states: "We feel that all the laws which restrict a woman's right to abortion deny us one of our basic rights—the right to control our own bodies, the right to control our own lives. We are also concerned with the repeal of restrictive contraception laws. We defend the right of every woman to decide for herself whether or not she wishes to bear children."[80]

A flyer from the Seattle Radical Women claims:

ABORTION IS A RIGHT! Fundamental to the liberation of women is our right as free individuals to exercise control over our own bodies on the basis of our own judgement.
We refuse to be considered "criminals" and forced to resort

to degrading and dangerous means when we attempt to control our own lives and prevent the birth of unplanned children that wreck the chances for economic independence and a decent standard of living for ourselves and our families. We bear the children, we bear the responsibility, and we demand and deserve the right to make such decisions.[81]

And in the preview issue of *Ms.* in 1972, fifty-three prominent American women, most of them writers and artists, published a statement declaring that they had had abortions: "To many American women and men it seems absurd, in this allegedly enlightened age, that we should still be arguing for a simple principle: that a woman has the right to the sovereignty over her own body. Still, there are tragically few places in the country where a woman can obtain an abortion without the expense and deception of conforming to inhuman laws, or the expense and physical danger of going outside the law."[82]

The right to control one's own body is a prowoman position. It leaves out of the decision on whether to have an abortion the state, the church, the medical profession, families, husbands, and lovers. Lucinda Cisler makes the case succinctly. Writing in opposition to those who would merely "reform" abortion laws and in favor of their outright repeal, she explains that important restrictions creep into reform efforts, namely, that abortions must be performed in hospitals, they must be performed only up to a certain point in pregnancy, and they must have the consent of the husband or parents of the pregnant woman or girl. In repudiating all these provisions, Cisler argues that the woman "belongs to herself and not to the state."[83]

Prowoman Antimasculinist Arts

In the world of the arts—painting, sculpture, and architecture; theater, poetry, and fiction—women have been a small minority of those receiving public acclaim. In relation to the new feminism, there has been a reassessment of women as artists, new attention to the works of women artists, and new feminist avenues for their public display and publication.

In literature, such works as Mary Ellman's *Thinking about*

Women and Carolyn Heilbrun's "The Masculine Wilderness of the American Novel" have offered a feminist literary criticism that gives new insights into assessing the literary treatment of women and literature by women. The Commission on Women of the Modern Language Association has done much to engender the teaching of college courses on literature written both by women and from the viewpoint of women. Feminist journals and newsletters provide opportunities for publication of poems and stories by women, aid to women in finding publishers for their work, and inspiration for women who have lacked the incentive to write before. A feminist literary journal, *Aphra,* staffed by women and publishing only women's work, has been flourishing since 1969.

New York has seen the birth of feminist theatrical events, beginning in 1969 with the New Feminist Theater, founded by Anselma dell'Olio. It first performed satirical reviews of feminist material and later a play by Myrna Lamb, "But What Have You Done for Me Lately?" A second play by Lamb, "The Mod Donna," was performed at the New York Shakespeare Festival Public Theater in 1970, and its script has been made available to the movement through feminist newsletters. A theater women's consciousness-raising group, the New York Tea Party, began in New York in 1970.[84]

In 1970 women painters and sculptors in New York City organized into a group called Women Artists for Revolution. They conducted a highly publicized confrontation with the Whitney Art Museum, which resulted in the museum mounting a show called "The Permanent Collection—Women Artists."[85] The January 1971 issue of *Art News* was devoted to women, feminism, and art. Women artists at the California Institute of the Arts in Los Angeles have developed a feminist art program with classes in female art history taught by women for women only. The women's liberation journals and newsletters have at times focused on art. For example, the May 7, 1971, issue of *Everywoman* was concerned entirely with painting and sculpture. Two feminist art journals have been started. The first, *Women and Art,* publishes women's photography and etchings as well as articles and news items on women artists and their works. It has demanded a major "Women Choose

Women" exhibit in New York's leading museums.[86] The second, *Feminist Art Journal*, was a breakaway from *Women and Art* because, as its editors claimed, the earlier magazine was more Marxist than feminist. It was so successful that its second issue had to go into a second printing.[87]

Much of the new assessment of women in art and of feminist artistic effort is women's liberationist in intent. The formation of women-only groups of artists is within the liberationist tradition. So was the confrontation of Women Artists for Revolution with the Whitney Museum, which was based on a conflict model and which insisted that women's work be shown. The inception of *Aphra* exclusively for the publication of women's work was a prowoman literary act.

Three examples of artistic production illustrate the artistic work being done under the women's liberationist banner. One is "Womanhouse," a product of the imagination of twenty-six women artists of the California Institute of the Arts in Los Angeles, led by Judy Chicago and Miriam Schapiro. They transformed a mansion about to be demolished into their vision and experience of what it meant to be a woman, turning what appeared to be a home into the horror of female reality. In their words, they demonstrated "the imprisonment of the female in a nurturing role."[88]

In the sheet closet, they showed a mannequin confined with the sheets behind the shelves-made-bars. A "Womb Room" depicted a tired uterus with a thicket of drooping fibers. At the top of the "Bridal Staircase" appeared a radiant and triumphant mannequin dressed in traditional white wedding satin before garlands of wedding flowers. The tableau continued to the bottom of the stairs where her backside disappeared into the gray woodwork. The "Nurturing Kitchen," flesh-colored, was covered wall and ceiling with sponge fried eggs, some of which had become breasts. A striking dramatization occurred in a bedroom, where a live woman sat amid odors of strong perfume, endlessly putting on and taking off makeup.[89]

"Womanhouse" made one kind of prowoman feminist statement. A number of others have been made by poets, some who would not be published outside of feminist circles, others who would. One poet who calls herself Alta expresses the rage of the antimasculinist side of the women's liberationist ideology and the heady exuberance of the prowoman side. In "penus envy," she attacks men and the male definition of femininity:

> penus envy, they call it.
> think how handy to have a thing
> that poked out; you could just shove
> it in any body, whang whang & come,
> wouldn't have to give a shit.
> you *know* you'd come!
> wouldn't have to love that person,
> trust that person.
> whang whang & come.
> If you couldn't get relief for free,
> pay a little $, whang, whang & come.
> you wouldn't have to keep. or abort.
> wouldn't have to care about the kid.
> wouldn't fear sexual violation.
> penus envy, they call it.
> the man is sick in his heart.
> that's what i call it.[90]

Defending the silent and nameless women left out of accounts of history and declaring the power of contemporary women to avenge the waste of past womanhood, Alta writes in "The Vow for Anne Hutchinson":

> sister,
> your name is not a household word.
> maybe you had a 2 line description
> in 8th grade history.
> more likely you were left out,
> as i am when men converse in my presence . . .
> you are dead, but not as dead as you
> have been, we will avenge you.
> you and all the nameless brave spirits.
> my mother, my grandmothers . . .
> it is too late for all you you. waste
> and waste again, life after life,

shot to hell, it will take more
than a husband with a nation behind him
to stop me now.[91]

And declaring what freedom means in a personal female
voice that might be speaking to a child, to a man, or to another
woman, Alta writes in "Poem";

i could not love you more
if i were in prison.
do not fear my freedom.
when i walk away it is only
because there is away
to walk. if you stopped me
i would have to fly & then
sometimes i don't come back.[92]

The women's liberationist view offers affirmation and
support of women and opposition to the masculine and
sometimes to men. It is a model of conflict and confrontation.
It places women over against men. It promotes a self-awareness
of women and supports women's confidence in themselves. In it
is an element of rage and antagonism against men as the enemy.
It calls for sweeping social change, using psychological and personal tools to bring it about. It is not a model adhered to only
by "castrating bitches." That is a male definition, which
feminists can turn around to say, "Bitch is beautiful." But the
women's liberationist ideology permits many stripes of women
to say to each other that together they will determine their own
destiny.

4

The Androgynous Perspective: Women and Men Equal to Each Other

For some of today's feminists an androgynous model is the operating paradigm. The word "androgynous" suggests "having some characteristics of both male and female." This is the pattern of women-and-men-equal-to-each-other. It is the most revolutionary of the concepts informing the new wave of feminism, for it implies the affirmation and cultivation of formerly sex-linked psychological and social characteristics in both men and women. It suggests that men should be equal to women as well as women equal to men. Proponents of this kind of thinking lay the blame for the inequality of women on attitudes and social institutions, and assert that equality can and must be achieved through a process of reshaping social attitudes and institutions by women and men together.

The androgynous position offers a model of cooperation and of rationality. Implied in it is a belief that both women and men can change once they see the inherent contradiction in a society that affirms human freedom yet circumscribes the roles to be played in it by males and females. The androgynous viewpoint assumes that rigidity in the male role expectation is as dehumanizing for the male as rigidity in the female role expectation is dehumanizing for the female. It assumes that the common area of humanity betwen males and females is a much wider dimension of their identity than sexuality per se. Regarding sexuality, it leaves open the question of what sexual complementarity will in fact mean between males and females when a broader range of social, vocational, and political options is available to them together.

A beginning point for understanding this approach is to investigate the framework of attitudes and beliefs that undergirds the status and role that women have had and continue to have in American society. An ideological analysis must be made of current views in order to create a new ideological base.

Although androgynous thinking has emerged as a full ideology for feminism in the new wave of feminism in the 1960s and early 1970s, it did not arise full-blown out of nothing. The germ of this concept and fragments of its current expression were present in the earlier history of American feminism. Therefore, in the treatment of aspects of androgynous thinking, connections must be made between the current feminist ideology and phases of historical feminism that seem to anticipate this framework.

Man's World, Woman's Place

Elizabeth Janeway, in her extensive 1971 study of the mythology of sex roles, *Man's World, Woman's Place,* attempts to present a temperate, reasonable analysis of the cultural belief system that dictates the roles to be played and the spheres of influence to be held by males and females. She defines the prevailing myth that governs our understanding of men's and women's identities in terms of the old adages "It's a man's world" and "Woman's place is in the home." The myth is prescriptive, not descriptive: "We declare its tenets to be true because we feel they ought to be true and that we should therefore behave in ways that will make them true . . . For it is the nature of myth to be both true and false, false in fact, but true to human yearnings and human fears and thus, at all times, a powerful shaping force. Myth is born out of psychological drives. What we do not have, that is what we need; and that is what we present to ourselves as desirable and, finally, as 'right.' "[1]

Looking at the level of social attitudes and discussing them in terms of myth, Janeway states, " 'Woman's place' is a short-hand phrase which sums up a whole set of traits and attitudes and ways of presenting themselves which we think proper to women, along with the obligations and restrictions we think it implies." Janeway believes that the set of assumptions about women that the myth incorporates is totally derived from the culture. The focus of those assumptions is the twin beliefs that she calls the myth of female weakness and the myth of female power. The myth of female weakness suggests that because women bear children, they must be protected, that they belong at home for the sake of their husbands and children, that the world runs more smoothly if women see themselves as subordinate to men and as persons whose duty is to please others—their husbands and children. Belief in and advocacy of this myth by women themselves is illustrated by Phyllis McGinley's *Sixpence in Her Shoe* "By and large . . . the world runs better when men and women keep in their own spheres. I do not say women are better off, but society in general is. And that is, after all, the mysterious honor and obligation of women—to keep this planet in orbit. We are the self-immolators, the sacrificers, the givers, not the eaters-up of life."[2]

The flip side of the myth of female weakness is the myth of female power, by which the primordial power of nurturing, of mothering, first of the helpless infant, then of the man, gives woman the authority for determining the manhood of man. In focusing her power in the private sphere, according to this myth, the woman holds the power to make of the man who he is. Unless she subordinates herself to him in public life, he will not be truly a man; his manhood is in reference to her "femininity." Thus, the mother's total power over the infant is extended into the adult world of authority so as to confer status on the man.[3]

The prevalence of these myths is graphically illustrated by Page Smith, a highly respected American historian. Smith claims that the key to understanding eminent women in American history is in their relationships with their fathers. Somewhat condescending toward public achievement by women at all, Smith takes upon himself the task of defining "the nature of women." The following quotation is typical of his assessment of what women are worth and what is their purpose: "It is the particular function of women . . . to create happiness and most of the happiness a man knows is the gift of a happy woman.

Women by the sensuous intensity with which they live in the moment, may teach the restlessly aspiring male the renewing pleasures of living a day at a time, of celebrating those things which are humble or useless. In such ways in a happy vivifying uselessness, a woman can save a man's soul and sanity."[4]

The effect of living by these myths is to see women as merely relational to men, to create a part-timeness and indirection to women's activities, and to look upon movements outside the limited boundaries of women's world as "unnatural" or "abnormal." Of the effects of women's role, Janeway writes:

> I think we must agree that we do in fact regard men as superior to women, if only because masculine goals urge men to do things, while femininity as an ideal attempts to stop women from doing them. This difference has a further effect: one runs into the limits of a restrictive role more often than into those of a wider and more diverse one. That is why the limits are there, to keep one in bounds. So women are more apt to be conscious of their role and its restrictions than men are to be aware of their role, with its manifold opportunities. The fence around woman's place is more apparent to the people who live inside it than to those outside in man's world.[5]

Normal people, in short, are men; and women who want a share in shaping their public world, who want to be "normal people," are seen as "abnormal women." It is a double bind.[6] The limits of the role determine the negative side of the role, for it is always easier to reverse a set of traits than to create a new configuration of traits. The positive aspects of woman's role are mother, worker, and wife. The negatives of these roles are witch, shrew, and bitch. The mother is the loving, self-effacing, giving nurturer; the witch carries the myth of female power to a point of destruction—domineering, manipulating, contriving in the private sphere. The worker is the server of needs, the comforter of woes, the subordinate to men's power; the shrew subordinates and denigrates men, in shrill, harsh defiance of them. The wife is the private, loving, charming, pleasing respondent to men; the bitch is the wife reversed, frivolous, foolish, secret-telling, wounding. The positive and negative sides of these aspects of women's role are the positive and negative manifestations of the myths of female weakness and female power. Both sides suggest that women live vicariously, that their reference point for identity is men. This polarity indicates that the mythology is too narrow, too constricting for a solid foundation for human society.

Janeway does not suggest a course of action for changing the mythology. She notes that women are breaking out of the old assumption that they must live vicariously, and that certain technological innovations, such as the contraceptive pill, have contributed to the greater possibility of proving that biology is not destiny. She observes, however, that the greatest criticism of the new feminism is that its advocates may not please men, an index of the continuing presence of the social mythology.

Janeway concludes that this mythology is false for the living of women's lives, for their own best interests as women, and for the mature development of society. Underlying her analysis is the call for a new configuration of traits to be assumed as the designations of male and female roles, and for breaking the old limitations of the social mythology of woman's place and man's world. She is under no illusion that mythic structure and role designations do not always exist in society in some form, but she would take a new look at what they should be for the betterment of all.

Toward a Recognition of Androgyny

The most thoroughgoing overt treatment of androgyny as a concept appears in Carolyn G. Heilbrun's *Toward a Recognition of Androgyny,* published in 1973. It is a splendid work of literary criticism, in which she makes the claim that currents of Western thought, myth, and literature have contained an understanding of androgyny which now, upon reexamination, can be recognized as having been there all along, a "hidden river of androgyny." She defines androgyny as woman-in-man and man-in-woman: "Androgyny suggests a spirit of reconciliation between the sexes; it suggests, further, a full range of experience open to individuals who may, as women, be aggressive, as men, tender; it suggests a spectrum upon which human beings choose their places without regard to propriety or custom."[7]

To demonstrate her thesis, Heilbrun focuses on three areas.

First, myth and literature from classical, Judeo-Christian, medieval, and Renaissance sources often express an androgynous vision, which is fully realized in Shakespeare. The woman as hero next emerges in the English novel, along with some fiction outside England. Finally, the Bloomsbury Group in London in the first decades of the twentieth century, illustrate people who have actually lived the androgynous life. Heilbrun feels that the creativity of those writers and thinkers was based on their emotional and spiritual courage to be androgynous. Only a part of their spirit was bisexual activity. They combined passion, which has been historically thought "feminine," and reason, which has been considered "masculine," in both their group and their persons, with a result of enormous intellectual and artistic productivity.

Deirdre's concern

Heilbrun finds in the tradition of androgyny the ideological basis for giving a new direction to the women's movement, for both women and men: "I believe that our future salvation lies in a movement away from sexual polarization and the prison of gender toward a world in which individual roles and the modes of personal behavior can be freely chosen. The ideal toward which I believe we should move is best described by the term 'androgyny.' This ancient Greek word—from *andro* (male) and *gyn* (female)—defines a condition under which the characteristics of the sexes, and the human impulses expressed by men and women, are not rigidly assigned. Androgyny seeks to liberate the individual from the confines of the appropriate." The recognition of androgyny includes the social recognition of the acceptability of homosexuality and bisexuality. Heilbrun points out that androgynous works have often been realized in societies and among artists who are homosexual and bisexual. She predicts that this will not be as frightening a realization to younger people as it has been to people of her generation.[8]

Throughout the book Heilbrun puts the terms "masculine" and "feminine" in quotation marks, to remind the reader that, though the use of these terms is pervasive in the language and thus difficult to avoid, she is not using them in the received sense. Instead, "masculine" is sometimes pejorative for her, standing for the distortions of "competitiveness, aggressive-

.ness, and defensiveness" that are found in men and which men and women have allowed to dominate our society. "Masculine" has become synonymous with "conventional." It is urgent, she believes, to temper these qualities with "the 'feminine' qualities of gentleness, lovingness, and the counting of cost in human rather than national or property terms."[9]

Social Organization

Moving from beliefs and values that have shaped the myth, advocates of androgyny plan for the realization in the social order of a new set of beliefs and values to regenerate social organization. Many of the new feminists have a social program or bits and pieces of a social program, ranging from requests for broad vocational and political involvement of women to intense efforts in specified areas to change such things as abortion laws or to establish child care facilities. The androgynous goal suggests a new basis for social formulations as well as social actions. Following the discovery of the roots of attitudes prejudicial against both women and men, these feminists consider a reconstruction of social institutions from the ground up.

While the feminist paradigm would indicate equal female participation in male-originated, already existing institutions, and the women's liberationist paradigm would call for new female-initiated institutions, the androgynous paradigm points to a new form of social order in which both women and men are involved in the inception and construction. In a sense, the social order of the androgynous model incorporates aspects of the other two, for the ideas and action of both women and men are involved in the creation and maintenance of structures of society.

The germ of this theory can be seen in the lives or writings of three famous historical feminists: Victoria Woodhull, Emma Goldman, and Charlotte Perkins Gilman. Although it is unlikely that any of the contemporary feminists would identify with these historical women in toto, a case can be made that some of the things they said and did anticipated what is being said and done by today's feminists who have an androgynous perspective.

Victoria Woodhull came close to advocating an antimasculinist viewpoint in her "Great Secession" speech in 1872, but the course of her life was nearer to an androgynous model.[10] In many of her acts—asserting herself as provider for her family when she was married to Canning Woodhull and later for the whole clan of her Claflin family, setting herself up with her sister Tennessee as the first women brokers on Wall Street, and declaring herself as a candidate for the presidency in 1872—she acted on her principle that women should go ahead and perform in public life without spending their energies on the effort to gain rights. She stated early in life: "women have every right. All they have to do is exercise them." In announcing her candidacy for President, she declared: "While others argued the equality of women with men, I proved it by successfully engaging in business; while others sought to show that there was no valid reason why women should be treated, socially and politically, as being inferior to men, I boldly entered the arena."[11]

Always having around her a coterie of admiring men, she not only made love with them but learned from them and made their ideas her own, so that eventually there was a merging of her own thought with that of Commodore Vanderbilt, Colonel James Blood, and Stephen Pearl Andrews.[12] Not concerning herself in her early years with the women's rights struggle that was going on through the National Woman's Suffrage Association and the American Woman's Suffrage Association, she entered briefly into its limelight when she maneuvered herself into the position of being the first woman to speak before a congressional committee on behalf of woman suffrage. Before the committee she argued that the proper interpretation of the word "person" in the Fifteenth Amendment would give the right to vote to women as well as to Negroes.

Victoria Woodhull's energetic self-assertion in plunging into public affairs, sordid though it sometimes was and self-serving always, coupled with her principle of woman's inherent capacity as public activator and leader, make her life an antecedent of the androgynous view. She was first of all her own person— self-actualizing, in today's psychological language. In the sexual, political, and economic spheres she was constructively aggressive and spontaneous. Yet she expressed her own personal female power in concert with men.

Emma Goldman, like Victoria Woodhull the object of much social opprobrium, anticipated the androgynous pattern in her life as much as in her feminist ideology. Emma Goldman was most renowned for her anarchist political philosophy, but her interests covered a wide range of political, social, and economic subjects, as well as literature. As a lecturer on the theater, she was one of the first persons to popularize the works of George Bernard Shaw in America. Like Victoria Woodhull before her, Emma Goldman proposed to attack the problem of prostitution at its root by exposing the hypocrisy of a society that punishes women prostitutes while men who buy their services go free. As some of today's feminists are doing, she drew an analogy between the situation of the prostitute who sells sex per se and the actual conditions of many a marriage, in which the woman exchanges sex and domestic services for security. She was opposed to monogamous marriage as simply an economic arrangement.[13]

Emma Goldman's feminism rose from her political anarchism. Her central belief was that all persons should be free and independent. Unlike most other feminists of her day, she did not favor women's suffrage, for she felt that it would further the power of the state, to which she was opposed. She was an early advocate of birth control as a means for greater freedom for women. She lectured and wrote about contraception soon after 1900, and there is evidence that she introduced the topic to Margaret Sanger, who later coined the term "birth control" and whose name has become synonymous with the birth control movement.

Emma Goldman advocated freedom for women from "internal tyrannies." She opposed other feminists such as Jane Addams and Charlotte Perkins Gilman on the basis that their battle was against "external tyrannies," but she thought "the internal tyrannies were far more harmful to life and growth." For Goldman, the object of feminism was to assure for women the widest possible range of experience and of participation in all of life, including sexual life. Suffrage would not gain this, nor would understanding woman merely as a "sexual vessel," nor would mere economic independence for women, of which the "tragedy of the self-supporting or economically free woman does not lie in too many but too few experiences."[14] While not necessarily adopting Emma Goldman's anarchism, feminists of the androgynous perspective do accept her view that women should have the widest possible freedom.

Charlotte Perkins Gilman, whose 1898 book was the source of Emma Goldman's attack on "mere economic independence," also made a contribution to the inception of the androgynous idea. In *Women and Economics,* Gilman essentially predated the argument made by Betty Friedan in *The Feminine Mystique* that the key to woman's freedom is having a vocation that yields both personal fulfillment and economic independence. This is the fundamental point of the feminist paradigm. However, Gilman's program for organizing domestic life on a social scale also looked forward to later social programs of an androgynous nature.

Gilman recommended a complex of city apartment houses for professional women and their families in which child care could be done communally. She proposed that cooking and household care be developed as vocations and services outside the family. The family apartment would have no kitchen, but nutritionally sound meals would be served in communal dining rooms where cooking would be developed as a specialized skill. Household maintenance would become an occupation with its own group of professionals serving the households of all.[15]

Although only a fragment of a social program, this particle of Gilman's thinking appears in revised form today in social plans being offered to realign the sexes. Two prominent exponents are the feminists Gloria Steinem and Alice Rossi, who give an overview of the possibilities for social reorganization within the androgynous framework.

Gloria Steinem has been an enigma to critics of the women's movement because she has been successful and adored by all the old standards and cannot be written off as a bitter, resentful, or deviant female. She is a beautiful woman by any criterion. What is more, she has a degree from Smith College where she earned a Phi Beta Kappa key. She has been a successful journalist, having published in such magazines as *Vogue, Harper's, Life,* the *New York Times Magazine,* and having been repeatedly interviewed on television talk shows. She has been accepted in chic New York social circles and has had romantic relationships with several men considered among the "very eligible."[16] Since 1968, she has been a contributing editor of *New York* magazine, and in the winter of 1972 she was one of the driving forces behind the emergence of the new feminist magazine, *Ms.,* assuming major editorial responsibility for this ambitious new publishing venture, which in its introductory issue sold out its 300,000 copies on the newsstands.[17]

In 1970 Steinem began to emerge as a symbolic national leader of the women's movement, a position she would prefer to deny on behalf of all women; nevertheless, her time has been filled with an exhausting schedule of public speaking before women's groups and on college campuses, answering phone and mail requests for help with women's problems, writing about women, and organizing women's groups. She was a central figure in the organization of the National Women's Political Caucus in the summer of 1971. Her face has appeared on the cover of *Newsweek* (Aug. 16, 1971), *Redbook* (January 1972), and *McCall's* (January 1972) as the symbol of the new woman.

The goals that Gloria Steinem wants realized in society are sketched out in an article she wrote for *Time,* titled "What It Would Be Like If Women Win." Her utopian vision is prefaced with the assertion that "Women don't want to exchange places with men."[18]

Making the analogy to blacks in our society that is so familiar in the women's movement, she argues that the same fear which whites have of blacks wanting to take over is operating in the male chauvinist's or social skeptic's fear that the objective of the women's movement is to rule men as men have ruled women. This fear carries with it the guilt that men have ruled women badly.

In Steinem's utopia, men and women would have equal economic opportunity, with access to jobs on the basis of merit and with adequate pay for the drudge jobs, including housework, that women have been doing all along. The option of being a housewife would not be abandoned if a woman wanted to function vocationally as her husband's housekeeper and hostess, but she would receive a legally determined percentage of his pay.

Women would hold half of the country's political offices, with a woman being President once in a while, which would weaken the notion that male identity depends on "violence and victory." While Steinem feels that women would not eventually govern any differently from the way men govern, she thinks that women at present are less acculturated to war games and fighting, less committed to competition and violence, so that when given political power, they would for the next generation temper men's war-making tendency.

Regarding role expectations, Steinem says that in her utopia, "Men will have to give up ruling class privileges, but in return they will no longer be the ones to support the family, get drafted, and bear the strain of power and responsibility. Freud to the contrary, anatomy is not destiny, at least not for more than nine months of the time."[19] For roles to be altered, changes in marriage laws and sex arrangements would have to take place. Sex could no longer be a barter for security for women, and men would no longer have to commit themselves for a lifetime to inferior, dependent persons. Marriage would not be abandoned, but alternative varieties of life-styles would be encouraged, and antiquated marriage laws revised. Divorce would be equivalent to dissolving a business partnership. Alimony laws that discriminate against men as well as state laws inhibiting the civil rights of a married woman in such matters as signing credit agreements, establishing her domicile, using her own name, and incorporating a business would have to be rejected.

In Steinem's utopia, child care and homemaking would be shared by men and women in the home and as a public occupation: "Free nurseries, school lunches, family cafeterias built into every housing complex, service companies that will do household cleaning chores in a regular, businesslike way, and more responsibility by the entire community for the children: all these will make it possible for both mother and father to work, and to have equal leisure time with the children at home. For parents of very young children, however, a special job category, created by Government and unions, would allow such parents a shorter work day.''[20] Educational arrangements would train according to talent, with teaching at all levels divided between men and women; and participation in athletics, school activities, and courses such as auto mechanics and home economics would be open to boys and girls together. Courses offered would be in sexual politics and women's history, at least until a balance was achieved with the current male-dominated politics and history.

Steinem believes that the realization of this women's utopia would have attendant results in liberating men, religion, literature, manners, and fashions. If women took a full share of financial responsibility, men would be freer from the stress-based diseases that now cause them to die younger than women. Changes that are already taking place in religion may bring about significant theological changes, such as a redefinition of sin as women cease to be considered the source of temptation. Literature for children and adults would change as sex roles were revised. Dress would be more alike between the sexes, and manners would hinge on according respect to persons rather than on prescribed niceties toward women on a sex role basis. Thus, Steinem's quick journey through a liberated utopia encapsulates androgynous objectives of the women's movement.

Alice Rossi, a family sociologist, professor, and researcher, has been chairperson of both the Women's Caucus of the American Sociological Association and Committee W on the Status of Women of the American Association of University Professors. She was a charter member of the National Organization of Women and has published widely in the field of the family.

For a special 1964 issue of *Daedalus* magazine on "The Woman in America," Rossi wrote an article called "Equality between the Sexes: An Immodest Proposal," which has become a classic of contemporary feminism. She states her thesis in androgynous terms:

By sex equality I mean a socially androgynous conception of the roles of men and women, in which they are equal and

similar in such spheres as intellectual, artistic, political and
occupational interests and participation, complementary only
in those spheres dictated by physiological differences between
the sexes . . . An androgynous conception of sex role means
that each sex will cultivate some of the characteristics usually
associated with the other in traditional sex role definitions.
This means that tenderness and expressiveness should be cultivated in boys and socially approved in men, so that a male
of any age in our society would be psychologically and socially
free to express these qualities in his social relationships. It
means that achievement need, workmanship and constructive
aggression should be cultivated in girls and approved in
women so that a female of any age would be similarly free to
express these qualities in her social relationships . . . this definition of sex equality stresses the enlargement of the common
ground on which men and women base their lives together
by changing the social definitions of approved characteristics
and behavior for both sexes.[21]

Rossi points out that, as is true in most social revolutions, in
the women's revolution the legal code had to be changed first,
and this reform was the work of the feminists of the nineteenth
and early twentieth centuries, but the change has not made sufficient difference in the social and personal realms. Americans
have been characteristically individualistic about their solution
to the woman problem, and the social sciences have supported
this individualism in their conservative assumption that sex is a
necessary determinant of family roles, thereby sending dissatis-
fied women to the most individualistic source for help: psycho-
analysis.

Rossi sees the solution to the inequality between men and
women in three areas of broad community institutional planning. First, child care in American society needs to be restruc-
tured. Rossi argues that the quality of care which parents give
their children is much more significant than the quantity. She
scoffs at the popular psychological notion of "maternal deprivation" of children whose mothers leave them under the care of
other people and asks why "paternal deprivation" is never
brought up. In her view, the love and attention of both parents
are important to a child's development, but parents need not

have exclusive responsibility for the care of their children. She proposes a network of public child-care facilities. These would have specially trained directors and a variety of kinds of equipment and opportunities for the children and would be open year round. They could also provide home-duty practical mothers to care for ill children. Such centers would provide occupational freedom for mothers and would free the American home from the dominance of women as well as give children a new range of experience:[22]

> Sooner or later . . . women have to face the question of who they are besides their children's mother . . . A major solution to this quest would be found in the full and equal involvement in the occupational world . . . A job *per se* does not provide a woman, or a man either, with any magical path to self-fulfillment . . . [but] I believe that occupational involvement of women would also be the major means for reducing American women's dominance in marriage and parenthood, and thus for allowing for the participation of man as equal partners in family life.[23]

The second social change Rossi proposes is a shift of the pattern of residence from suburban to urban. Life in the suburbs takes men out of the family into a distant and isolated work area in the city, while it isolates mothers in the suburbs with the children, where they require a disproportionate effort for transportation and other necessities. Rossi proposes the development of housing units near the centers of work so that there can be an interplay between work and home and so that child care centers and other facilities can be more accessible.[24]

Rossi's third proposal is to change the educational pattern of boys and girls so that sex stereotypes for occupations and activities are no longer inculcated. Under the present system, boys are taught to fix mechanical things, girls to cook and sew. Sex education and family care instruction are usually given in sexually separated classes. Boys and girls have separate gym classes. Adults are pictured and described in textbooks as having separate sex roles vocationally. Rossi proposes that boys and girls have sex education, mechanical training, gym, and occupational training together, that they take field trips to laboratories and publishing houses, hear and observe men and women dancers, doctors, and business executives, to develop an attitude that activities and vocations of every sort are open to all.[25]

Rossi emphasizes vocation as a potential for fulfillment, but she sees it in relation to a total pattern of men and women relating to each other as similar persons in all areas of life. The entire community is responsible for effecting change, from the quest of women to be like men to the search for equality *between* the sexes. A humanizing change for men that encourages their tender participation in family life is just as important as a humanizing change for women that allows their aggressive participation in vocational and political leadership in society.

Women and the American English Language

The androgynous approach, which aims to erase prejudice against women at the root, to seek equality between women and men, and to replace inadequate mythology about the proper place of women or the proper definition of women, incorporates within its field of operations all those aspects of the culture that have a contributing or determining effect on our view of persons as human beings and as sex-differentiated persons. One such powerful aspect of culture is the language we speak, the way we talk about ourselves and one another.

A seven-year-old girl child brought home a note from school that said, "Help your child with his reading. He will learn to love books if books are a regular part of his home atmosphere."

Her serious response was, "That note isn't about me. I'm not a 'he.' "

This child's response is a part of the new feminist consciousness about the language. The word "mankind" is the label applied to the composite of humanity. Human energy is known as "manpower." "Man" is generic for person: "he" is the generic pronoun. We are supposed to understand that "man" as a suffix is supposed to mean "person" in such words as statesman, spokesman, chairman, congressman, postman, handyman, policeman. Yet there is ample room for ambiguity. If "man" means "male human being" and also "human being," there is room for the interpretation that standard humanity is male, with the female being some kind of appendage, an afterthought, an other-than-standard version of humanity. If a "he" is definitely male, and a "she" definitely female, the use of "he" for an indefinite reference weights the symbolic image in the hearer's or reader's mind toward the male.

The linguistic relativity theory, an hypothesis developed by Edward Sapir and Benjamin Lee Whorf and widely credited, holds that language is the articulation of the particular notions which define a culture. Language is a cultural product, and beyond that, language is the labeling of concepts that identify the values, experiences, and beliefs which make up the components and boundaries of a particular culture. Language is a symbol system, and it provides the means by which a culture segments its reality, that is, the mode by which the culture frames its conceptualization of things and sequences, processes and events. Whorf uses as the image for language a pair of glasses with somewhat warped lenses, through which perspective the participants in a given culture must get their picture of reality.[26] On the relationship between language and thought, Edward Sapir further states:

> The modern psychology has shown us how powerfully symbolism is at work in the unconscious mind. It is therefore easier to understand . . . that the most rarefied thought may be but the conscious counterpart of an unconscious linguistic symbolism . . . We may assume that language arose pre-rationally but we must not imagine that a highly developed system of speech symbols worked itself out before the genesis of distinct concepts and of thinking, the handling of concepts. We must rather imagine that thought processes set in, as a kind of psychic overflow, almost at the beginning of linguistic expression; further, that the concept, once defined, necessarily reacted on the life of its linguistic symbol, encouraging further linguistic growth . . . Not until we own the symbol do we feel that we hold a key to the immediate knowledge or understanding of the concept. Would we be so ready to die for "liberty," to struggle for "ideals," if the words themselves were not ringing within us? And the word, as we know, is not only a key; it may also be a fetter.[27]

It is in the spirit of this kind of linguistic theory that some of the feminists are attacking prevailing American English language usage. A feminist named Varda One writes a regular column titled "Manglish" for the newspaper *Everywoman*. In one column she attacks *Time* magazine for deriding the movement usage of "herstory" for "history," "girlcott" for "boycott," "sheroes" for "heroes," and other deliberately feminine substitutions for male-defining words, and for presuming that to be the point to "manglish." The purpose of her analysis of the language is rather "to make us realize that language is the basis of thought and that our own thought patterns are steeped in sexism, racism, class snobbery, and adult chauvinism." As Kate Millett observes in *Sexual Politics:* "In many patriarchies, language, as well as cultural tradition, reserves the human condition for the male. With the Indo-European languages this is a nearly inescapable habit of mind, for despite all the customary pretense that 'man' and 'humanity' are terms which apply equally to both sexes, the fact is hardly obscured that in practice, general application favors the male far more often than the female as referent, or even sole referent, for such designations."[28]

In another "Manglish" column on the need to stop using "man" generically, Varda One defines the problem as people having the choice of which meaning to give it. She proposes three possible solutions:

1. Use man specifically only, use a word for woman, use person or human to refer to both sexes.
2. Use man generically only, specify when referring to one sex by using a modifier such as male man or female man.
3. Use man generically only, invent a new word for man in the specific sense and for woman.[29]

On the generic use of the masculine pronoun, Kate Miller and Casey Swift reported a trend among people in 1972 to try to avoid the problem of using "he" in speaking and writing by using "he/she" or "he or she." They note that, on the ideological question of grammar discriminating against females, Lynn T. White pointed out fifteen years earlier:

The grammar of English dictates that when a referent is

either of indeterminate sex or both sexes, it shall be considered masculine. The penetration of this habit of language into the minds of little girls as they grow up to be women is more profound than most people, including most women, have recognized: for it implies that personality is really a male attribute, and that women are human subspecies . . . It would be a miracle if a girl-baby, learning to use the symbols of our tongue, could escape some wound to her self-respect: whereas a boy-baby's ego is bolstered by the pattern of our language.[30]

Miller and Swift therefore propose a new set of pronouns to desex the language and to overcome the awkwardness of using "he or she" in every context calling for indefinite sex or both sexes:

Distinct Gender	Singular Common Gender	Plural Common Gender
he and she	tey	they
his and her (or hers)	ter (or ters)	their (or theirs)
him or her	tem	them[31]

Varda One also compiled a list of suggested pronouns for use when persons need not be distinguished by gender:

Present usage	Varda One	Mary Arovan	Dana Densmore	Anonymous
he and/or she	ve	co	she	they
his and/or her	vis	cos	heris	their
him and/or her	ver	co	herm	them
himself and/or herself	verself	coself		theirself[32]

The list by Dana Densmore adopts the feminine pronoun for the generic and derives her proposed usage from the existing feminine words "she" and "her." This replacement of the existing feminine for the generic is in line with the women's liberationist ideology of asserting female superiority. The rest of the lists indicate an operation of the androgynous viewpoint so as to bring about a new equality in the language, a new linguistic neutrality.

Another feminist language concern has been the forms of address. Unmarried women are addressed as ''Miss,'' married women as ''Mrs.,'' and even divorced women as ''Mrs.,'' while there is no linguistic distinction between married and unmarried men. Again, is embedded in this linguistic practice an assumption that a man's identity is individual in manhood, while woman's identity is dependent on her relationship to a man. For naming her, calling her who she is, identifying her, woman must indicate whether or not she is or was married. This linguistic problem is related to the legal and social problem of the woman being expected to assume her husband's name at marriage, while the male continues to have the same name throughout his lifetime. In the last few years, feminists have popularized the form of address ''Ms.,'' to be used by all women as a parallel to ''Mr.'' It has caught on more rapidly in written communication than in speaking, but many persons see it as a kind of code form of address for a wide range of people sympathetic with the women's movement. In naming its new magazine *Ms.,* the editors wrote, ''In practice Ms. is used with a woman's given name: Ms. Jane Jones, say, or Ms. Jane Wilson Jones. Obviously, it doesn't make sense to say Ms. John Jones: a woman identified only as her husband's wife must remain a Mrs. . . . The use of Ms. isn't meant to protect either the married or the unmarried woman from social pressure—only to signify a female human being. It's symbolic, and important. There's a lot in a name.''[33]

As a further step in the question of naming, some feminists have given themselves new liberation names. Rejecting both use of both the husband's surnames and father's surnames as masculine-derived, women have given themselves new names such as Laura X, Kathie Sarachild, Gail Witch, Anna Q, Ellen Eumenides, and Sara Savage.[34] Early feminists did not go this far, but it is clear that some of them were conscious of the problem. When Lucy Stone married Henry Blackwell in 1855, their marriage contract assured her of keeping her name. Victoria Woodhull took the married name of ''Woodhull'' when she married at sixteen, but in her subsequent marriages she retained the Woodhull name. Margaret Sanger took her husband's name on her first marriage, but kept the Sanger name when she married Mr. Slee. It has become usual for famous women or professional women to remain known by their original or "maiden" name or the name under which they came into prominence.

In the "Manglish" column Varda One identifies several other linguistic practices that seem to discriminate against women. We use a number of nouns to designate vocation or activity or condition, such as "actor" or "poet," but maintain a set of feminine suffixes that set apart such an actor if she is female—"-trix," "-ess," "-enne," "-euse."[35] Varda One suggests that such feminine suffixes be dropped, for a poet is a poet with no distinction necessary for sex, and anyone who flies an airplane is an aviator, without any need to differentiate a she-plane-flier as an "aviatrix."

One "Manglish" column deals with the metaphors of woman as food and woman as animal commonly used in American English speech. It is common to hear women referred to as "dish," "peach," "plum," "tomato," "cookie," "cheesecake," and "sugar," but never as anything solid like meat and potatoes. As animal, women are "chick," "quail," "squab," "pigeon," "filly," "bunny," or "goose," but never anything indicating strength like a lion or tiger or bear.[36] To labor the obvious, the image of softness and weakness as attributes of woman is maintained in this aspect of language usage.

There is a growing interest in the gender-specific use of language, that is, in vocabularies, inflections, and syntactical patterns that are used exclusively or dominantly by members of one sex. Robin Lakoff writes of a larger range of color words belonging to women—"mauve, beige, ecru, aquamarine, lavender"—signifying that fine discriminations of this sort are women's province. She points out the female use of the questioning inflection, to indicate the speaker's reservation about making a flat statement until her respondent can affirm what she has to say: "Dinner will be ready around six o'clock?" Lakoff regards the feminine use of the tag question—"isn't it? don't we?"—as showing female uncertainty.[37]

Varda One has a theory that women's names and words referring to women have degenerated in the history of the language. Since language in general is continually changing, it
would take considerably more linguistic evidence than she has
given to prove this point, but it would be a study worth serious
attention in linguistics. On names, Varda One lists the following: "maudlin," from the name Mary Magdalene, has come to
mean "excessively sentimental." "Moll," from the name
Molly, has come to mean "thief's mistress." "Betty," a woman's nickname, is now applied to "a man who busies himself
with household duties of a woman." "Lazy Susan" is an assembly of dishes that saves a maid work, "Susan" being a name
that used to be the label for "maid." With respect to the general
degeneration of words that refer to women, Varda One lists the
word "hysterical," which comes from the Greek "hysterikes,"
meaning "suffering from the womb," and now means "a high
level of uncontrolled emotion." The word "mistress" originally
was an equivalent to "master," meaning a woman of authority,
but by the seventeenth century it meant "illicit sweetheart."
"Hussy" came from the Old English "huswife," but it now
means "lewd or brazen woman." "Harlot" once meant "a fellow of either sex," but it is now a woman prostitute.[38]
The practice of a suitor asking for a woman's "hand,"
Varda One suggests, is associated in linguistic history with the
terms of slavery. The Latin word "manus," meaning "hand,"
is embedded in the word "mancipation," the laying on of the
hand as the symbol of possession, and "emancipation," re-
moval from under the hand.[39]
Language favoring the man, however, is typified by such
words as "virtue" and "virile," coming from the Latin root
"vir," meaning "man." Virtue and virility are manly qualities.
The male testicles are symbols for praise, as is apparent in the
slang phrases "He's got balls" and "He's a ballsy guy." Masculine insults in all-male groups put down other men by equa-
ting them with the receiver of sexual intercourse: "Fuck you,"
"Up yours," "Screw you," or the familiar nonverbal finger
signs for intercourse or for cuckoldry. Women, in contrast, have
no profanity and no insulting language of their own. Further-

more, women still are often considered unwomanly ("unlady-like") if they use the male-derived put-down language.[40]

Today there is uncertainty in a fairly wide portion of the population over a few areas of linguistic usage, and this kind of uncertainty is the beginning point for language change, though it is impossible to predict what linguistic matters will be permanently altered. Newspapers and correspondents are increasingly picking up "Ms." as a form of address; and since NOW initiated "chairone," numerous formally structured meetings have struggled with calling the presiding officer the "chairperson" or "chairone," though more often when the presiding person is female than when he is male. The *Spokeswoman* periodical has contributed the neologisms "congresspersons" and "fore-mothers." No change in the generic pronoun seems to be coming into practice beyond the awkward "he/she" and "he or she," reminding us that the language has a life of its own and very little intentional change can be brought about by a group of ideological advocates.

The investigation of language's impact on sexism or on discrimination against women is itself an aspect of the androgynous approach. The androgynous or men-and-women-equal-to each-other model compels investigators and advocates to go to the roots that make women unequal in our society. The English language is layered with values and beliefs that over the centuries have created our culture. It provides our way of saying who we are. By investigating it thoroughly, we can find one kind of evidence for the cultural definition of who woman is. The investigation has only touched the surface, but already there is evidence that women are spoken of as secondary human beings, dependent on men for their central identity.

The feminists' advocacy of change in the language falls dominantly under the androgynous label. Their request is essentially not that we talk about humanity as female, as "she" any more than as "he," but that we search for and use comprehensive terms which denote humanity first and subordinate sex-designation. A "chairperson" is male or female by definition; a "Ms." is equivalent to a "Mr." The central ideological ingredient in such advocacy of language change is to recognize the prejudices

in the way we say things and to replace them in our consciousness with a neutrally human way of speaking.

Androgyny in Religion

In *Beyond God the Father,* Mary Daly provides philosophical
and theological underpinnings for a feminism in the androgynous mode. Her training and language are explicitly Christian, but she seeks to open up the predominant doctrines so as
to allow for a new and comprehensive focus. She acknowledges
a radicalization in her life since writing *The Church and the
Second Sex;* and *Beyond God the Father* is indeed conceptually
more brittle.

Ontology is the paramount theological framework for Daly.
In this, she is a spiritual daughter of Paul Tillich, but the
daughter has gone a far different route from the sons. Daly
claims that women have been excluded from Being; but apply-
ing the Christian doctrine of a Second Coming in a new way,
she advises that women must do nothing less than bring about a
Second Coming of New Being for humanity. Women must lead
the world to a new participation in Being, which will shatter the
hierarchical structure of patriarchy which the Church has
helped to make. In being excluded by men, women have known
separation from their rightful human share of being and will
not reenact the male pattern of hierarchy. She calls on women
to transcend their separation: "Women generally can see very
well that the movement will self-destruct if we settle for ven-
geance. The more imminent danger, then, is that some women
will seek premature reconciliation, not allowing themselves to
see the depth and implications of feminism's essential opposition to sexist society. It can be easy to leap on the bandwagon of
'human liberation' without paying the price in terms of polarization, tensions, risk, and pain that the ultimate objective of
real human liberation demands."[41]

Daly maintains that women have had a primary power stolen
from them, the power of naming. In the biblical account of
creation, God gave man (generic) the right to name. Daly uses
jarring linguistic juxtapositions to remind women and men as
"man" of this power. In a generic sense, she calls for the "sisterhood of man." She insists on a "castration of phallocentric

values." She would have the image of God be neither Father, Son, Master, nor Lord, but "God the Verb," the active power of Being.

Daly insists that historical Christianity has been Christolatrous, that is, has maintained a veneration of maleness of Jesus. There has been no feminine presence in the Christian deity. Daly believes that women must form the Antichurch, and that in the bonding of a new sisterhood they can be the force to *no longer* liberate the church from these distortions and idolatries.

Androgyny is one of her words for the wholeness potential in New Being: "Such independence means the becoming of psychologically androgynous human beings, since the basic crippling 'complementarity' has been the false masculine/feminine polarity. Androgynous integrity and transformation will require that women cease to play the role of 'complement' and struggle to stand alone as free human beings."[42]

Psychic Identity

Evidence is accumulating that sexual stereotypes are held as assumptions in psychological studies of the nature of women and in psychological and psychiatric treatment of women with problems. In a 1968 test given at Worcester State Hospital in Massachusetts by Inge K. Broverman and others to male and female clinical psychologists to examine their assumptions about mental health, it was shown that "those traits stereotypically masculine . . . are more often perceived as socially desirable." In the test, the psychologists were divided into three groups and given three identical lists of 122 traits, the first group being instructed to choose those traits that showed a clinically healthy male, the second choosing a clinically healthy female, and the last choosing a clinically healthy adult. The male-valued items included such qualities as "very aggressive," "very independent," "not at all emotional," "very logical," "very direct," "very adventurous," "very self-confident," and "very ambitious." The female-valued items were "very talkative," "very tactful," "very gentle," "very aware of feelings of others," "very religious," "very quiet," "very strong need for security." When the lists were correlated, the set of traits valued for males was identical to the set of traits valued for the

clinically healthy adult. Thus, it was demonstrated that for the
clinical psychologists tested, what was perceived as a clinically
healthy woman contradicted what was seen as a clinically
healthy adult. The model for adult mental health was masculine, with a double standard of mental health applied to
women.[43]

Another clinical psychological study by Matina Horner
shows women to be in a double bind regarding achievement.
According to Horner's findings, published as "Fail: Bright
Women," a bright woman "is caught in a double bind. In
achievement oriented situations she worries not only about failure but also about success."[44]

Horner began work on her study with the recognition that
recent testing on the "achievement motive" had been done with
men. Her task was to study sex differences in achievement motivation:

> My first clue came from the one consistent finding on the
> women that they get higher test anxiety scores than do the
> men. Eleanor Maccoby has suggested that the girl who is
> motivated to achieve is defying conventions of what girls
> "should" do. As a result, the intellectual woman pays a price
> in anxiety. Margaret Mead concurs, noting that intense intel-
> lectual striving can be viewed as "competitively aggressive
> behavior," and of course Freud thought that the whole es-
> sence of femininity lay in repressing aggressiveness (and
> hence intellectuality).

> Thus consciously or unconsciously the girl equates intellec-
> tual achievement with loss of femininity. A bright woman is
> caught in a double bind. In testing and other achievement-
> oriented situations she worries not only about failure, but
> also about success. If she fails, she is not living up to her own
> standards of performance; if she succeeds she is not living up
> to societal expectations about the female role. Men in our
> society do not experience this kind of ambivalence, because
> they are not only permitted but actively encouraged to do
> well.[45]

Horner conducted her empirical study in three parts with

bright male and female undergraduates at the University of Wisconsin. The first part involved administering the Thematic Apperception Test as well as asking the subject to tell a story about a person who found himself or herself at the head of a medical school class—the person being a male for the males and a female for the females. This test was designed to uncover the motive for avoiding success. Sixty-five percent of the girls, but fewer than ten percent of the boys, made up stories to avoid success. The young women made up stories of a female's loneliness, unhappiness, and worry following achievement, while a large majority of the young men expressed unambiguous delight at a male's success.

The second part of the test compared individuals working alone both with individuals working in competition with members of their own sex and with individuals in competition with members of the opposite sex. The data indicate that far more men did much better in competition of either kind, while women worked less well in any kind of competition and least well in competition with men.

The final test required each individual subject to score on a 1-to-100 scale the importance to her or him of doing well in the three different kinds of work situation. The majority of girls who had tested as having a high fear of success reported that it was much more important to succeed when they were working alone. Horner concludes:

> These findings suggest that most women will fully explore their intellectual potential only when they do not need to compete—and least of all when they are competing with men. This was true of women with a strong anxiety about success. Unfortunately, these are often the same women who could be very successful if they were free from that anxiety. The girls in my sample who feared success also tended to have high intellectual ability and histories of academic success . . . We can see from this small study that achievement motivation in women is much more complex than the same drive in men. Most men do not find many inhibiting forces in their path if they are able and motivated to succeed. As a result, an opponent is a source of pride and enhanced masculinity.

If a woman sets out to do well, however, she bumps into a number of obstacles. She learns that it really isn't ladylike to be too intellectual. She is warned that men will treat her with distrustful tolerance at best, and outright prejudice at worst, if she pursues a career. She learns the truth of Samuel Johnson's comment, "A man is in general better pleased when he has a good dinner upon his table, than when his wife talks Greek." So she doesn't learn Greek, and the motive to avoid success is born.[46]

Another important contribution to the psychology of women is Naomi Weisstein's "Psychology Constructs the Female, or the Fantasy Life of the Male Psychologist." It first appeared in the magazine *motive,* in a special issue on women titled "Kinder, Kuche, Kirche As Scientific Law,"[47] and has appeared in *Psychology Today* and in numerous anthologies of feminist writings, which suggests that it holds wide credence or strikes a responsive chord among numerous and various adherents to the women's movement as well as raising a provocative question for the field of psychology.

Weisstein proposes that in looking to psychology for a definition of woman, we have found a reflection of the cultural consensus that woman's nature is to be identified as sex object for men and as nurturer in the home. Further, research by psychologists and psychiatrists into the nature of woman has led to "theory without evidence," since it is based on case studies of women who have been perceived as sick merely because of deviance from the status quo. Moreover, some of the generalizations about the proper nature of women have been made from nonhuman primate studies, which have dubious results when applied to human beings and which have also been selective in the range of primates studied. Weisstein concludes that psychological studies up to this time have not told us in any comprehensive way what a woman would be like if she were to realize her full potential. In short, we do not know the kind of psychological definition of woman that would be possible if sufficient studies were made.

Citing Bruno Bettelheim, Eric Ericson, and Joseph Reingold, Weisstein shows them all to be in the tradition of Freud's

"Anatomy is destiny." Bettelheim writes, "We must start with the realization that, as much as women want to be good scientists or engineers, they want first and foremost to be womanly companions of men and to be mothers." Ericson's study of inner and outer space concludes: "Much of a young woman's identity is already defined in her kind of attractiveness and in the selectivity of her search for the man (or men) by whom she wishes to be sought . . . Mature womanly fulfillment rests on the fact that a woman's . . . somatic design harbors an 'inner space' destined to bear the offspring of chosen men, and with it, a biological, psychological, and ethical commitment to take care of human infancy." And Reingold turns the biological determinism of women into a social program: "Anatomy decrees the life of a woman . . . when women grow up without dread of their biological functions and without subversion by feminist doctrine, and therefore enter upon motherhood with a sense of fulfillment and altruistic sentiment, we shall attain the goal of a good life and a secure world in which to live it."[48]

Focusing on the failure of clinicians to look at the social context of women's experience, Weisstein describes a group of clinical experiments that demonstrates the effect of social pressure on subjects. Subjects do a number of things under social pressure that they would not normally be expected to do, such as administer shock to a subject to a point that is believed lethal, or identify faces as high or low success on the basis of suggestion from the experimenter, or express belief that rats are intelligent in running a maze at the suggestion of the experimenter. Weisstein applies these findings to the understanding of women's experience:

If subjects under quite innocuous and non-coercive social conditions can be made to kill other subjects and under other types of social conditions will positively refuse to do so; if subjects can react to a state of physiological fear by becoming euphoric because there is somebody else around who is angry; if students become intelligent because teachers expect them to be intelligent, and rats run mazes better because experimenters are told the rats are bright, then it is obvious that a study of human behavior requires, first and foremost, a study of the social contexts within which people move, the expectations as to how they will behave, and the authority which tells them who they are and what they are supposed to do.[49]

Weisstein maintains that the biologically based theories can be refuted in two ways. Studies which show that men and women are biologically different, that physiological states are different, tell us nothing about the resulting varieties of behavior, for a multiplicity of felt emotional states is still possible. Second, the nonhuman primate studies have not taken into account all the variations of nonhuman primate life, much less the variations in behavior that take place in altered physical and social settings.

Weisstein poses the question:

How are women characterized in our culture, and in psychology? They are inconsistent, emotionally unstable, lacking in a strong conscience or super ego, weaker, "nuturant" rather than productive, "intuitive" rather than intelligent, and if they are at all "normal," suited to the home and the family. In short, the list adds up to a typical minority group stereotype of inferiority; if they know their place, which is in the home, they are really quite lovable, happy childlike, loving creatures. In a review of the intellectual differences between little boys and little girls, Eleanor Maccoby has shown that there are no intellectual differences until about high school, girls begin to do worse on a few intellectual tasks . . . and beyond high school, the achievement of women now measured in terms of productivity and accomplishment drops off even more rapidly. There are a number of other, non-intellectual tests which show sex differences: I choose the intellectual differences since it is seen clearly that women start becoming inferior. It is no use to talk about women being different but equal; all of the tests I can think of have a "good" and a "bad" outcome. Women usually end up at the "bad" outcome. In light of social expectations about women, what is surprising is not that women end up where society expects they will; what is surprising is that little girls don't get the message that they are supposed to be stupid until high school.[50]

She concludes, "I do not know what immutable differences exist between men and women apart from differences in their genitals; perhaps there are some other unchangeable differences; probably there are a number of irrelevant differences. But it is clear that until social expectations for men and women are equal, until we provide equal respect for both men and women, our answers to this question will simply reflect our prejudices."[51]

Weisstein's conclusion represents a courageous kind of intellectual humility. The direction she opens for research in psychology as well as for ordinary women's and men's assessment of themselves is an androgynous one. Everyone who has attempted to make a rational, objective study of any topic knows the difficulty of recognizing and attempting to obliterate one's prejudices, the difficulty that makes pure objectivity impossible. Women doing psychological testing to "prove" women's superiority or to "prove" equality would be just as suspect as those who time and again "prove" the status quo assumptions about women in the cultural consensus. Indeed, it was a woman psychiatrist, Maryna Farnham, who "demonstrated" in the 1940s that woman was "the lost sex" because of her striving to leave the home for occupations unnatural to her. Testing such as that done at the Worcester State Hospital and by Matina Horner gives some idea of what is the status of women in women's assessment of themselves and in the psychological professional's assessment of them. Naomi Weisstein's suggestion is that we take a new look at how our psyches operate, a new look at what is human and at what is male or female.

Female Sexuality and the Revolution

The meaning of sexuality per se has been a locus of much feminist debate, with the results of the sex researchers being examined and contested on many fronts. The central question as to which human attributes are essentially sexual emerges in both polemical and scientific confrontations. Most feminists would reject a double standard of sexual morality. The androgynous paradigm implies a recognition that a sexual ingredient of human personality is present and vital but not definitive. The masculine-equalitarian paradigm places the emphasis more firmly on discarding a double standard of sexual morality or on repudiating the consideration of sexuality in matters of social, political, or vocational consequence. The prowoman, antimasculinist argument focuses on the presence of a specific female sex organ in anatomy; and the extreme antimasculinist form of the women's liberationist paradigm, which abandons relationships and interaction with men, suggests an even more irreconcilable difference between men and women.

Only a few of the historical feminists spoke out on the forbidden topic of sexuality, and they were considered by their more conservative sisters of the women's rights movement to be more enemies than friends of the cause, which in fact they often were in their social context. Yet these advocates of what was anathematized as "free love" were the forebears to some extent of the androgynous ideology with its affirmation of a sexual dimension to personality and its posture of support for freeing men as well as women from restrictive social roles. Frances Wright, the wealthy Scotswoman who came to America and lectured on sexual freedom, Negro emancipation, and atheism in the 1820s and 1830s when it was shocking for a woman to appear on a public platform, made her case for female emancipation partly on the basis that men were no freer than women when their wives and sisters were subjected to educational and legal bondage.[52]

Wright was following that English foremother of modern feminism, Mary Wollstonecraft, in her principle of sexual freedom, which she spoke for from the platform and practiced in her several relationships. That is, passionate love is one kind of relationship with a man, companionship is another, both of which should be based on the character of the relationship. Women should be as free as men to participate in passionate love as they desire. It was this principle, probably laced with an element of vindictiveness, that led Victoria Woodhull to expose the affairs of Henry Ward Beecher in one of the most notorious scandals of the nineteenth century. It was hypocrisy, Woodhull charged, for Beecher's seduction of his women parishioners to go unnoticed when women who were prostitutes or who had love affairs or who, like herself, proclaimed themselves free lovers were punished by society.[53]

In addition to regarding sexual freedom as an aspect of the full freedom of persons, historical feminists affirmed the woman's right to choose her own sexual partner for the pleasure of a sexual relationship as much as the man had such a right. A similar kind of validation of the woman's right to sexual pleasure was made by Margaret Sanger, who held a romantic view of the contrast between male and female sexuality. Influenced by Freud and more explicitly by Havelock Ellis, Sanger accepted the notion of different "natures" in women and men; but her birth control crusade was based in part on a feminism that called for releasing the "feminine spirit" by allowing woman to participate more actively in sexual intercourse for love's sake, free from the possibility of pregnancy. Sanger saw aggression and enjoyment in the sex act on the woman's part as an avenue for her personal fulfillment, and she thought such fulfillment could become a reality through the use of birth control methods and devices. She strongly felt that birth control was a woman's problem. This feminist focus on personal fulfillment anticipated the androgynous ideology.[54]

Australian-born Germaine Greer, read widely in America, articulates an androgynous view of female sexuality for today. Popular magazine reviewers of her book *The Female Eunuch* billed her as "the feminist men like," and *Playboy* called her a "ballsy female," for in its interview of her she made quite clear that she not only likes sexual intercourse but likes it with lots of different men and with lots of variations.[55]

The Female Eunuch centers on what female sexuality means, and Greer's treatment of the topic leads to a conclusion that a completely realized sexual identity is essential for a fully developed independence and autonomy as a person. Spontaneity, to Germaine Greer, is the mark of the free person, and heterosexual spontaneity is the central ingredient for human emancipation. Hence, it is essential for maximum freedom in human interaction that both men and women experience intense, creative, aggressive sexual relationships.

A justification for placing her analysis under the androgy-

nous heading is her statement, "If women understand by emancipation the adoption of the masculine role, then we are lost
indeed."[56] Rather, she suggests that they both strike out in a
new direction:

> The surest guide to the correctness of the path that women
> take is *joy in the struggle* . . . For a long time there may be no
> perceptible reward for women other than their new sense of
> purpose and integrity . . . To be emancipated from helpless-
> ness and need and walk freely upon the earth that is your
> birthright . . . To be freed from guilt and shame and the tire-
> less self-discipline of women. To stop pretending and dis-
> sembling, cajoling and manipulating, and begin to control
> and sympathize. To claim the masculine virtues of magnan-
> imity and generosity and courage. It goes much further than
> equal pay for equal work, for it ought to revolutionize the
> conditions of work completely. It does not understand the
> phrase "equality of opportunity," for it seems that the op-
> portunities will have to be utterly changed and women's souls
> changed so that they desire opportunity instead of shrinking
> from it. The first significant discovery we shall make as we
> racket along our female road to freedom is that men are not
> free, and they will seek to make this an argument why nobody
> should be free. We can only reply that slaves enslave their
> masters, and by securing our own manumission we may show
> men the way that they could follow when they jumped off
> their own treadmill. Privileged women will pluck at your
> sleeve and seek to enlist you in the "fight" for reforms, but
> reforms are retrogressive. The old process must be broken,
> not made new. Bitter women will call you to rebellion, but
> you have too much to do. What will you do?[57]

Greer's central thesis is that women have been castrated, that
the status quo notions of femininity have created in women an
asexuality that is the source of their disability to experience
personal freedom. The notions of femininity which now guide
their lives and maintain their identity have denied that women
have a sex organ:

> The acts of sex are themselves forms of inquiry, as the old
> euphemism "carnal knowledge" makes clear: it is exactly the

element of quest in her sexuality which the female is taught to deny. She is not only taught to deny it in her sexual contacts, but (for in some subliminal way the connection is understood) in all her contacts, from infancy onward, so that when she becomes aware of her sex the pattern has sufficient force of inertia to prevail over new forms of desire and curiosity. This is the condition which is meant by the term *female eunuch.* In traditional psychological theory, which is after all only another way of describing and rationalizing the status quo, the desexualization of women is illustrated in the Freudian theory of the female sex as lacking a sexual organ . . . On these grounds we can, indeed we must, reject femininity as meaning *without libido,* and therefore incomplete, subhuman, a cultural reduction of human possibilities, and rely upon the indefinite term female, which retains the possibility of female libido.[58]

Greer deals with four aspects of the subject of castrated femininity: body, soul, love, and hate. In each context she describes what the situation and effects of women's conditioning have been and suggests what the possibilities of emancipation might be. But first she points out the conservatism of the reforming groups in the women's movement today, which essentially "follow the tracks" of the suffragists and are "not certain about the degree of inferiority or natural dependence which is unalterably female."[59] Greer, in contrast, is sure that women are not inferior and that there is nothing unalterably female. It is her contention that all of our assumptions about what it means to be female *"could be otherwise."*[60] That is, the composite of characteristics and behavior patterns that make up femininity are culturally derived, and they mask the outlines of what a female person might be. It is essential to make the distinction between femininity and a female person—femininity being a patterning, a stereotype that is constricting and negative; a female person being a not-yet-realized possibility.

Greer argues that, whatever else we are, we are our bodies, beginning with the chromosome determination of gender at conception. Of the forty-eight chromosomes that program a person, only one differs between males and females, and that is for the determination of sex. Yet the classification of bone structure made by archeologists, to take one of Greer's examples of female castration, calls female bones "pedomorphic" or infantilized, while male bones are called "gerontomorphic" or aged. Greer cites the cultural norm of standardizing female curves, recognizable at any cocktail party by a gesture of male hands, which makes individual women with either buxom bosoms or flat chests feel alike inadequate to fit the norm. Body hair, long recognized as a secondary sexual characteristic, comes under scrutiny as an arbitrary division between the hairy male and the smooth female, an artificial division that makes ridiculous the feminine practice of shaving and plucking body hair.

Regarding sexual intercourse, Greer objects to the terms of the recent controversy over the locus of the female orgasm—the clitoris or the vagina—as well as to the leveling result in the sex act of the advice of such clinicians as Masters and Johnson. This makes dull sex for dull people. She regards the adoption of a technique, a standardized plan for sexual intercourse, whether portrayed in fiction or developed in a laboratory situation, as a mechanization of the act, which at its best is spontaneous, exploratory, and infinitely varied. Orgasm takes place in the whole sex organ. In her statement that "the cunt must come into its own" lies the nub of her argument.

Menstruation is a biological reality that has been characterized as a deterrent to women's productivity in public life and a source of shame for one's femaleness, but Greer considers it a minor nuisance, which is neither shameful nor any more counterproductive than men's tension or ulcers or drinking habits. It is an index of the fact that women are no more perfect than men.

Tracing the conditioning of the girl to a role of passivity and dependence, Greer shows the development of a polarity between love and hate. The girl is taught in puberty to wait for the boy's aggressive action, to subordinate her will and her ability to the boy's. If this does not take, she is sent to the counselor or doctor or priest or psychiatrist for "the psychological sell" on femininity. This fantasy of a sex of the mind continues to be perpetrated in spite of years of testing that would indicate there is no such thing. Women are subjected to notions of romance that suggest the male mastery of female weakness, and they are finally acculturated to a sense of sacredness about the nuclear family centered around the mother, in which a kind of metaphysical sanction is given to woman's destiny in motherhood and homemaking. The cumulative effect is to produce a form of cultural masochism in the female and of sadism in the male, which is prohibitive of full human interaction. Greer feels that the nature of the current rebellion in the name of the new radical feminism represents a further acting out of the masochist/ sadist enmity, with the women confronting or attacking men in identifying them as the enemy. Her sympathies are with neither the Freudians nor the Marxists.

The revolution that she calls for is based on cooperation, on a wrecking of the stereotype, and on the self-assertion of women as female persons. For her, this means abandonment of monogamy and the nuclear family, but such a goal would not have to be so for all persons participating in the revolution:

why?

> *Revolution* ought to entail the correction of some of the false perspectives which our assumptions about womanhood, sex, love and society have combined to create. Tentatively it gestures towards the redeployment of energy, no longer to be used in repression, but in desire, movement and creation. Sex must be rescued from the traffic between powerful and powerless, masterful and mastered, sexual and neutral, to become a form of communication between potent, gentle, tender people, which cannot be accomplished by denial of heterosexual contact. The Ultra-feminine must refuse any longer to countenance the self-deception of the Omnipotent Administrator, not so much by assailing him as by freeing herself from the desire to fulfill his expectations. It might be expected that men would resist female liberation because it threatens the foundations of phallic narcissism, but there are indications that men themselves are seeking a more satisfying role. If women liberate themselves, they will perforce liberate their oppressors: men might well feel that as sole custodians of sexual energy and universal protectors of women and children they have undertaken the impossible, especially now that their misdirected energies have produced the ultimate weapon . . . If women could think that civiliza-

tion would come to maturity only when they were involved in it wholly, they might feel more optimism in the possibilities of change and new development. The spiritual crisis we are at present traversing might be just another growing pain.[61]

In that her objective for achieving full female personhood is cooperation between women and men and that her identification of women's enemy is society's stereotyped attitudes about women's identity, Greer is arguing for the androgynous pattern. Although she speaks to the questions of social and political identity, her central contribution to the ideology is the affirmation of female sexuality.

Family Structure, Child-Rearing, and Education

There are women's liberationists who claim that the nuclear family must be abolished if women's full humanity is to be achieved, that the institution of the family is an oppressive force for women. Other advocates see a variety of alternative units already in existence, which must be affirmed socially and legally in a pluralistic conception of what constitutes a ''family''—one-parent families, two-adult childless families, extended interest groups living together, communal marriages or communal living arrangements of several adults of both sexes with or without children or of single sex groupings, and homosexual marriages with social and legal sanction, alongside the traditional nuclear family of two parents and children.

Short of abolition of the family, attacks have been made on the idea of motherhood as the singular route to woman's fulfillment. One finds considerable advocacy of day care centers for tending the children of working mothers. The terms of marriage contracts indicating the agreement of husband and wife to share equally in the work of the household and the care of children are being published, and considerable discussion has been engendered regarding men assuming an equal share of domestic work as women take on an equal share of public involvement.

The androgynous ideology can incorporate most of these alternatives for family organization. With its goal of making women and men equal to each other, it can encompass varieties of choice about how to structure families and rear children.

Central to an androgynous view, however, must be abandonment of the belief that motherhood is the singular or primary means for a woman to realize her identity, to achieve her personal fulfillment. It is sometimes called "the myth of motherhood." Counteracting this myth is the evidence that men as well as women are fully capable of loving and nurturing children, given a sense of personal freedom to do so and a social context where the intimate care of children by both men and women is granted social approval. Further, the population problem in today's world suggests a need to break a pronatalist mentality which dictates that procreation is a necessity for human fulfillment. Also, it has been shown again and again that there is no necessary determining link between the fact of procreating and the ability to nurture children capably. Adoption of children is a familiar demonstration of this, as are the works of child development professionals such as Sigmund Freud's daughter, Anna Freud, who had no children of her own.[62]

In an empirical study showing that American women do not spend the largest portion of their time on mothering and supporting the argument that women need not focus primarily on motherhood, Alice Rossi reports:

> A young woman can, but typically does *not,* anticipate three characteristics of her adulthood: (1) she will actually spend almost twice as many years with neither husband nor dependent children than she will carrying responsibility for preschool children (23 vs. 12 per cent): (2) almost two-thirds of her adult years will be spent either alone or living with a husband but no children under 18 years of age: and (3) of the remaining 36 per cent of her adulthood, 25 per cent will be largely part time parenting and only 12 per cent full time mothering of pre-kindergarten age children. For a two child family, only seven of the woman's 56 adult years will go to rearing pre-school children. One would never get any suggestion of the significance of these changes from most of the literature available to college students in either human development or the sociology of the family, for both fields are steeped in a focus on maternity as the primary adult role of women.[63]

Rossi shows that home maintenance is much more time-consuming for the housewife than is mothering. It is on this point that many feminists are arguing that care of the home should become the joint responsibility of husband and wife. Joint responsibility for the house creates equality at the point of doing tasks that at best contribute to the order and maintenance of the family and at worst are repetitious drudgery. Joint responsibility in housekeeping also grants a kind of equality in domestic life to the man who often in the home is found to be subordinate to the woman's decision-making about the domestic style of life and ordering of the private existence of the family. Joint responsibility between man and woman in the home also furnishes positive role models for the children, as they see adults of both sexes assume a variety of tasks that do not suggest sex segregation or sexual stereotypes.

Letty Cottin Pogrebin testifies on the basis of experience with her own family about raising children without sex stereotypes: "In our household, whoever can, does. Call it convenience plus ability. I make dinner because I like to and because I cook better. My husband makes breakfast because I simply cannot get up that early in the morning and the children love his pancakes."

Under the androgynous heading, the goal of equality between the sexes must start early. Pogrebin suggests a number of factors of sex stereotyping that begin in the family and under social pressure. One of the first signals is dressing a baby girl in pink and a baby boy in blue, then cooing and cuddling the baby girl while roughhousing with the baby boy. Next follows the selection of toys, books, and games, which are nonverbal signals of sex role expectations: "Do-it-yourself crib games for boys. Delicate mobiles for girls. And later—he gets baseballs, model ships, Erector sets, chemistry sets. She gets Barbie dolls, tea sets, nurse kits, minimops. And still later—he goes skiing, camping, skin-diving and plays football with Dad. She goes to ballet class, piano lessons, art exhibits and bakes brownies with Mom."[64] Pogrebin quotes Sirgay Sanger, a New York child psychiatrist, on the disadvantage of sex stereotyping of the very young:

In the child's earliest years, masculine or feminine differences are a fake issue. Until three or four years of age children have the same needs. Beyond that age, what they require most is individual differentiation, not gender differentiation. To highlight differences only denies one sex the advantages permitted to the other. Such gender differences can be alarming and threatening to children. Unisex clothes and relaxed dating rituals among the young indicate that there's a natural tendency to minimize sex differences and to find comfortable common areas of human communication.[65]

Even when children come from families where sex role stereotyping is minimized, they meet it in public encounters, as when Pogrebin's son was told in his father's law office that they needed more lawyers around there, while her twin daughters were told that they needed more legal secretaries. Still more do children meet sex stereotyping in the educational system. Children's work is defined as "girl tasks" and "boy tasks." Children are often sex segregated for gym classes, sex education, manual training, and home economics. Girls get the message early that they are not supposed to excel in mathematics and science, while boys learn that literature and art are "girl stuff." Boys are players and girls are cheerleaders in school athletic contests. The books in their libraries and the textbooks assigned to them indicate the expectations of boys and girls. Florence Howe reports on her study of books classified by the National Council of Teachers of English under the headings "Especially for Girls" and "Especially for Boys":

> Verbs and adjectives are remarkably predictable through the listings. Boys "decipher and discover," "earn and train" or "foil" someone; girls "struggle," "overcome difficulties," "feel lost," "help solve," or "help out." One boy's story has "strange power," another moves "from truancy to triumph." A girl, on the other hand, "learns to face the real world" or makes a "difficult adjustment." Late or early, in catalogues or on shelves, the boys of children's books are active and capable, the girls passive and in trouble.[66]

There is a considerable body of literature, produced by librarian researchers as well as by feminists, bearing out the claim that children's literature and textbooks minimally involve girls in contrast to boys' activity and productivity, show boys as dominant and active and girls as passive and receiving, portray boys as achieving and adventurous and girls as either struggling or uninvolved, and routinely show mothers as domestic and fathers as publicly active.[67] Feminists are beginning to counter this literary discrimination against girls by publishing lists of nonsexist children's books and writing or publishing books of their own about creative and responsible women and girls. They are also meeting with book publishers, writers, and developers of school curricula to help make them aware of the sexism implicit in such a wide range of materials children are given to read.

A cursory view of the dominant attitudes in home and school that promulgate the inferior status of women and sexist ideology suggests that a number of specific kinds of viewpoint need to change and be followed by specific practices to achieve a goal of women-and-men-equal-to-each-other in the society. While empirical evidence indicates that the majority of people are still choosing to live in the nuclear family,[68] the affirmation of a plurality of possible forms for the family is in order, so as to open up male/female roles. Within the family, a new assessment of who performs what household tasks needs to be made. Mature adult male/female interaction and positive role models for children can best result from a sharing in domestic decision-making, household jobs, and the development of a life style. In education, individual personal possibility and growth toward a socially human maturity should be the goal, with the abandonment of sex stereotypical activities or assumptions.

Realization of Artistic Identity

It is often the case that artists, particularly writers, first experience and portray a problem that receives wide social attention only many years later. Just so, Anne Bradstreet in her poetry in the seventeenth century defined the contemporary woman problem. Margaret Fuller raised the question of the place of the woman, particularly the literary artist, in her mid-nineteenth century work *Woman in the Nineteenth Century*. In spite of her numerous classical literary references, she phrased her point that women's identity is primarily human in surprisingly contemporary terms. Virginia Woolf in 1929, writing *A Room of One's Own,* recognized the dilemma for women in that all the books about them were written by men, and called for the realization of the private, professional, and creative possibilities of the female identity in an explicitly androgynous framework.

The contribution of women literary artists has in some cases been brought to feminist attention by members of the women's movement, but in other instances the artists themselves have spoken outright on behalf of the movement. The works of Doris Lessing and Anaïs Nin are deliberate expressions of female humanity that furnish models for feminist identification. The literary works of Sylvia Plath are viewed by the feminists as expressions of the particular agony of the female experience. Anne Sexton, whose reputation as a poet is growing in literary circles and whose subject matter is specifically female experience, is a favorite writer for anthologizing in feminist publications.

From the androgynous viewpoint, the possibility of an artist doing her work primarily as a human being is the central question—a question at least as old as Anne Bradstreet. The way we actually look at the literary creations of female writers and the possibilities for the artist under an androgynous system have been articulated by the fiction writer, essayist, and literary critic Cynthia Ozick. Two essays describe her consciousness raising as a woman writer. Although she does not call it "consciousness raising," her ire arose as she realized the preconceptions she had to confront about "feminine" writing and the female writer. She would have much preferred just to be a writer, to create the literature that her talent and energy drove her to create; but there was the stereotype, eclipsing her; so she used her considerable creative skill to write of it. One such article on her experience, her insight, and her views about breaking the stereotype is "We Are the Crazy Lady and Other Feisty Feminist Fables," published in the first issue of *Ms.*

Ozick's fables are vignettes of her particular experiences of the contradiction between her own sense of her individuality and unique ability as a human being and writer and her encounters with the cultural preconception of what a woman is. In the first fable she describes being a student at Columbia University in a famous critic's class, where the other woman student was a crazy lady "with wild tan hair, a noticeably breathing bosom, eccentric gold-rimmed old-pensioner glasses and a tooth-crowded mouth that seemed to get wilder the more she talked." The crazy lady behaved in a bizarre fashion, offered weird and ostentatious literary statements, and made the other students and the critic uncomfortable with her references to institutions in which she had been a patient. Ozick understood herself as a significant contrast to the crazy lady, psychologically, physically, and academically; but at the end of the term she got back her paper from the critic with comments addressed to the crazy lady. The critic could not tell the two women apart. The fable has two morals: "All cats are gray at night, all darkies look alike," and "Even among intellectual humanists, every woman has a *Dopplegänger—every other woman.*"[69]

Another fable tells of Ozick's invitation to speak at a book-author luncheon for a women's group, and her statement to the program leader on the telephone that she would talk about "The Contemporary Poem." When she rose to talk at the luncheon and began to speak on poetry, the women began to rattle their programs and look at them confusedly. Finally, she picked up her program to discover that it read, "Topic: The Contemporary Home." The moral suggested here is, "Even our ears practice the caste system."[70]

The subject of another fable is "Hormones," in which Ozick tells of an encounter with a commissioner of health who described to her a set of facts about the endocrinal make-up of women and the differences between men and women. She re-joined with the assertion that "a congeries of facts is not equivalent to an idea." Her sense of her own humanity was supposed to be refuted by hormonal research, a set of "facts" determining what is standard humanity:

> My psychology, you tell me, which in your view is the source of my ideas, is the result of my physiology. It is not I who express myself, it is my hormones which express me. A part is equal to the whole, you say. Worse yet, the whole is simply the issue of the part: my "I" is a flash of chemi-

cals . . . Who can prove what is "standard" humanity, and which sex, class, or race is to be exempted from whole participation in it? On what basis do you regard female hormones as causing a modification from normative humanity? And what better right do you have to define normative humanity by what males have traditionally apperceived than by what females have traditionally apperceived?[71]

The doctor's response was, "Why are you so emotional about all this? . . . You see how it is? Those are your female hormones working on you right now." The moral of this fable is, "Defamation is only applied research."[72]

The final fable is called "Ambition." It tells of the thirteen years of incubation and effort that produced her novel *Trust*. In the early years, she had read and written extensively. She saw herself as a writer who had not published; her relatives saw her as a wife who had not produced a child. She and the relatives agreed that her life was a failure, but her sense of failure was of herself as an artist, theirs of her as a woman. The novel took six years to complete, and when it was finished, she thought she had left nothing out: "Though I did not imagine the world would fall asunder at its appearance, I thought—at the very least—the ambition, the all-swallowingness, the wild insatiability of the writer would be plain to everyone who read it. I had, after all, taken History for my subject: not merely History as an aggregate of events, but History as a judgment on events. No one could say my theme was flighty."[73]

Ozick had been especially conscious of the narrator's "sensibility." The narrator, a young woman, was designed to have not a shred of "sensibility": "My machine-narrator was there for efficiency only, for flexibility, for craftiness, for subtlety, but never never, as a "woman." I wiped the "woman" out of her."[74] But when the reviews of *Trust* were published, the *New York Times Book Review* focused on the longing for femininity of the narrator, accompanying its review with a backside picture of a naked woman, and titling the article "Daughter's Reprieve." *Time's* review of the book called Ozick a housewife.

Ozick is so angry in this fable that she cannot produce as glib a moral as she was able to attach to her other tales. She knows she has to wrestle with the question of whether she did indeed produce meritorious art, but also she knows she has evidence of being sold out as a "woman writer." The first moral is: "If you look for it, there will always be a decent solution for female ambition. For instance, it is still not too late to enroll in a good secretarial school." The second moral is: "In conceptual life, junk prevails. Even if you do not produce junk it will be taken for junk . . . The products of women are frequently taken for junk."[75]

The second article about Ozick's experience with the assumption that a woman writer is "different" is called "The Demise of the Dancing Dog," published in *motive* in 1969. The title comes from an eighteenth century remark by Dr. Johnson, on hearing a woman preacher, that it was like "a dog dancing on its hind legs; one marvels not at how well it is done, but that it is done at all."[76] The woman writer in Ozick's experience is still today seen as the dancing dog—a novelty to be amused by but not to be taken seriously. She presents what she calls the Ovarian Theory of Literature: if the writer is female, the reader and the critic see her work as sentimental, soft, and intuitive.

Ozick tells of her experience as a teacher in a university English department. She was neither a writer nor a teacher, but a "woman writer," a "woman teacher." All her students believed that men and women thought and wrote differently. They did not know that Flannery O'Connor was a woman when they first read her stories, but when Ozick told them, they began to talk of her "woman's sentences," saying that they were not concrete, not tough. Ozick's colleagues, all male, confronted her with such arguments as an analogy between women's sex affecting them and Keats' struggle with tuberculosis affecting his last writings. Being a woman is a disease. Ozick points out that it is an insult to a male writer to say his work sounds like a woman writer's. The other side of the coin of derogating women in literature is to regard woman as the writer's Muse: woman does not have to write because she is the inspiration of the high art. Furthermore, the woman creates babies in her body and has no need for other creativity. Ozick views this equation of physiology with creativity as a cheap escape: "All this is, one would think almost stupefyingly obvious. It is embarrassing, it is humiliating, to be so obvious about the quality either of literature or of women. She, at any rate, is not a Muse, nor is she on the strength of her womb alone an artist. She is—how stupidly obvious!—a person.''[77]

Ozick moves to the social definition of women as belonging in the home, of society's separate minority culture for women devoted primarily to caring for helpless babies. Since the care of babies takes up only a few years of a woman's life, and because there is not enough meaningful work available in the society for this group of the population, society has created a culture of products and attitudes to focus women's lives on the home:

> That is why there are in our society separate minority cultures for adolescents and for women. Each has its own set of opinions, prejudices, tastes, values, and—do not underestimate this last—magazines. You and I are here concerned only with the culture of women. Society, remember, is above men and women; it acts *in* men and women. So you must not make the mistake of thinking that the culture of women is the conspiracy of men. Not in the least . . . The culture of women is believed in by both men and women, and it is the conspiracy of neither, because it is the creature neither of men alone, nor of women alone, but of society itself—that autonomous, cunning, insensitive sibling of history.[78]

This is the problem with which we are faced, Ozick says, but no one has even stated the question. She believes that the genuine formulation of the question, and the facing of the question with seriousness and passion, will produce the answer. What she calls "tracts," like *The Feminine Mystique,* will not raise the question, nor will the feminists: "Well, what *is* the question? Who will formulate it? 'Feminists' will not because it is not a feminist question. It is not a group question or a conspiratorial question. It is a humanist question. (And yet note how questions that long ago began as purely 'feminist,' such as birth control with Margaret Sanger, eventually became the foremost and profoundest of humanistic concern . . .)"[79]

The way Ozick sees the issue is that artists must grasp why there are no female creators—"architects, painters, playwrights, sailors, bridgebuilders, jurists, captains, composers''—in the society and turn the problem over to the scientists-humanists. The resolution will come in terms of persons using their full creative capacity for the benefit of society without any qualifications regarding sex. A sexual stereotype will be eradicated when the society says to its persons that it needs creative contributions and humanistically invites all to participate. Of the voice issuing the invitation, Ozick asks: "Is it a man's voice or a woman's voice? Students, colleagues, listen again; it is two voices. 'How obvious,' you will one day reply, and if you laugh, it will be at the quaint folly of obsolete custom, which once failed to harness the obvious; it will not be at a dancing dog."[80]

From her particular stance as a literary artist, Ozick reveals the workings of the androgynous ideology. The source of the stereotyping of women is in the society, through its attitudes and organization. The solution to the problem is a shift in attitudes, effected by artistic questioning of where women belong. The problem will be solved, as Ozick sees it, by men and women together creating the new society.

Historiography

In 1962, David M. Potter published an essay titled "American Women and the American Character." In it, he asks the question, Do we take into account in our writing of history about the American people and our generalizations about the American character the experience of women? His answer is no. Rather, generalizations in American social history, though made about "the American," upon close examination are based on the experience of the American male. He illustrates with Frederick Jackson Turner's description of the frontier colonist who, as Turner describes him, has increasingly clear male attributes. Yet Turner's thesis was that the frontier with the economic opportunity it offered was the basic force in shaping the American character. Potter points out that a parallel opportunity for the economic independence of women did not occur until urban clerical and secretarial work became available to them.[81]

In like manner, when generalizing about the direction of change in American identity, commentators say that the American's occupational life has moved increasingly from the independence and self-employment of the farmer to employment in a firm for pay: that Americans have become extremely specialized; that the pattern of work is an eight-hour day, five-day week, from age twenty to age sixty-five; and that Americans have become, as David Riesman describes them in *The Lonely Crowd,* other-directed individuals. Yet these kinds of social statements can be applied broadly only to males; for two-thirds of all women live their lives primarily in the home as homemakers and child rearers, follow a schedule that is self-determined; do their work without pay, spend their lives in an array of nonspecialized activities, and pursue an unbroken occupation, not segmented into hours and years, throughout their adult life. Further, their primary nurturing role made them other-directed long before social scientists began to observe that men were becoming other-directed.[82]

Speaking of the need to include women in the assessment of American social history and of the ambiguity in the emancipation of women, Potter writes:

> Clearly, we are still a long way from having arrived at any monotonous unanimity of opinion about the character of American women. Yet if we will focus carefully upon what we really know with some degree of assurance, we can perhaps begin the process of striking a balance. We certainly know, for instance, that many of the trends of American history have been operative for both men and women in somewhat the same way. The emphasis upon the right of the individual has operated to remove legal disabilities upon women, to open many avenues to gainful employment, to confer the suffrage, and so on . . . On the other hand, we also know that the experience of women remains in many ways a distinctive experience.[83]

Since the year when Potter wrote his essay, and to some extent motivated by the rise of the contemporary feminist movement, a move has taken place among scholars of history, especially among women historians, to look at the history of women. These historians are saying that historiographical questions must be asked in new ways to get at the reality of women's past, to acknowledge the presence of women, and to show how women have lived as half of humankind. Such questions include: What kind of documents can be found written by and about women? What kind of questions and assumptions does the historian researcher bring to the documents being examined? What kind of contemporary social and analytical frameworks can be applied for insight into women's past? Historians like Anne Firor Scott are saying that we need to turn to private documents, such as diaries and letters, and to the private institution of the family as well as to records of women's organizations to find out more about women in history. Scott observes that women have been overlooked in history often because historians are men:

> Poets and novelists rarely overlook women. Historians often do. Frequently they write as if half the human race did not exist . . . There are fat textbooks in American history which mention women three or four times . . . It is particularly intriguing that social and economic historians of the past century have overlooked women, for during that time one of the most impressive social and economic facts has been the rapid change in the part women have played in the society and the economy.
>
> One day perhaps an inquiring psychologist will explain the extreme reluctance of American historians to recognize that women have been here too, and when that time comes the answer will be, in part, that the historians were men. Male historians share society's attitudes toward women, and add a few of their own. They carry a heavy baggage of assumptions, usually unacknowledged and unexamined, about the importance of women in history. It is time they began to examine these assumptions, to correct the biases built into their work, and to revise their accounts of historical events accordingly.[84]

In her own splendid study *The Southern Lady: From Pedestal to Politics, 1830-1930,* Scott revises the understanding of Southern womanhood in the United States. She contrasts the image of the antebellum southern woman as demure, dependent, dumb, and decorative with the record of domestic, political, social, and religious activism of a century of southern women. Significant to her study is an examination of the reasons for the need to maintain the image while engaged, sometimes surreptitiously, in the action.[85]

Another woman historian, Gerda Lerner, has been a prolific writer on the history of American women. Her books include *The Grimké Sisters from South Carolina: Rebels Against Slavery* and *The Woman in American History,* the latter having been prepared as a high school textbook for American history. In an essay on historiography, Lerner writes that the study of women has been vastly underrepresented in American history, largely because the subject of historians has been the transmission and exercise of power. She observes that there have been two strands of work on women's history. One is the study of feminism, greatly influenced by the availability of the six-volume *History of Woman Suffrage*; and the other is the attempt to offer a corrective to the feminist view that women have always been oppressed, as in Mary Beard's contention that women have been a large and significant force in history, particularly in economic history.

Lerner insists that a new conceptual framework is necessary for the study of women's history. It should be viewed in the context of reform history, family history, and the history of education. The old feminist history approach is now empty, but the view of women's history as equivalent to men's is equally invalid. Although women have been powerless as a group, as individuals they have been nearer to power or more influential upon the exercise of power, quite unlike the ethnic or radical minorities to which they are compared. The psychology of women in their social context is a valid consideration in the study of women, for women's lives have been different from men's, but the reduction of women's history to a study of psychological attributes and relationships is incomplete. Lerner feels that the records for a fuller account of women's history are available in conventional sources for social history—local historical records, labor union records, government archives, magazines—but these sources have hardly been tapped for the information they could supply.

Lerner suggests five points as a framework for looking at women's history. First, the subject should not be so vast as "women," but rather the variety of aspects of women's status at any given time—economic, family, political-legal, class. Second, in addition to the women's rights movement, the actual contribution of women to society at specific times must be investigated. Third, the model of "oppressed group" must be discarded. Lerner believes that women have wielded power in American society, but it has taken different forms from the male use of power. Fourth, the influence of access to education must be studied in relation to women's participation or lack of it in intellectual and cultural leadership in society. Fifth, investigation should be made of the correlation or lack of it between the social expectations of "woman's place" and women's actual status and role at given times. Lerner concludes:

> The fact remains that women are different from men and that their role in society and history is different from that of men. Different, but equal in importance. Obviously their achievements must also be measured on a different scale. To define and devise such a scale is difficult until the gaps in our historical knowledge about the actual contributions of women have been filled. This work remains to be done . . . It is an endeavor that should enlist the best talents of the profession and, hopefully and at long last, not primarily female talent.[86]

An historiographical essay with a more deliberately contemporary feminist stance is the first half of "Women in American Society" by Ann D. Gordon, Mari Jo Buhle, and Nancy E. Schrom. In reviewing a large body of historical literature about women, they find:

> The contours of women's history have been determined in large part by the questions historical writers have been interested in exploring, the assumptions researchers have brought to their work, and the sources available for examining the lives women led in previous centuries . . . Most historical studies fall into one of three categories: institutional histories of women's organizations and movement; biographies of important suffragists and "token" women . . . and "prescriptive history"—that is, discussions of class or societal ideals rather than actual cultural practices.[87]

The authors discredit these types of history as inadequate for a full knowledge of who women have been in the American past, and they look to the development of a new historical approach: "Perhaps now, with a renewed feminist consciousness and with better, more sophisticated tools of historical analysis, we can begin to ask new questions about the actual historical experience of women, about the social and economic forces which shaped and changed women's lives, and about the nature of and factors involved in shaping feminist consciousness."[88]

In the second half of their essay Gordon, Buhle, and Schrom offer an account of the cultural experience of women, with the purpose of helping women to understand their present situation, to be able to make personal and collective connections with their own past.

The androgynous paradigm, a model of women and men being equal to each other, is operative for some of the feminists in the contemporary women's movement. It is articulated in a number of writings that have come to be considered major works of the movement, and it can be perceived as the ideological framework for many of the activities aimed at changes in behavior and attitudes. The focus for identifying the enemy of the women's movement is on cultural forces, attitudes, and institutions, rather than on men, as in the women's liberationist ideology, or on one particular male-derived political and economic system, capitalism, as some feminist socialists maintain. The androgynous paradigm is built on the groundwork of awareness not only of female experience but of both the cultural mythology of the roles of women and men and the embedding of those cultural expectations in language, psychological investigation, family structure, and education. Its premise is that the awareness of sex-based sources and of the practice of limiting personal qualities and behavior by the criterion of sex will be a force in breaking cultural sexual stereotyping and in changing men's and women's conceptions of themselves and of what is possible for them to do. It affirms sexuality as an aspect of human life which is powerful and fulfilling, but denies that one's sex is determinative of what is psychologically or socially productive for an individual or of what contributions can be made collectively to humanity by males and females. Its key lies in Alice Rossi's use of the word "between" in her immodest proposal for "Equality between the Sexes," which generated so much support in the women's movement. Equality between the sexes means that women are equal to men and men are equal to women. It requires both sexes to be "equal" before one is equal to the other. Women have traditionally held power over the home, the children, and private life, while men have held power in public life. The androgynous position is an invitation for power to be shared by women and men in both the private and the public spheres.

5

A Perspective for the Future

In the last decade, a new feminism has risen in the land, affecting virtually every level of American life. Dormant for many years, feminism since the early 1960s has begun to color interpersonal relations, the language we speak, family life, the educational system, child-rearing practices, politics, business, the mass media, religion, law, the judicial system, the cultural value system, and intellectual life. The last dimension—the force of its ideas, their variety, the shape they give to action, and the aspects of our lives to which they speak—is the most fundamental to understanding contemporary feminism. During the seventies the women's movement has mushroomed, literature of it and and about it has multiplied, and feminist changes have been effected throughout American life. Yet the underlying pattern of feminist thought has remained the same, involving three distinct ideologies. A wide spectrum of variations on these themes exists, in cogently expressed or inarticulately felt manifestations of feminism. And not all of everybody's feminism can be squeezed into neat categories of thought. The broad concepts informing feminist thinking and values nevertheless persist: the feminist, the women's liberationist, and the androgynous.

The feminist paradigm echoes the thinking that led early feminists to focus finally on suffrage, the idea that women should be equal-to-men. Rights and opportunities open to men should be open to women. Women should receive equal pay for equal work. Women should have equal work. Newspaper advertising, television programming, universities, banks, and real estate firms should not discriminate against women. Votes should be cast for women for public office, and it should not be unthinkable for women to hold high leadership positions alongside men.

The women's liberationist paradigm is a new idea arising from rage and the perception that men have oppressed women as a class. It is a conflict and confrontation model, whereby women collectively assert their own importance, call for solidarity among women, and assert a new politics whereby the male definition of woman as sex object is turned into a political tool for forging a new political order out of the special experience of women. It is a pattern of women-over-against-men, in which new norms will come from women.

The androgynous paradigm is a design of women-and-men-equal-to-each-other. It is essentially a cultural model, although it also takes into account the social and political spheres. It is a pattern of conversion, based on a belief that people—women and men—can shift their beliefs and behavior when they recognize the injustice and intolerance prevalent in their social sexual roles and in the attitudes based on them.

The three ideas exist simultaneously in the feminism that our nation has watched grow over the last decade and in which many of us have participated. The future of today's feminism is anybody's guess. Events that shape history most dramatically are usually unforeseen. The backlash against feminism that has been stirring in the early 1970s is testimony to its effectiveness, but the backlash could also mount to such proportions as to redirect public support for women's rights and women's liberation and to make the advocates of women's liberation more timid. The achievement of some gains, such as passage of the Equal Rights Amendment and the Supreme Court abortion decision, could lessen the movement's momentum and bring undue satisfaction with less than women's complete freedom. Still, some prophets are saying that the women's revolution is the most significant ever to occur in American life, that the whole direction of our culture will be reoriented because of

what women have done. Surely, the course of our politics and
work, our values, ideas, and homes, will never again be quite
the same.

The three feminist ideologies characterize the different historical stages in feminism, besides representing the potential
stages in the feminism of the individual. In the past, when
women did not have men's access to property, education, vocation, or political leadership, the masculine-equalitarian vision
was profound. When the vote as well as entry into male educational, professional, and political domains still did not bring
women an equal share of influence and opportunity, it was
again appropriate to raise the standard that women should be
equal to men. The goal was so simple as to be obvious; but it
was never tried as an operating principle for American social
institutions until the early 1960s, when Betty Friedan published
The Feminine Mystique and the President's Commission on the
Status of Women prepared its report declaring equal opportunity for women to be a national concern.

Having achieved a little but not enough, younger women up
from the ranks of civil rights and the peace protest, seeking
justice and humane concern in certain areas of society, were
enraged that there was so little for themselves. They shaped a
new model, which held that drafting new legislation and going
to work one by one at new jobs was too slow and not comprehensive enough to combat what they called male chauvinism
and the class oppression of women. The women's liberationist
ideology, coming as a stage of the new feminism, broke open a
new concept of women-over-against-men. Women had to believe in women, to unite with women, and to confront masculinist claims and male antagonism, in order to spell out their
own identity in their own terms, for themselves and for the
social order. They had to develop, many of them believed,
something equivalent to a class consciousness. Such unity in
anger and readiness for confrontations was little conceived of in
the nineteenth century, when the hope was a progressive one for
achieving gradual change by persuasion, but in the late 1960s
this bold attitude impressed women's liberation onto the
American consciousness in a way that nothing before had done.

Some of the feminists who had been involved in the formation of NOW and of other primary women's rights groups, some of the original women's liberationists, and some other feminists whose impulse for feminism sprang largely from within themselves and their daily lives, together shaped still another concept, the androgynous ideology. It caught some flickering sparks from the past, through such women as Victoria Woodhull, Emma Goldman, Margaret Sanger, and perhaps Margaret Fuller, Jane Addams, and Florence Kelley. Perceiving that domestic effort and power must be shared with men and that public effort and power must be shared with women, the adherents of androgyny established a new view of equality, of women-and-men-equal-to-each-other. The shift of the female role in society, they argue, must necessarily effect a shift of the male role, hopefully toward a new humanist inconclusiveness. Taking into account the inequity of the existing female subordination and expressing indignation that women should not count for as much as men in the current scheme of things, they hold that our cultural beliefs, our myths and values, must change to equalitarian ones. Changes in law and the political process, patterns of work and family life, will follow upon such a shift in the fundamental beliefs to which we adhere.

These three viewpoints sometimes also define the stages in the development of an individual woman's feminism. Handed a typing test after college and seeing her male counterpart sought for management, watching the astute president of the local League of Women Voters manage a school board campaign for her husband, observing her mother dominated by her father's whims, a woman can be moved to adopt a masculine-equalitarian feminism. Then, in the fray over what she sees as a reasonable value of equality, in combat with her man about how to achieve equality in the bedroom, the kitchen, or the head, in confrontation with groups at work or in the community with which she is involved, she can become outraged at the massiveness of the inequality, at the obdurateness of many men, at the intransigence of society, and she can be moved to a prowoman, antimasculinist feminism. Finally, when she learns that she can move herself, that women believing in themselves and acting jointly can direct their rage to constructive change, that female recognition brings about male and social recognition, she can shift to an androgynous feminism. Thus, it is as possible for the three types to be personal stages of feminism, as for them to be historical stages or stages of social realization.

A responsible historian does not take upon herself the authority to predict the future. My task in this study of recent history has been merely to try to discern and demonstrate the intellectual strands that have existed and do exist in the women's movement. My thesis is that in the current feminism the three ideologies are in competition. One of them may prevail as the dominant concept during the last quarter of the twentieth century; or a new model encompassing parts of all three may emerge; or if some horrendous course of events stifles its current momentum, feminism may die out altogether and no longer have use for any ideology. My own preference as an individual would be for androgyny to prevail, notably in the areas of sexuality, the family, work, politics, society, education, and religion.

She really doesn't cover this

7 areas

Sexuality

The contemporary women's movement must deal with sexuality, for the genesis of the whole montage of female and male identifications and expectations rests in the society's presuppositions about sexuality. And whatever the outcome when the last word has been uttered on the subject, sexual feeling and experience are the sine qua non of being human. They are the surd on which human life is posited, the means for procreating and recreating humanity, and the chief force of irrationality that interpenetrates the rationality of humankind.

meaning of sexual (relational? (genital?)

The perspectives on female sexuality are distinct under the three feminist modes, all of them making a contribution to a revised version of what is appropriately female. In the feminist view, what has for decades been called the sexual double standard must be abandoned. The freedom of men to have sexual relations before and outside of marriage must be open to women. It should be no more disgraceful for a girl than for a boy to experiment with sex, no more stigmatizing for a woman than for a man to have what is called an affair.

In the women's liberationist mode, a much fuller redefinition of female sexuality is offered. Women must trust their experience with their own bodies and define the locus of their own sexual pleasure. Women have a sex organ, the clitoris, which has been neglected in male clinical descriptions of women's sexuality and in male sexual interaction with women. In masturbation, in homosexual relations, and in heterosexual lovemaking, the recognition of a specifically female sex organ can make a considerable difference in the nature of the sexual experience, in the demands and expectations of women about their sexual nature, and in the definition of women physically.

Under the androgynous label, the affirmation is made that women are fully sexual creatures, no more, no less than men. The declaration of full female sexuality is one more aspect of women's common humanity with men. Men are not somehow "more" sexual than women, do not have any greater need or drive for sexual activity; and women are not mere objects of men's higher level of sexual force, nor the passive receivers of male sexual attention and the vessels for delivering the products of sexual intercourse, babies. Rather, it is basic to human identity, both female and male, to be charged by sexual impulse, to desire sexual interaction, and to be active sexually. Male and female sexual anatomy is human complementarity.

Regarding sexuality, the androgynous view transcends and comprehends the feminist and the women's liberationist views. Recognition of the root humanness of sexuality implies that the avenues of its expression should be open alike to women and men, and that the particulars of physiology and the feelings of female and male alike should be authenticated.

Even the sexual definition of persons, then, starts at the point of human commonality. It is human to be a sexual creature. Sex is an extremely significant aspect of all human beings. Its level of importance and manner of expression vary from person to person in the same way as do all other dimensions of personhood.

Sexual expression is a choice people make about themselves. Since it is a serious and significant choice, there is all the more reason that it be based on a considered ethic. Such an ethic would apply evenly to females and males. It is perhaps only now possible to conceive of such a moral principle, since for the first

ethic arises only if something is viewed as a "choice".
? We don't have a pro-life ethic if we don't con... choice

time in history it is possible, because of the medical development of contraception, to engage in sexual relations without the fear or expectation of pregnancy. Because pregnancy can now be a choice for a woman, it is only in the present time that a double standard regarding the factor of different potential consequences of sexual intercourse for women and men need not be operative.

So basic a human choice as whether to enter into sexual intercourse with another person should not be made lightly, should not be done merely for the sake of experimentation, should not be a competitive match for what other people are doing, and should not be bought or sold. Since sexuality permeates personality, its expression in the sexual act should represent a commitment of the persons engaging in the act to each other, should be a manifestation of love, of shared lives. Some such commitments are short-term; the richest are for a lifetime; but the norm for sexual partnership should be a total human relationship.

Precisely because sex is so central to humanness, the option to live without sexual activity is a meaningful one. To give up something good for another purpose is a sign of one's strength and clarity of resolution. The model of the Roman Catholic nun, who is celibate for her religious vocation, or her secular counterpart, the "old maid" schoolteacher who has been derided rather than esteemed, can now be seen as a valid and sacrificial mode of acting out one's humanity. Virginity or celibacy is proper for a lifetime if it is chosen for one's self-proclamation and one's service to the world, as it is also decent for a period while waiting for the fullness of a relationship.

Sexuality is a wellspring of human nature. It has female and male courses, but the determination of its expression can be made and sanctioned by females and males together. The principles governing sexual choices can be human standards.

Marriage and Family

It is hard to live without any norm as a ruling principle for life, and most of us like to think that our own principle ought to be the guiding principle for everybody. In the area of marriage and the family, the most intimate of social institutions, this is especially true. We Americans live under the long-standing norm that the marriage of one man and one woman, sanctioned by law and religion, is the foundation of the only centrally significant family structure in society and the only legitimate locus for the bearing and nurturing of children to adulthood. According to this norm, the numerous other patterns of private life that do exist are considered abnormal, temporary, or even devious—single persons living alone, groups or pairs of persons of the same sex, childless couples, communal families of chosen adults of both sexes with or without children, even kinship groups of more than two generations, which are viewed as the declining family pattern of a former era, having now given way to the nuclear family. It is within the nuclear family that the most abiding definitions of roles, of what is proper for woman and man to be and to do, have coalesced, been acted upon, and been promulgated by example, custom, and law.

need

The need for a primary and private group for intimate life is real for both adults and children. All people need a cushion from the stress and exhaustion of their various publics. It is fundamental to being human to need to give and receive love, trust, and emotional support from other human beings, and most of us wish to live in a home where such love and trust are shared. Children must have their physical and emotional needs met by adults in òrder to survive; and to survive well, they must live with adults who care deeply, even sacrificially, who are committed to the children in time and energy as well as love, and who are models of creative humanity for the children's personhood.

What is needed in our society is the affirmation of a new pluralism of marriage agreements and organizations of private life. Marriage as it now stands is a legal and ecclesiastical recognition of the commitment of a man and woman to share their sexual life, their domestic life, and the responsibility for any children they may have. There are layers of law and custom that proclaim the man the head of the household, the man economically responsible for the unit, and the woman domestically responsible for the unit and dependent on the man for the family's geographic location, social status, and economic viability. Most powerful of all, tradition has it that the woman as the bearer of children is fundamentally responsible for the nurture of children in the family; for her, no other identity is so strong as this one.

To sanction a pluralism of marriage and family arrangements would not necessarily mean a reorganization of social sex roles, but it would be a beginning for persons who want to make more deliberate choices about how they will live, with whom, and by what standards. It should be legitimate, for example, for a professional woman and a professional man to be married to each other and choose not to have children, and to share equally in the household tasks and expenses of the marriage partnership for the sake of their professions. This arrangement, though legal, is not fully legitimated socially. There is something stigmatizing about a choice not to have children. It should also be legitimate for homosexual couples to marry, or for groups of three, six, or ten adults to form a family, making their own contracts regarding the sexual and domestic arrangements to be followed.

One adult, or two or more adults of the same sex who are friends and not sexual partners, might form a family for the sake of rearing children or for emotional and economic support and social benefits. There have long been and will continue to be informal living arrangements for companionship or sex or both, but socially and publicly recognized contracts of marriage and family need to be made both for society's sake and for that of the persons involved. Legally contracted family units should exist as a microcosm of social values, as a location for economic distribution, as a source of protection and support for individuals, and as a basis for dependable security and permanence for children. Children might come into new family forms by childbirth, by adoption, or not at all, but children when they do come have a right to legitimacy as persons in the eyes of the state and in the eyes of their adults. Divorce should be possible, for persons do discover that others with whom they thought they had a full commitment to a life together turn out to be the wrong ones; but divorce might be less necessary if a precontract period for couple marriages or group marriages of one or more years could be entered into by persons wishing to become families. Still, the goal of the family should be a permanent relationship, for persons flourish most readily in the security of *stability* knowing that their loved ones' commitment to them will be stable over time, and the society is stabilized by a foundation of homes.

To hold up new family forms for public justification does not signal the demise of marriage and the family as we now know it. Not only because of the momentum of tradition, but also because of the ever-renewing impulse of heterosexual love and the female and male's desire to sanctify and make public their private mutual commitment, marriages will continue to take place between one man and one woman; and to many of them, children will be born. The nuclear family is alive and well as one valid family option, but within it women and men are not equal today. For husband and wife to be equal in the family, a spate of laws and government regulations about the family needs to be changed, ranging from domicile law stating that the wife is domiciled wherever her husband lives, to laws defining the legal age for marriage, to Census Bureau regulations requiring that all Americans check one and only one box for the head of the household. Likewise, assumptions in business and other places of employment have to be challenged. Business must give women real work, real titles, and real pay, and must not ask beforehand who are their husbands and children. Employers must also give up the power to manipulate their employees' families either by using wives as company decoration or by moving the family for the company's sake without regard to the personal cost to the family. A couple who really want to live together equal-to-each-other are caught in a molasses-like network of social attitudes and expectations about how they should live, sometimes making it impossible for them to be equal when they want to be. For the couple who are not sure, there are plenty of ways to rationalize that man as pivotal and woman as relational is the way it ought to be.

Still, there are a host of ways in which married couples can live with each other as true equals and thereby have some impact on the world, provide a model for an androgynous society, and come closer to a full humanity for both woman and man. The first step is for each marriage partner honestly to believe that the other person is equal to herself/himself in her/his mundane as well as exalted life. This is not so much a step as a process, undergirded by a belief that both women and men are variegated in their abilities, interests, and feelings, and that the particular personalities of a certain woman and a certain man shape the dynamic of their unique marriage relationship.

One possibility for androgynous marriage is to divide the domestic tasks fifty-fifty and to divide the breadwinning fifty-fifty, so that there is nothing he does that she does not also do, nothing she does that he does not also do. Thus, both parents care for the children; both adults cook and clean house and take out the garbage; both adults work at meaningful vocations that provide the family's income, personal growth in the world for each individual, and contributions from outside the home to the family. Gone is the dichotomy between housewife and bread-winner, replaced by an adult social role, rather than by a sexual one, blending the responsibility for home and children with the responsibility for making a public contribution through voca-tion. A number of graduate student couples with children live this way quite happily and successfully, and it is the model in Alix Shulman's celebrated marriage contract.

Yet a strictly fifty-fifty arrangement of all things is not essen-tial for an androgynous life. In an atmosphere of mutual trust and support, wife and husband can decide to work and stay home in stages, each being primarily responsible in one sphere at one time, in another sphere at another time. They can decide to do what is most important for one partner in one decision, such as making a move to another city, and what is most im-portant to another partner at a later time when what is mutually best cannot be reached. They can make a mutual choice about a place in which to live and shape other factors around it. For example, a woman professor and her businessman husband could make a joint decision to stay put, he telling his company he is unavailable for any promotion that involves a move, and she turning down leads for jobs in other cities. This would be an androgynous choice.

The essential factor is mutuality. In such a marriage, it can-not be predetermined that the woman or the man ought to make more money, ought to have the higher public status, ought to serve on the community committee, ought to get up for the baby at night, ought to wash the clothes, ought to shovel the

snow, ought to take the children to the dentist. The discovery of
the mutual best for the woman and the man and the family unit
is an internal struggle as well as a social one, for women and
men have been socialized to believe that manhood rests on his
performance and status in a vocation, and that womanhood
rests on her man's status and on her own performance in the
nursery and the kitchen. To say that homemaking is a joint
enterprise and that vocation knows no sex is a radical departure
toward a new and richer humanity.

Vocation

Without question, identity in American society is based on
work. This principle is grounded in the Protestant ethic, and is
primary in the American way of life. The considered worth of a
human being is based on what she/he does. One of the first
questions asked a stranger with whom one is becoming ac-
quainted is, "What do you do?" When the interlocutor receives
an answer, she/he has a satisfaction that she/he "knows" the
other. The social status of a family is directly indicated by the
occupation of the man of the family; and even when inherited
wealth and family standing make conventional work unneces-
sary, the most honored of the wealthy are the ones who employ
their time in business or politics, social service or education.
The American social class structure is based on income and
vocation, with the lower class including those who do the least
valued jobs—home and industrial cleaning, agricultural cultivation and harvesting, industrial packing, lifting, and hauling—
and have the most tenuous security. The bulging American
middle class ranges from the truck driver to the investment
banker, but it has specific subclass gradations. Blue collar work
is at the bottom of the middle class, white collar work at the
middle of the middle class, professional work at the top of the
middle class. But it is the man's work that stratifies the family.
The woman medical doctor who is married to an electronics
technician belongs to a lower middle class family; the cleaning
lady, lower class by occupation, is lower middle class when she
is married to a carpenter. It is small wonder that women seeking
liberation look to vocation as an avenue for its realization.

The argument is made by some that the most essential worth

of persons is not in the work they do but in themselves, simply in being human. Being alive is credit enough for human authenticity. But the people making this argument are psychiatrists and counselors, professional writers, philosophers, teachers, and ministers, all of whom have a center of work in their own humanity.

[margin note: not work but self.]

For a time, especially during the period of the 1940s and 1950s, women were told that housewifery was a vocation, a calling in the old sense of social duty and personal fulfillment. Eloquent rhapsodies were written by the scores about the fullness of her generalist occupation—creative cook, nurse, home manager, schedule arranger, cleaner, teacher, hostess, decorator. It was a separate but equal doctrine in which the argument was made that women's work in the home was a career on a par with men's work in public. To turn that argument upside down, all that is needed is the question, "Then why not househusbandry as a career for men?" In stark relief, this question shows that work for which one is not paid is not a vocation, that relegation to the home is no basis at all for social status, and that, as with black people, separate is not equal. Homemaking is a functional task for ordering and making comfortable and pleasurable our private lives, but it is not a vocation until people are paid for doing it, until it is validated by the community as a legitimate social position, and until it is equally suitable as an occupation for women and for men. It may never need to be a vocation. It is something everybody has to do or have done for them; and the arrangement may be for women, men, and children to share such tasks as a part of our common lives; but the possibility should be left open that either women or men might see it as their central life focus for a period or a lifetime.

The androgynous life cannot be realized until the work world is sex blind. What is currency for half the population should be currency for the whole. We need to reexamine the notion that the basis for human identity and the chief component of social class and position lie in work; but until those values are reshuffled, women must have the same access to work that men have.

[margin note: but until...]

The work that is available is both demanding and drudgery, both creative and stultifying, both boring and exciting. Women need to share with men alike the drudgery and boredom, the responsibility, the means to personal fulfillment, and the involvement in decisions that shape society, which are the several faces of vocation. There are no real sex-linked vocational qualifications. If there were, gynecologists would all be women. Professional singing is enhanced by the variation of male and female voices. Likewise, professional sports could be reoriented to variations in the size, shape, and movement of female and male bodies.

What has been absent is a belief that women or men can work at any kind of jobs. We have believed that women must be confined to certain kinds of labor and men to others. Women cannot pump gas; it is unladylike. Man cannot teach little children; they only supervise those who do. Women cannot drive a truck, for they are mechanically inept; they only drive automobiles. Women cannot lift heavy boxes, only heavy children. Women cannot make buildings stand up; they do not have the mathematical aptitude. Men cannot nurse sick people; they are weak at nurturing. Women cannot manage corporations; they are indecisive and flighty. Men cannot type other people's letters; they are bad at details. All of these things have been true because we believed they were true and taught our children to live by these assumptions and acted on them in our applications for jobs, our policies for hiring people for jobs, our training of people for their future employment, and our support of people in their work. Yet none of them is a form in a Platonic heaven. Each of them, on being tested, proves false for some women and some men. They can be socially false if we choose as a society to make them so.

Work is at least a means to human dignity, for whatever the nature of the work, it enables one to earn an income for oneself and one's closest loved ones. It is also a route to personal fulfillment and social service. It is further a locus of public power and decision-making. At every level, it should be shared by women and men who are equal to each other.

Politics and the Social Order
In the short run, the masculine-equalitarian objective of getting women into elective and appointive public office in proportion to their numbers in the population is worth pursuing.

Women have to run for public office, campaign for women, vote for women, put up women for appointive positions, pressure office-holders to attend to women's issues. Men too can easily be such masculine-equalitarian feminists if they set their minds to it. Certainly after almost two hundred years, it is women's turn to have one of their number in the oval office at the White House, and after the same two hundred years the next four or five or nine appointees to the Supreme Court ought to be women, and each state should bear in mind that of its two United States senators, one should be a woman, one a man, and on down the political line.

Given the fact that not one President, Supreme Court justice or United States senator in 1973 was female, it does appear that gradualism takes forever, that sexual politics is established, and that tokenism puts only the exceptional woman in political leadership, as in the case of Yvonne Braithwaite, who co-chaired the 1972 Democratic National Convention so much more skillfully than her male counterpart and went on to win a seat in the House of Representatives. Among Democratic Kennedy devotees, the mantle of John and Robert has fallen only on Ted, not on Eunice or Patricia, Jackie or Ethel. Neither ability nor blood nor marriage is usually enough in life for a woman to gain high office, though several women have succeeded their husbands as widows to seats in Congress, making it clear that women can serve, but pushing no further the question of why women cannot serve "in their own right." The Kennedy women believe something about "women's place," as do most of the American people. It is still so unusual for women to lead politically that recognition is given to only the stalwart and pioneering, like Bella Abzug, whose daughters campaigned to "get her out of our house into the House," and Sissy Farenthold, who demanded that Texans take her seriously as a gubernatorial candidate. Both Margaret Chase Smith and Shirley Chisholm have presented themselves to their parties as candidates for the presidency; but the most telling "liberal" argument against Chisholm's candidacy was that it would be worse for black men to have a black woman in the White House than to keep "whitey" there.

More is required than simply to request that women have a

share in political leadership. Sexual politics is an accurate reading of the status quo for the ordering and directing of our national affairs. From the village council to the Supreme Court, phallic ascendancy is in firm control. Men dominate politics by biological right, and a prowoman, antimasculinist challenge to that right is in order. Self-centeredness and self-righteousness are human attributes, and it is time for a collective female self-assertion to enter politics. Women have loved men into the present state of affairs; it is time that we loved ourselves as much and took over the tables in the smoke-filled rooms. Sexual politics must be exposed and banished. National and international affairs may be grounded in biology, but biology has female and male dimensions.

In the long run, androgynous politics would be the better way. Men along with women should demand that political order be made by women and men together. Probably women would ultimately consider the same range of political choices as do men; but women's particular experiences up to the present might also give rise to some new priorities. Political divergence might become real with the actuality of political female and male equality.

Although not inevitable, androgynous politics is more likely under democratic socialism. If women and men together were really thought of as "the people," both would probably fare better under democratic socialism. Androgynous democratic socialism could influence the state meaningfully to decrease production and increase service. The state could give priority to distributing nutritious food, developing public transportation, and conducting research in preserving life and cleaning air, not in making more kinds of aerosol cans and motored equipment, or more new automobile models and ugly buildings from which to sell them. The state could effect a decrease in defense spending, an increase in spending on health, education, and welfare.

The androgynous democratic socialist state need not be a monster central state. It could have layers of community power, achieved through local control of funds for production, health, and welfare, and based on strong, viable, active voluntary associations—interest and professional groups, political parties, religious groups. The state could provide a floor under and ceiling over family and personal incomes, which would provide greater economic equality and would obviate the need to derive status and security entirely from work. The state, as the people, could own the mass media, airlines, and oil companies, but authority over them could be held by the local community users.

By their experience, women have become nurturers rather than planners, servers rather than producers, reconcilers rather than aggressors. Given equality, they might eventually behave politically like men, and men might behave like women—but for the moment, because of women's special respect for ecology, service, and peace, they have a unique contribution to make to politics.

Learning and Believing

Mathematics and geography are not sexual; teachers and children are. The American educational system needs a vast overhauling to abandon sex-role prescriptions for children and adults and to affirm sexuality as only one human attribute. Textbook and library book pictorial and verbal representations of men and women contribute to the learner's view of male and female roles. Teacher attitudes contribute even more. The mere presence of both women and men in the classroom speaks further. Curricular counseling and prevailing custom in education constitute still another dimension. Both women and men need to be trained, encouraged, and employed as teachers from preschool to the university. The fact of the presence of men on the nursery school faculty and women on the graduate faculty will affirm the androgynous view that women and men can both train the very young and investigate mature ideas. Even in the minute details of writing first readers and preparing problems for the math books, attention needs to be paid to the fact that both Dick and Jane climb trees, love Spot, sleep with their teddy bears, draw pictures of horses, and have use for prowess at addition. Children need to be taught that they all have an open-ended future, and assigning the boys to run the projector and the girls to clean up after the class party, sending boys to higher math and girls to higher home economics, putting boys only on the competitive swimming team and girls only in the flute section of the orchestra, will close in the future for both of them.

teachers &
scholars

Not only in the transmission of knowledge but in the discovery of knowledge, an androgynous affirmation has far-reaching implications. The writing of history is an example of what might be true for all the disciplines. In history, scholars such as Anne Firor Scott and Gerda Lerner are asking: What is the reality of women's past? Who has woman been and what did this half of humankind do back then? New sources and new methods have to be used to discover a new part of the past, and it is no longer acceptable for a historian to publish a book with only five pages touching on women. For biology and the medical sciences, the question may be, What is the significance of anatomical and endocrinal differences between human females and males? For psychiatry, What are the implications of women's and men's social roles for their psychic order or disorder? Are there any feelings which women have that men do not, or which men have that women do not? Has the standard of mental health been a sexual standard? For literature, How do we write about women and men as first of all fundamentally human? How have women and men been treated in literature? How has the woman writer fared in the literary establishment? Are elements of the woman writer's biography as relevant or irrelevant to her literary assessment as the man's? For theology, Is God male? Who indeed is God if the masculine and the feminine are equally significant in human experience? For linguistics, How has language discriminated against women, reflected male superiority? How can we swear and make love with words that are androgynous? These questions, phrased from an androgynous perspective, are new ones to ask, and from them volumes of new ideas can be generated.

Women's studies is quickly becoming a new academic discipline, holding out enormous possibilities as a focus within traditional disciplines, as a means for rectifying academic neglect, and as a way of increasing knowledge of and esteem for women as persons and as a group worthy of academic attention. The androgynous ideal requires that women's studies eventually come to permeate all intellectual endeavor as a full, creative, and sound component of the search for truth.

In the final analysis, what is true is what we believe, individually, academically, and socially. The androgynous concept is offered as a new belief system around which old myths and values can be rearranged, new attitudes and myths can arise. The assertion that "women and men are equal to each other" is an empty claim to be dismissed or ridiculed, unless we take it into ourselves as a belief. What we believe shapes what we do, the questions we ask, the way we vote, and what is published in the morning paper. The network of action and inquiry, politics and events, is vastly complicated; but it is rooted in personal and social conviction. The feminist revolution must take place in the creed of the American people. It will not come without anguish and sacrifice; but if it does come, and if it is androgynous, we shall not ask whether it is feminine or masculine, but will know that it is human.

Bibliography
Notes
Index

Bibliography

Books

Adams, Elsie, and Briscoe, Mary Louise, eds. *Up Against the Wall, Mother . . .* Beverly Hills, Cal.: Glencoe Press, 1971.

Adelstein, Michael E., and Pival, Jean G., eds. *Women's Liberation.* New York: St. Martin's Press, 1972.

Altback, Edith Hoshino, ed. *From Feminism to Liberation.* Cambridge, Mass.: Schenkman, 1971.

Anthony, Susan B., Stanton, Elizabeth Cady, Gage, Matilda Joslin, and Harper, Ida Husted. *The History of Woman Suffrage.* 6 vols. Vols. I-IV. New York: Fowler and Wells, 1881-1902. Vols. V-VI. New York: National American Woman Suffrage Association, 1922.

Babcox, Deborah, and Belkin, Madeline, eds. *Liberation Now! Writings from the Women's Liberation Movement.* New York: Dell, 1971.

Beard, Mary. *Woman As a Force in History.* New York: Macmillan, 1946.

Beauvoir, Simone de. *The Second Sex.* Trans. and ed. H. M. Parshley. New York: Bantam Books, 1961.

Bernard, Jessie. *The Future of Marriage.* New York: Bantam Books, 1972.

————. *Women and the Public Interest.* Chicago: Aldine, 1971.

Bird, Caroline. *Born Female.* New York: Pocket Books, 1969.

Bolinger, Dwight. *Aspects of Language.* New York: Harcourt, Brace and World, 1968.

Bosmajian, Hamida, and Bosmajian, Haig. *This Great Argument:*

The Rights of Women. Menlo Park, Cal.: Addison-Wesley, 1972.

Bradstreet, Anne. *Poems of Anne Bradstreet.* Ed. Robert Hutchinson. New York: Dover, 1969.

Brown, Helen Gurley. *Sex and the Single Girl.* New York: Pocket Books, 1962.

Cade, Toni, ed. *The Black Woman.* New York: Signet Books, 1970.

Chafe, William Henry. *The American Woman: Her Changing Social, Economic, and Political Roles, 1920-1970.* New York: Oxford University Press, 1972.

Chambers, Clarke A. *Seedtime of Reform.* Ann Arbor: University of Michigan Press, 1967.

Chmaj, Betty E. *American Women and American Studies.* Pittsburgh: KNOW, 1971.

Cott, Nancy F., ed. *Root of Bitterness.* New York: E. P. Dutton, 1972.

Dahrendorf, Ralf. *Class and Class Conflict in Industrial Society.* Stanford, Cal.: Stanford University Press, 1959.

Daly, Mary. *Beyond God the Father.* Boston: Beacon Press, 1973.

_____. *The Church and the Second Sex.* London: Geoffrey Chapman, 1968.

Dector, Midge. *The New Chastity and Other Arguments Against Women's Liberation.* New York: Coward, McCann and Geoghegan, 1972.

Doely, Sarah Bentley. *Women's Liberation and the Church: The New Demand for Freedom in the Life of the Christian Church.* New York: Association Press, 1970.

Dollard, John. *Caste and Class in a Southern Town.* 3rd ed. Garden City, N.Y.: Doubleday Anchor Books, 1957.

Drinnon, Richard. *Rebel in Paradise: A Biography of Emma Goldman.* Boston: Beacon Press, 1961.

Ermarth, Margaret Sittler. *Adam's Fractured Rib.* Philadelphia: Fortress Press, 1970.

Fairchild, J. E., ed. *Women, Society and Sex.* Greenwich, Conn.: Fawcett, 1956.

Figes, Eva. *Patriarchal Attitudes.* Greenwich, Conn.: Fawcett, 1970.

Firestone, Shulamith. *The Dialectic of Sex: The Case for Feminist Revolution.* New York: Bantam Books, 1970.

Flexner, Eleanor. *Century of Struggle: The Woman's Rights Movement in the United States.* New York: Atheneum, 1968.

_____. *Mary Wollstonecraft.* Baltimore: Penguin Books, 1973.

Friedan, Betty. *The Feminine Mystique.* New York: Dell, 1963.

Fuller, Margaret. *Margaret Fuller, American Romantic: A Selection*

from Her Writings and Correspondence. Ed. Perry Miller. Gloucester, Mass.: Peter Smith, 1969.

Gilman, Charlotte Perkins. *Women and Economics.* Ed. Carl Degler.
New York: Harper and Row, 1966.

Goldman, Emma. *Living My Life.* 2 vols. New York: Alfred A.
Knopf, 1931.

Gornick, Vivian, and Moran, Barbara K., eds. *Women in Sexist Society.* New York: New American Library, 1971.

Graebner, Alan. *After Eve: The New Feminism.* Minneapolis: Augsburg, 1972.

Greer, Germaine. *The Female Eunuch.* New York: McGraw-Hill,
1971.

Grimke, Sarah. *Letters on the Equality of the Sexes and the Condition
of Woman.* New York: Burt Franklin, 1970.

Hays, Elinor Rice. *Lucy Stone: One of America's First and Greatest
Feminists.* New York: Tower, 1961.

Heilbrun, Carolyn G. *Toward a Recognition of Androgyny.* New
York: Alfred A. Knopf, 1973.

Herschberger, Ruth. *Adam's Rib.* New York: Harper and Row, 1970.

Hole, Judith, and Levine, Ellen. *Rebirth of Feminism.* New York:
Quadrangle Books, 1971.

Horney, Karen. *Feminine Psychology.* New York: W. W. Norton,
1967.

Howe, Florence, and Ahlum, Carol. *Female Studies III.* Mimeographed. Pittsburgh: KNOW, 1971.

——. *The Guide to Current Female Studies II.* Mimeographed. Old
Westbury, N.Y.: The Feminist Press, 1972.

Irwin, Inez Haynes. *Up Hill with Banners Flying.* Penobscot, Me.:
Traversity Press, 1964.

Janeway, Elizabeth. *Man's World, Woman's Place: A Study in Social
Mythology.* New York: William Morrow, 1971.

Jenness, Linda, ed. *Feminism and Socialism.* New York: Pathfinder
Press, 1972.

Johnston, Johanna. *Mrs. Satan.* New York: G. P. Putnam's Sons,
1967.

Kanowitz, Leo. *Women and the Law: The Unfinished Revolution*
Albuquerque: University of New Mexico Press, 1969.

Kennedy, David M. *Birth Control in America: The Career of Margaret Sanger.* New Haven: Yale University Press, 1970.

Kraditor, Aileen S. *The Ideas of the Woman Suffrage Movement,
1890-1920.* Garden City, N.Y.: Anchor Books, 1971.

——, ed. *Up from the Pedestal: Landmark Writings in the Ameri-*

can *Woman's Struggle for Equality.* Chicago: Quadrangle Books, 1968.

Kuhn, Thomas S. *The Structure of Scientific Revolutions.* Chicago: University of Chicago Press, 1962.

Laird, Charlton, and Gorrell, Robert M., eds. *Reading about Language.* New York: Harcourt, Brace, Javanovich, 1970.

Lerner, Gerda. *The Woman in American History.* Menlo Park, Cal.: Addison Wesley, 1971.

Lloyd, Trevòr. *Suffragettes International: The World-wide Campaign for Women's Rights.* New York: American Heritage Press, 1971.

Maccoby, Eleanor E., ed. *The Development of Sex Differences.* Stanford, Cal.: Stanford University Press, 1966.

Martin, Wendy, ed. *The American Sisterhood.* New York: Harper and Row, 1972.

Marx, Karl, *et al. The Woman Question: Selections from the Writings of Karl Marx, Frederick Engels, V. I. Lenin, Joseph Stalin.* New York: International, 1951.

Mill, John Stuart, and Mill, Harriet Taylor. *Essays on Sex Equality.* Ed. and intro. Alice S. Rossi. Chicago: University of Chicago Press, 1971.

Millett, Kate. *Sexual Politics.* Garden City, N.Y.: Doubleday, 1970.

Mitchell, Juliet. *Woman's Estate.* New York: Pantheon Books, 1971.

Montagu, Ashley. *The Natural Superiority of Women.* New York: Collier Books, 1970.

Morgan, Robin, ed. *Sisterhood Is Powerful: An Anthology of Writings from the Women's Liberation Movement.* New York: Vintage Books, 1970.

National American Woman's Suffrage Association. *Victory: How Women Won It.* New York: H. W. Wilson, 1940.

New York City Commission on Human Rights. *Women's Role in Contemporary Society.* New York: Avon Books, 1972.

Newman, Charles, ed. *The Art of Sylvia Plath.* Bloomington: Indiana University Press, 1970.

Nisbet, Robert A. *The Social Bond.* New York: Alfred A. Knopf, 1970.

O'Neill, William L. *Everyone Was Brave: The Rise and Fall of Feminism in America.* Chicago: Quadrangle Books, 1969.

Plath, Sylvia. *Ariel.* New York: Harper and Row, 1961.

———. *Winter Trees.* New York: Harper and Row, 1972.

Potter, David M. *History and American Society.* Ed. Don E. Fehrenbacher. New York: Oxford University Press, 1973.

Reed, Evelyn. *Problems of Women's Liberation.* New York: Pathfinder Press, 1971.

Riegel, Robert E. *American Feminists.* Lawrence: University of Kansas Press, 1963.

Rossi, Alice S. ed. *The Feminist Papers.* New York: Bantam Books, 1974.

Roszak, Betty, and Roszak, Theodore, eds. *Masculine/Feminine.* New York: Harper and Row, 1969.

Salper, Roberta, ed. *Female Liberation.* New York: Alfred A. Knopf, 1972.

Sanger, Margaret. *Woman and the New Race.* New York: Blue Ribbon Books, 1920.

Schneir, Miriam, ed. *Feminism: The Essential Historical Writings.* New York: Vintage Books, 1972.

Scott, Anne Firor, ed. *The American Woman: Who Was She?* Englewood Cliffs, N.J.: Prentice-Hall, 1971.

_____. *The Southern Lady: From Pedestal to Politics, 1830-1930.* Chicago: University of Chicago Press, 1970.

_____, ed. *Women in American Life.* Boston: Houghton Mifflin, 1970.

Sexton, Anne. *All My Pretty Ones.* Boston: Houghton Mifflin, 1961.

_____. *To Bedlam and Part Way Back.* Boston: Houghton Mifflin, 1960.

Showalter, Elaine, ed. *Women's Liberation and Literature.* New York: Harcourt, Brace, Jovanovich, 1971.

Shulman, Alix Kates. *Memoirs of an Ex-Prom Queen.* New York: Alfred A. Knopf, 1972.

Sinclair, Andrew. *The Better Half.* New York: Harper and Row, 1965.

Smith, Page. *Daughters of the Promised Land.* Boston: Little, Brown, 1970.

Smuts, Robert W. *Women and Work in America.* New York: Schocken Books, 1971.

Stambler, Sookie, ed. *Women's Liberation: Blueprint for the Future.* New York: Ace Books, 1970.

Stern, Karl. *The Flight from Woman.* New York: Farrar, Straus and Giroux, 1965.

Tanner, Leslie B., ed. *Voices from Women's Liberation.* New York: Signet Books, 1970.

Thompson, Mary Lou, ed. *Voices of the New Feminism.* Boston: Beacon Press, 1970.

Tyler, Alice Felt. *Freedom's Ferment.* New York: Harper and Row, 1962.

Ware, Cellestine. *Woman Power: The Movement of Women's Liberation.* New York: Tower, 1970.

Woolf, Virginia. *A Room of One's Own.* New York: Harcourt, Brace and World, 1957.

Periodicals: Special Issues

Aphra 1-3 (Fall 1969-Spring 1972).

Atlantic March 1970: "Women Against Men.

College English 34 (Oct. 1972): "Women Writing and Teaching," ed. Elaine Hedges.

Congressional Digest 50 (January 1971): "Controversy over the 'Equal Rights for Women' Amendment: Pro and Con."

Daedalus 93 (Spring 1964): "Women in America."

motive 29 (March-April 1969): "On the Liberation of Women," 32 (1972): "Lesbian/Feminist Issue."

Ms., Spring 1972-March 1973.

New Woman, April/May 1972.

The Spokeswoman, June 5, 1970-Mar. 15, 1973.

Time, Mar. 20, 1972: "The American Woman."

Women: A Journal of Liberation, Fall 1969.

Women's Studies Newsletter, Winter 1972.

Articles

Anderson, Brian. "Women on 'U' Faculty Organize To Fight for Rights." Minneapolis *Tribune,* Mar. 14, 1971.

Ash, Mildred. "Freud on Feminine Identity and Female Sexuality." *Medical Aspects of Human Sexuality,* 6 (July 1972): 101, 105-107, 112.

Barry, Herbert, III, Bacon, Margaret K., and Child, Irvin L. "A Cross-Cultural Survey of Some Sex Differences in Socialization." *The Journal of Abnormal and Social Psychology* 55 (1957).

Beauvoir, Simone de. "The Question of Fidelity." *Harper's,* November 1964, pp. 57-64.

Benson, Ruth Crego. "Women's Studies: Theory and Practice." *AAUP Bulletin* 58 (September 1972): 283-286.

Berkwitt, George J. "Corporate Wives: The Third Party." *Dun's,* August 1972, pp. 61-62.

Bernard, Jessie. "Minnesota Women: One Alumna's Story." *Alumni News: University of Minnesota,* October 1971, pp. 8-13.

Broverman, Inge K., Broverman, Donald M., and Clarkson, Frank E. "Sex-Role Stereotypes and Clinical Judgments of Mental Health." *Journal of Counselling and Clinical Psychology* 34 (1970): 1-7.

Brownmiller, Susan. "Sisterhood Is Powerful." *New York Times Magazine,* Mar. 15, 1970, pp. 26 ff.

Calderone, Mary. "It's Really the Men Who Need Liberating." *Life,* Sept. 4, 1970, p. 26.

Chisholm, Shirley. "A Visiting Feminine Eye." *McCall's,* August 1970, p. 6.

Cook, Alice H. "Sex Discrimination at Universities: An Ombudsman's View." *AAUP Bulletin* 58 (September 1972): 279-282.

Cully, Iris V. "On Woman and Liberation." *The Review of Books and Religion,* Jan. 15, 1972, pp. 1 ff.

Dector, Midge. "The Liberated Woman." *Commentary,* October 1970, pp. 33-44.

Didion, Joan. "The Women's Movement." *New York Times Book Review,* July 30, 1972, pp. 1-2, 14.

Dudar, Helen. "Women's Lib: The War on 'Sexism.' " *Newsweek,* Mar. 23, 1970, pp. 71-78.

"Faculty Backlash." *Newsweek,* Dec. 4, 1972, p. 127.

Farrell, Barry. "You've Come a Long Way, Buddy." *Life,* Aug. 27, 1971, pp. 52-59.

Farson, Richard E. "The Rage of Women." *Look,* Dec. 16, 1969, pp. 21-23.

"Feminists Look at Children's Books." *Library Journal* 46 (Jan. 15, 1971): 235-240.

"Five Passionate Feminists." *McCall's,* July 1970, pp. 52-55, 111-117.

Fleming, Thomas. "Sex and Civil Rights." *This Week Magazine,* Mar. 19, 1967, pp. 4-6.

Gilman, Richard. "The 'Woman Problem.' " *Life,* Aug. 13, 1971, pp. 40-55.

"Gloria Steinem: A Liberated Woman Despite Beauty, Chic and Success." *Newsweek,* Aug. 16, 1971, pp. 51-55.

Goodman, Ellen. "The Movement: They Act the Part." *Boston Sunday Globe,* Aug. 10, 1969.

"Goodwill Toward Women." *New Republic,* Dec. 25, 1971, pp. 5-6.

Gordon, Ann D., Buhle, Mari Jo, and Schrom, Nancy E. "Women in American Society." *Radical America* 5 (July-August 1971): 1-66.

Grossman, Edward. "In Pursuit of the American Woman." *Harper's,* Feb., 1970, pp. 47-69.

Hancock, Brenda Robinson. "Affirmation by Negation in the Women's Liberation Movement." *The Quarterly Journal of Speech* 58 (October 1972): 264-271.

Harris, Ann Sutherland. "The Second Sex in Academe." *AAUP Bulletin* 56 (Fall 1970): 283-295.

Harrison, Barbara. "Feminist Experiment in Education." *The New Republic,* Mar. 11, 1972, pp. 13-17.

Hartley, Ruth E. "Some Implications of Current Changes in Sex-Role Patterns." *Merrill-Palmer Quarterly of Behavior and Development* 6 (1959-1960): 153-164.

Heide, Wilma Scott. "What's Wrong with Male-dominated Society." *Impact of Science on Society* 21 (1971).

Heilbrun, Carolyn. "The Masculine Wilderness of the American Novel." *Saturday Review,* Jan. 29, 1972, pp. 41-44.

Hoffman, Nancy Jo. "Sexism in Letters of Recommendation." *MLA Newsletter,* September 1972, pp. 5-6.

Hollinger, David A. "T. S. Kuhn's Theory of Science and Its Implications for History." *American Historical Review* 78 (April 1973): 370-393.

Hovik, Suzanne. "Moderates Try To Change Women's Lot Through Education, Legislation." *Minneapolis Star,* Apr. 28, 1970.

————. "Radicals Doubt System, Say Change in Attitude Needed for Equality." *Minneapolis Star,* May 1, 1970.

————. "Women's Lib Message: 'I Am a PERSON.' " *Minneapolis Star,* Apr. 27, 1970.

Howard, Jane. "Is Women's Lib a Dirty Word in Milwaukee?" *Life,* Aug. 27, 1971, pp. 46-51.

Howe, Florence. "Feminism, Fiction, and the Classroom." *Soundings* 55 (Winter 1972): 369-389.

————. "Sexual Stereotypes Start Early." *Saturday Review,* Oct. 16, 1971, pp. 76-82, 92-94.

Howe, Irving. "The Middle-Class Mind of Kate Millett." *Harper's,* December 1970, pp. 110-129.

Janeway, Elizabeth. "Skeptical Report on the Experts Who Tell Women How To Be Women." *McCall's,* April 1966, pp. 94-95 ff.

Kern, Edward. "Women's Fight for the Vote." *Life,* Aug. 20, 1971, pp. 40-50.

Komisar, Lucy. "The New Feminism." *Saturday Review,* Feb. 21, 1970, pp. 27-30, 55.

Lakoff, Robin. "You Are What You Say." *Ms.,* July 1974, pp. 65-67.

Lear, Martha Weinman. "The Second Feminist Wave." *New York Times Magazine,* Mar. 10, 1968, pp. 24 ff.

Lerner, Gerda. "New Approaches to the Study of Women in American History." *Journal of Social History* 3 (Fall 1969): 53-62.

_____. "Women's Rights and American Feminism." *The American Scholar* 40 (Spring 1970): 235-248.

"Liberation of Women." *New Left Notes,* July 10, 1967.

Loercher, Diana. "Books on Women's Lib a New Genre." *Christian Science Monitor,* Jan. 15, 1973.

Luce, Clare Booth. "Woman: A Technological Castaway." *Britannica Book of the Year, 1973,* pp. 24-29. Chicago: Encyclopedia Britannica, 1973.

MacEoin, Gary. "Unequal in the Sight of God." *McCall's,* June 1971, pp. 78 ff.

"Margaret Mead on Family Life, Sex Roles." *Minneapolis Tribune,* Dec. 10, 1972.

"Making Transfers Less Painful." *Minneapolis Tribune,* December 13, 1972.

Mead, Margaret. "What Shall We Tell Our Children?" *Redbook,* June 1970, pp. 35 ff.

Mitchell, Juliet. "Women: The Longest Revolution." *New Left Review,* November-December 1966, pp. 11-37.

Murray, Alice. "Feminist Press Creating What It Couldn't Find." *New York Times,* Dec. 10, 1972.

"The New Feminists: Revolt Against 'Sexism.' " *Time,* Nov. 21, 1969, pp. 53-54, 56.

"A New Ms. at *Ms.*" *Newsweek,* Mar. 13, 1972, p. 50.

Pifer, Alan. "A Fuller Role for Women." *The Chronicle of Higher Education,* Jan. 3, 1972, p. 12.

"Playboy Interviews Germaine Greer." *Playboy,* January 1972, pp. 61-82.

Porter, Sylvia. Untitled column. *Minneapolis Tribune,* May 29, 1972.

Potter, David M. "American Women and the American Character." *American Character and Culture,* ed. John A. Hague, pp. 65-84. Deland, Fla: Everett Edwards Press, 1964.

Rich, Adrienne. "The Anti Feminist Woman." *The New York Review of Books,* Nov. 30, 1972, pp. 34-40.

Rossi, Alice S. "Abortion and Social Change." *Dissent,* July-August 1969, pp. 338-346.

_____. "Discrimination and Demography Restrict Opportunities for Academic Women." *College and University Business,* February 1970.

_____. "Job Discrimination and What Women Can Do About It." *The Atlantic Monthly,* March 1970.

_____. "Sentiment and Intellect: The Story of John Stuart Mill and Harriet Taylor Mill." *Midway* 10 (Spring 1970): 29-51.

_____. "Sex Equality: The Beginnings of Ideology." *The Humanist,* September/October 1969, pp. 3-16.

_____. "Sex Segregation and the Women's College." *The Quarterly* (Goucher College), Winter 1971, pp. 10-13.

_____. "Status of Women in Graduate Department of Sociology, 1968-1969." *The American Sociologist* 5 (February 1970): 1-12.

_____. "Transition to Parenthood." *Journal of Marriage and the Family* (February 1968): 26-39.

_____. "Women—Terms of Liberation." *Dissent,* November-December 1970, pp. 531-541.

Rostow, Edna G. "Feminism and Femininity." *Yale Review* 51 Spring 1962): 384-399.

Scott, Anne Firor. "Women, Religion, and Social Change in the South, 1830-1930." *Religion and the Solid South,* ed. Samuel S. Hill, Jr., pp. 92-121. Nashville: Abingdon Press, 1972.

"Senate Approves Amendment for Women's Rights." *Minneapolis Tribune,* Mar. 23, 1972.

Sennett, Richard. "Women: What Is To Be Done?" *The New York Review of Books,* Apr. 20, 1972, pp. 22-26.

"Sex Stereotypes in Readers." *Library Journal* 46 (Feb. 15, 1971): 680.

Shainess, Natalie. "Images of Woman: Past and Present, Overt and Obscured." *American Journal of Psychotherapy* 23 (January 1969): 79-97.

Shanahan, Eileen. "Lack of Funds Cripples Women's Political Group." *Minneapolis Tribune,* Sept. 4, 1972.

_____. "Opposition Rises to Amendment on Equal Rights." *New York Times,* Jan. 15, 1973.

Smith, Liz. "Gloria Steinem, Writer and Social Critic Talks about Sex, Politics and Marriage." *Redbook,* Jan., 1972, pp. 60-76.

"Sound and Fury at Assembly of Methodist Women." *Christian Century,* June 17, 1970, pp. 773-774.

Stavan, D. G. "Reducing the Miss Muffet Syndrome: An Annotated Bibliography." *Library Journal* 97 (Jan. 15, 1972): 256-259.

Steinem, Gloria. "What It Would Be Like If Women Win." *Time,* Aug. 31, 1970, pp. 22-24.

_____. "What *Playboy* Doesn't Know about Women." *McCall's,* October 1970, pp. 76-77, 139-140.

Sternhell, Carol Ruth. "A March in the Dark." *McCall's,* November 1970, pp. 8 ff.

"Stewardesses Start Drive Against 'Sexism' on Jobs." *Minneapolis Tribune,* Dec. 13, 1972.

Swidler, Leonard. "Jesus Was a Feminist." *Catholic World,* January 1970, pp. 177-183.

Trecker, Janice Law. "Woman's Place Is in the Curriculum." *Saturday Review,* Oct. 16, 1971, pp. 83-86, 920.

Trible, Phyllis. "Depatriarchalizing in Biblical Interpretation," *Journal of the American Academy of Religion* 41 (March 1973): 30-48.

Weissman, Myrna M., Nelson, Katherine, Hackman, Judith, Pincus, Cynthia, and Prusoff, Brigitte. "The Faculty Wife: Her Academic Interests and Qualifications." *AAUP Bulletin* 58 (September 1972): 287-292.

"Who's Come a Long Way, Baby?" *Time,* Aug. 31, 1970, pp. 16-21.

Wilson, Richard. "Women's Lib Amendment—A Pandora's Box?" *Minneapolis Tribune,* Mar. 22, 1972, p. 11A.

"Women 'Crash' History Books." *Minneapolis Tribune,* Feb. 21, 1971.

Women's Caucus, American Sociological Association. "Statement and Resolutions." *The American Sociologist* 5 (February 1970): 62-65.

"Women's Legal Rights in Fifty States." *McCall's,* February 1971, pp. 90-95.

"Women's Lib and the Liberated Woman" (Letters to the editor and replies by Midge Dector). *Commentary,* February 1971, pp. 12-36.

"Women's Lit." *Newsweek,* Apr. 26, 1971, p. 65.

"Women's Rights in the Professions." *Ford Foundation Letter,* June 1, 1972, p. 1.

Woodward, Kenneth L. "Women and the Church: From Adam's Rib to Women's Lib." *McCall's,* June 1971, pp. 77 ff.

Wrenn, Marie-Claude. "Women Arise." *Life,* Sept. 4, 1970, pp. 16 B-23.

Zack, Marg. "Contract Spells Out Marriage Terms." *Minneapolis Tribune,* Dec. 17, 1972, pp. 1E ff.

Feminist Group Newspapers, Newsletters, Pamphlets, and Papers

Ain't I a Woman? Iowa City: June 30, 1971-June 16, 1972.

Arrow, Jeanne. "Dangers in the Pro-Women Line and Consciousness-Raising." Mimeographed. New York: The Feminists, n.d.

Atkinson, Ti-Grace. "The Institution of Sexual Intercourse." Mimeographed. New York: The Feminists, 1968.

————. "Radical Feminism." Mimeographed. New York: The Feminists, 1969.

————. "Radical Feminism and Love." Mimeographed. New York: The Feminists, 1969.

————. "Vaginal Orgasm As a Mass Hysterical Survival Response." Mimeographed. New York: The Feminists, 1968.

Bread and Roses untitled information sheet. Mimeographed. Boston-Cambridge: n.d.

Bread and Roses Newsletter. Boston-Cambridge: November, Dec. 4, 1970.

Brown, Judith, and Jones, Beverly. *Toward a Female Liberation Movement.* Boston: New England Free Press, 1968.

Champagne, The Rev. Emily A., ed. "Women and Religion." Mimeographed. Oakland, Cal.: National Organization for Women's Ecumenical Task Force on Women and Religion, 1972.

Cleary, Josephine. "Notes from the Lower Classes II." Mimeographed. New York: The Feminists, 1969.

Columbia and Harvard New University Conference (Ellen Cantarow *et al.*). "I am Furious (Female)." Mimeographed. Detroit: Radical Educational Project, n.d.

Cronan, Sheila. "Marriage." Mimeographed. New York: The Feminists, n.d.

Densmore, Dana. "Speech Is the Form of Thought." Mimeographed. Pittsburgh: KNOW, 1970.

Diner, Helen. "The Story of the Amazons." Mimeographed. New York: The Feminists, n.d.

Dunbar, Roxanne, and Grizzard, Vernon. "Caste and Class: The Key to Understanding Female Oppression." Mimeographed. Cambridge, Mass.: Female Liberation—Cell 16, n.d.

————. "Female Liberation As the Basis for Social Revolution." Boston: Female Liberation—Cell 16, n.d.

————, and Grizzard, Vernon. "Students and Revolution." Mimeographed. Boston: Female Liberation—Cell 16, n.d.

Edmiston, Susan. "The Psychology of Day Care." Pittsburgh: KNOW, 1971.

Everywoman, May 8, 1970-May 1972.

Faust, Jean. "Words That Oppress." *Women Speaking,* April 1970.

Female Liberation—Cell 16. "Dialectical Materialism As a Tool For Female Liberation." Mimeographed. Boston, n.d.

————. " 'Motherhood' and Subordination of Females and Children." Mimeographed. Boston, n.d.

————. "Petition to the State of Massachusetts for Infant and Child

Care." Mimeographed. Boston, n.d.

———. "Self Defense and the Preservation of Females" Mimeographed. Boston, n.d.

Female Liberation Newsletter (Minneapolis), March 1970-June 1971.

The Feminists. "History of the Feminists." Mimeographed. New York, 1970.

———. "Organizational Principles and Structure." Mimeographed. New York, n.d.

———. "Statement of the Feminists on the Equal Rights Amendment." Mimeographed. New York, 1970.

Gross, Louise, and MacEwan, Phyllis. "Day Care." Chicago: New University Conference Women's Caucus, n.d.

Heide, Wilma Scott. "New York Times Guest Editorial." Mimeographed. Pittsburgh: KNOW, n.d.

———. "The Reality and Challenge of the Double Standard in Mental Health and Society." Mimeographed. Pittsburgh: KNOW, n.d.

Jordan, Joan. "The Place of American Women: Economic Exploitation of Women." Boston: New England Free Press, 1968.

Joreen. "The BITCH Manifesto." Mimeographed. Pittsburgh: KNOW, n.d.

A Journal of Female Liberation (Boston Female Liberation—Cell 16), February 1969-April 1970.

Kearon, Pamela. "Man-Hating." Mimeographed. New York: The Feminists, 1969.

———. "Power As a Function of the Group—Some Notes." Mimeographed. New York: The Feminists, 1969.

———. "Rules and Responsibility in a Leaderless Feminist Revolutionary Group." Mimeographed. New York: The Feminists, 1969.

Koedt, Anne. "The Myth of the Vaginal Orgasm." Mimeographed. Boston: New England Free Press, n.d.

The Ladder (Daughters of Bilitis), October 1964-September 1965, October/November 1970-August/September 1971.

Letter from Cell 16 (Dana Densmore, Lisa Lezharn, Abby Rockefeller, Betsy Warrior, Jane West), Nov. 25, 1970. Mimeographed.

Letter from Florence Howe and Carol Ahlum, Commission on the Status of Women, Modern Language Association of America, June 21, 1971. Mimeographed.

Letter from Florence Howe and Joanna Miller, The Feminist Press, Jan. 23, 1973. Mimeographed.

Mainardi, Pat. "The Politics of Housework." Mimeographed. Boston: Female Liberation—Cell 16, n.d.

Mann, Nancy. "Fucked-up in America." Mimeographed. Boston:

New England Free Press, n.d.

McAfee, Kathy, and Wood, Myrna. "Bread and Roses." Detroit: Radical Education Project, 1969.

Mehrhof, Barbara. "Class Structure in the Women's Movement." Mimeographed. New York: The Feminists, 1969.

———, and Cronan, Sheila. "The Rise of Man." Mimeographed. New York: The Feminists, 1970.

Michaels, Sheila. "The Archetypal Woman." Mimeographed. New York: The Feminists, n.d.

National Organization for Women. "Action Resolutions." Passed at the fourth annual conference, Mar. 20-22, 1970. Mimeographed.

———. "Bill of Rights," n.d. Mimeographed.

National Organization for Women. "National Organization for Women" pamphlet, n.d.

———. "Statement of Purpose." Adopted at the organizing conference in Washington, D.C., Oct. 29, 1966. Mimeographed.

———, "Task Force Reports" (Task Force on the Image of Woman, Task Force on Education, The Right of a Woman To Determine Her Own Reproductive Process, Task Force on Women in Poverty, Task Force on Political Rights and Responsibilities, Task Force on Legal and Political Rights, Task Force on Women and Religion). 1970.

National Women's Political Caucus. Membership brochure, 1971.

———. *Newsletter* 5-6 (June-December 1972.

———. "State Contacts." Washington, D.C., 1972.

———. "Statement of Purpose." Mimeographed. Washington, D.C., n.d.

———. "What Is a Women's Caucus?" Washington, D.C., n.d.

———. "Why Join the National Women's Political Caucus?" Mimeographed. Washington, D.C., July 1972.

New University Conference. "Women's Caucus Perspective." Adopted at the National Convention of the New University Conference, June 1969.

Notes from the Second Year: Women's Liberation. New York: Radical Feminists, 1970.

Notes from the Third Year: Women's Liberation. New York: Radical Feminists, 1971.

NOW Acts, Winter 1970-Fall 1971.

NOW Newsletter (Twin Cities Chapter), January 1971-June 1972.

Off Our Backs (Washington, D.C.), June 26, 1970-September 1971.

Peslikis, Irene. "Resistances to Consciousness." Mimeographed. Boston: Female Liberation—Cell 16, n.d.

Robinson, Patricia. "Poor Black Women." Boston: New England Free Press, n.d.

Sade, Janine. "History of the Equality Issue in the Contemporary Women's Movement." Mimeographed. New York: The Feminists, 1969.

Schwartz, Rosalind. "Notes from the Working Class: A Jewish Woman Speaks Her Mind." Mimeographed. New York: The Feminists, n.d.

Seattle Radical Women. "Program and Structure." Mimeographed. October 1969.

_____. "Radical Women—Support Minority-Race Workers and Contractors in Their Struggle for Equal Job Opportunity." Mimeographed. Seattle, n.d.

_____. "Seattle Women Speak Out!" *Seattle Post Intelligencer,* January 1970.

Something Else! issue on "Man's World and Welcome to It!" Detroit: Radical Education Project, January-February 1970.

Warrior, Betsy. "The Quiet Ones." Mimeographed. Boston: Female Liberation—Cell 16, n.d.

Wells, Lynette. "On Sisterhood." Mimeographed. Boston: Female Liberation—Cell 16, n.d.

Wendoffer, Melba. Letter to Noreen Bagnall from Seattle Radical Women, Apr. 25, 1970.

Willis, Ellen. " 'Consumerism' and Women." Mimeographed. Boston: Female Liberation—Cell 16, n.d.

Women's Action Committee, Minneapolis. "Women Unite." Minneapolis, n.d.

Women's Caucus, Modern Language Association. "Resolutions." (Dittoed.) 1969.

Women's Collective, Stratford, Conn. "Consciousness-Raising." Mimeographed. Pittsburgh: KNOW, n.d.

Women's Equity Action League. "1971 National Committee Reports." State College, Pa., 1971.

_____. Press release, Novelty, Ohio, April 1969. Mimeographed.

Women's Equity Action League. "WEAL—Women's Equity Action League" (membership pamphlet). State College, Pa., 1972.

Government Documents

Congress, House of Representatives, Special Subcommittee on Education of the Committee on Education and Labor. *Discrimination Against Women.* 2 parts. 91st Cong., 2nd sess., 1970.

Labor Department, Women's Bureau. *Handbook on Women Workers. 1969.*

President's Commission on the Status of Women. *American Women.* Washington: Government Printing Office, 1963.

President's Task Force on Women's Rights and Responsibilities. *A*

Matter of Simple Justice. Washington: Government Printing Office, 1970.

Congress, Senate. Committee on the Judiciary. *Equal Rights for Men and Women.* 92nd Cong., 2nd sess., 1972. Senate Report 92-689 to accompany S. J. Res. 8, S. J. Res. 9, and H. J. Res. 208.

Unpublished Papers

Clarenbach, Kathryn. "Women *Are* People." Symposium on Behavioral Sciences, American Psychological Association, 1969.

Conrad-Rice, Joy Belle. "Religion, Language, Psychology—Women Left Out." KNOW, 1971. Mimeographed.

Dean, Everett. Notes on speech by Patricia Carbine of *Ms.* Magazine to Minnesota Press, Feb. 22, 1973.

Phipps-Sanger, Susan, and Alker, Henry A. "Dimensions of Internal-External Locus of Control and the Women's Liberation Movement." Cornell University, 1971. Mimeographed.

Rossi, Alice S. "Family Development in a Changing World." Presented to the American Psychiatric Association, Washington, D.C., May 5, 1971.

————. "Women in the Seventies: Problems and Possibilities." Keynote speech, Barnard College Conference on Women, Apr. 17, 1970.

Truax, Anne. "Women's Rights As a Social Change Movement." Minnesota Planning and Counseling Center for Women, University of Minnesota, Minneapolis, July, 1971. Typescript.

Way, Peggy. "You Are Not My God, Jehovah." Sermon preached at Rockefeller Memorial Chapel, March 1970. Mimeographed.

Bibliographies

Chambers, Clarke A., and Martin, Judith. *Woman in America: A Bibliographic Essay on a Complex Historical Problem and Current Issue.* 2d ed. rev. Minneapolis: University of Minnesota, General Extension Division, 1972.

Cisler, Lucinda. *Women: A Bibliography.* Rev. New York: by the author, 1969.

Laura X. "Log of Laura's Labyrinthic Libe" (catalogue for Women's History Research Center). Dittoed. Berkeley, Cal.: by the Author, 1969.

Tuning in to the Women's Movement. Mimeographed. Pittsburgh: KNOW, 1971.

Notes

1. The History and Framework of the Women's Movement

1. Lucy Komisar, "The New Feminism," *Saturday Review,* Feb. 21, 1970, p. 55.

2. Robert W. Smuts, *Women and Work in America* (New York: Schocken Books, 1971), p. xiii.

3. Diana Loercher, "Books on Women's Lib a New Genre," *Christian Science Monitor,* Jan. 15, 1973, p. 8.

4. "Women's Lit," *Newsweek,* Apr. 26, 1971, p. 65.

5. "Faculty Backlash," *Newsweek,* Dec. 4, 1972, p. 127.

6. Betty Friedan, *The Feminine Mystique* (New York: Dell, 1963), ch. 8.

7. Anne Truax, "Women's Rights As a Social Change Movement," Minnesota Planning and Counseling Center for Women, University of Minnesota, Minneapolis, July, 1971, p. 2.

8. William L. O'Neill, *Everyone Was Brave: The Rise and Fall of Feminism in America* (Chicago: Quadrangle Books, 1969), p. 340.

9. U.S., President's Commission on the Status of Women, *American Women* (Washington, D.C., 1963), p. 57.

10. "Executive Order 10980," *American Women,* p. 76.

11. Caroline Bird, *Born Female* (New York: Pocket Books, 1969), pp. 1-15.

12. Alice S. Rossi, "Women—Terms for Liberation," *Dissent,* November-December 1970, p. 534.

13. Eileen Kraditor, ed., *Up from the Pedestal* (Chicago: Quadrangle Books, 1968), p. 363.

14. National Organization for Women, "Statement of Purpose," mimeographed, Washington, D.C., 1966, p. 1.

15. Linda Seese, "You've Come a Long Way, Baby," *motive,* March-April 1969, p. 70.

16. Seese, p. 70.

17. Seese, p. 70.

18. "Liberation of Women," *New Left Notes,* July 10, 1967, p. 4.

19. Cellestine Ware, *Woman Power: The Movement for Women's Liberation* (New York: Tower Public Affairs Books, 1970), p. 19.

20. Ware, p. 19.

21. Ware, pp. 20, 32-50.

22. "Redstockings Manifesto," in Robin Morgan, ed., *Sisterhood Is Powerful* (New York: Vintage Books, 1970), pp. 533-535.

23. Ware, pp. 24-29.

24. Letter from Melba Windoffer of Seattle Radical Women to Noreen Bagnall of the Majority in Minneapolis, Apr. 25, 1970, p. 1.

25. "Women's Lib: The War on 'Sexism,' " *Newsweek,* Mar. 23, 1970, pp. 71-76.

26. Ware, p. 175; "Tuning in to the Women's Rights Movement," Women's Caucus, American Sociological Association, Summer 1970.

27. Women's Equity Action League, Press release, Novelty, Ohio, April 1969.

28. Morgan, p. xxv.

29. Seese, p. 71; Carol Ruth Sternhall, "A March in the Dark," *McCall's,* November 1970, p. 8.

30. Morgan, p. xxiv.

31. National Women's Political Caucus, "Statement of Purpose," mimeographed, n.d.

32. Letter from Florence Howe and Joanna Miller, The Feminist Press, Jan. 23, 1973 (mimeographed).

33. O'Neill, pp. vii-x.

34. Friedan, p. 37; Women's Caucus, New University Conference, *I Am Furious—Female* (Detroit: Radical Education Project, n. d.), pp. 3-4.

35. Marlene Dixon, "The Restless Eagles: Women's Liberation, 1969," *motive,* March-April 1969, p. 23.

36. Alice S. Rossi, "Equality Between the Sexes: An Immodest Proposal," *Daedalus* 93 (Spring 1964): 608.

37. Ware, p. 17; Seese, p. 71.

38. Sarah Grimke, *Letters on the Equality of the Sexes and the Condition of Woman* (New York: Burt Franklin, 1970), pp. 82-83.

39. Grimke, *Letters on the Equality of the Sexes,* p. 51.

40. Margaret Fuller, "Woman in the Nineteenth Century," in Perry Miller, ed., *Margaret Fuller: American Romantic,* (Gloucester, Mass.: Peter Smith, 1969), p. 150.

41. Marlene Dixon, "The Rise of Women's Liberation," in Betty and Theodore Roszak, eds., *Masculine/Feminine* (New York: Harper and Row, 1969), p. 191.

42. Kate Millett, *Sexual Politics* (Garden City, N.Y.: Doubleday 1970), p. 24.

43. For my method of paradigm analysis I found guidance in Thomas S. Kuhn, *The Structure of Scientific Revolutions* (Chicago: University of Chicago Press, 1962). I found useful the suggestion of David W. Noble in his American intellectual history course at the University of Minnesota that Kuhn's analysis of scientific revolution can be applied to a social or ideological one such as the woman revolution. Kuhn says that the scientist joins a field where persons are committed to the same rules and standards, and follow concrete models where there is wide agreement on fundamental attitudes and concepts. This is the state of normal science following an established paradigm. The questioning of the paradigm comes with the discovery of anomalies. The presence of enough anomalies leads to suspecting the old paradigm but may not lead immediately to a new paradigm. There might be a period in which the old paradigm is in flux but no single new hypothesis has emerged as the controlling paradigm of the field. In this situation no controlling model seems to work and all evidence seems equally important. A theory that accounts for most of the facts better than other hypotheses emerges as the dominant paradigm, but it may not account for all the facts, and for a while it exists as a concurrent competing paradigm or paradigms with the old one. The formulation of the new paradigm is the work of a community of scientists or a composite of discoveries, not the single, simple discovery of one person. People's acceptance of the paradigm can be an immediate kind of understanding that this paradigm is more comprehensive and relevant than the old paradigm, after a period of their being puzzled about what adequately explains the phenomena before them. In this frame of reference I see the contemporary feminist movement, by analogy with Kuhn's scientific framework, in a state of paradigm flux with three competing paradigms operating as the ideological mode for achieving equality for women. For further discussion on Kuhnian method and history, see David A. Hollinger, "T. S. Kuhn's Theory of Science and Its Implications for History," *American Historical Review* 78 (April 1973): 370-393.

44. Andrew Sinclair, *The Better Half* (New York: Harper and Row, 1965), p. 24.

45. Sinclair, p. 24.

46. Sinclair, p. 24.

47. Anne Bradstreet, "The Prologue," in Kraditor, pp. 29-30.

48. Sinclair, p. 9.

49. Gerda Lerner, "Women's Rights and American Feminism," *The American Scholar* 40 (Spring 1971): 238.

50. Friedan, p. 77.

51. Eleanor Flexner, *Century of Struggle* (New York: Atheneum, 1968), p. 15. See also Abigail Adams papers in Alice Rossi, ed., *The Feminist Papers* (New York: Bantam Books, 1974), pp. 7-15.

52. Sinclair, pp. 49-50. See also the biography by Eleanor Flexner,

Mary Wollstonecraft (Baltimore: Penguin Books, 1973).

53. Flexner, p. 16. See also Murray, "On the Equality of the Sexes," in Rossi, p. 21.

54. Sinclair, pp. 35-37. See also Flexner, p. 27.

55. Sinclair, p. 41.

56. Sinclair, p. 25.

57. Angelina Grimke, "Letter to Catharine Beecher," in Kraditor, pp. 62-63.

58. Sinclair, p. 47.

59. Kraditor, pp. 148-149.

60. Sinclair, p. 67.

61. Sinclair, pp. 83-84, 88.

62. Sinclair, pp. 86-87.

63. Sinclair, pp. 87-89.

64. Sinclair, p. 93.

65. Flexner, p. 25.

66. Sinclair, pp. 96-97.

67. Flexner, pp. 29-30.

68. Bird, pp. 21-22.

69. Flexner, pp. 71-77.

70. Kraditor, pp. 184-186.

71. Sinclair, pp. 102, 105.

72. Lerner, p. 241.

73. Sinclair, pp. 148, 156-159.

74. Sinclair, p. 141.

75. National American Woman Suffrage Association (NAWSA), *Victory: How Women Won It* (New York: H. W. Wilson, 1940), p. 55.

76. Fuller, pp. 149-150.

77. NAWSA, pp. 35-41.

78. Flexner, pp. 105-108.

79. NAWSA, pp. 51-52; Flexner, pp. 152-153.

80. NAWSA, p. 55.

81. NAWSA, p. 66.

82. Flexner, pp. 153-154.

83. NAWSA, pp. 74-75.

84. Flexner, pp. 264-267; Sinclair, pp. 328-329.

85. Sinclair, pp. 333-335.

86. Sinclair, p. 339.

2. The Feminist Perspective: Women Equal to Men

1. Betty Friedan, *The Feminine Mystique* (New York: Dell, 1963), pp. 37-38.

2. Friedan, pp. 109-112.

3. Friedan, pp. 134-138.

4. Friedan, pp. 162-163.

5. Friedan, p. 364.

6. Ann D. Gordon, Mari Jo Buhle, and Nancy E. Schrom, "Women in American Society: An Historical Contribution," *Radical America* 5 (July-August 1971): 47-50.

7. Page Smith, *Daughters of the Promised Land* (Boston: Little, Brown, 1970), pp. 133-135.

8. Barbara Welter, "The Cult of True Womanhood," in Wendy Martin, ed., *The American Sisterhood* (New York: Harper and Row, 1972), p. 245.

9. Betty Friedan, "Our Revolution Is Unique," in Mary Lou Thompson, ed., *Voices of the New Feminism* (Boston: Beacon Press, 1970), pp. 35-36.

10. Friedan, pp. 36-37.

11. Caroline Bird, *Born Female* (New York: Pocket Books, 1969), pp. 72-73.

12. Bird, pp. 148, 150, 151.

13. Judith Hole and Ellen Levine, *Rebirth of Feminism* (New York: Quadrangle Books, 1971), pp. 77-107.

14. National Organization for Women (NOW), "Action Resolutions," Fourth Annual Conference, Mar. 20-22, 1970 (mimeographed). "National Organization for Women," n.d.; "NOW Challenges License Renewal for ABC-TV," *The Spokeswoman* 2 (June 1, 1972): 7; "National Organization for Women," *The Spokeswoman* 3 (July 1, 1972): 9; "National Organization for Women," *The Spokeswoman* 3 (Sept. 1, 1972): 8; Emily A. Champagne, ed., *Women and Religion* (Oakland, Cal.: National Organization for Women Ecumenical Task Force on Women and Religion, 1972), mimeographed; Hole and Levine, pp. 81-95.

15. NOW, "Statement of Purpose," adopted at organizing conference, Washington, D.C., Oct. 29, 1966, pp. 1, 5 (mimeographed). Italics mine.

16. "Bill of Rights," n.d. (mimeographed).

17. NOW, "Bill of Rights" (italics mine).

18. Hole and Levine, p. 96.

19. WEAL, "1971 National Committee Reports."

20. WEAL, "WEAL—Women's Equity Action League," n.d.

21. "National Women's Political Caucus," *The Spokeswoman* 2 (Aug. 1, 1972): 1.

22. Eileen Shanahan, "Lack of Funds Cripples Women's Political Group," *Minneapolis Tribune,* Sept. 4, 1972, p. 2B.

23. "NWPC Is Full-Blown Body Politic," *The Spokeswoman* 3 (Aug. 1, 1972): 1.

24. National Women's Political Caucus, "Women's Plank," *Newsletter* 5 (June 1972): 1-2.

25. Gerda Lerner, *The Woman in American History* (Menlo Park, Cal.: 1971), pp. 159-171; Flexner, pp. 262-270; Inez Haynes Irwin, *Up*

Hill with Banners Flying (Penobscot, Me.: Traversity Press, 1964).

26. Susan B. Anthony, "Letter to Elizabeth Cady Stanton, October, 1902," in Ida Husted Harper, ed., *History of Woman Suffrage* (New York: National American Woman Suffrage Association, 1922), V, 741.

27. "Senate Approves Amendment for Women's Rights," *Minneapolis Tribune,* Mar. 23, 1972, p. 1.

28. William Henry Chafe, *The American Woman: Her Changing Social, Economic, and Political Roles, 1920-1970* (New York: Oxford University Press, 1972), p. 112.

29. Chafe, pp. 112-132.

30. "Earlier Efforts to Win Equal Rights," *Congressional Digest* 50 (January 1971): 3.

31. "Earlier Efforts," p. 3.

32. "Earlier Efforts," p. 3.

33. Hole and Levine, pp. 55-56.

34. "'Equal Rights' Action, 1969-70," *Congressional Digest* 50 (January 1971): 9.

35. U.S. Congress, Senate, Committee on the Judiciary, *Equal Rights for Men and Women,* 92nd Cong., 2nd sess., 1972, S. Rept. 92-689 to accompany S.J. Res. 8, S.J. Res. 9, and H.J. Res. 208, pp. 4-5.

36. Hole and Levine, p. 57.

37. U.S., Congress, Senate, *Equal Rights,* pp. 2-4.

38. U.S., Congress, Senate, *Equal Rights,* pp. 6-15.

39. U.S., President's Task Force on Women's Rights and Responsibilities, *A Matter of Simple Justice* (Washington, D.C.: U.S. Government Printing Office, 1970), p. 5.

40. U.S., Congress, Senate, *Equal Rights,* p. 13.

41. U.S., Women's Bureau, Department of Labor, *Handbook on Women Workers,* 1969, pp. 96, 137, 139, 141. Reprinted in Elsie Adams and Mary Louise Briscoe, eds., *Up Against the Wall, Mother* (Beverly Hills, Cal.: Glencoe Press, 1971), pp. 264-267.

42. "Working Women," *Daedalus* 93 (Spring 1964): 677-678.

43. See testimony in the New York City Commission on Human Rights, *Women's Role in Contemporary Society* (New York: Avon Books, 1972), particularly Mary Dublin Keyserling, "The Socioeconomic Waste: Underutilization of Women," pp. 67-73; Dorothy Height, "To Be Black and a Woman," pp. 82-85; Florynce Kennedy, "To Be Black and a Woman," pp. 85-89; Elizabeth Koontz, "Women in the Labor Force," pp. 184-189; Frank White, "Women in Private Industry," pp. 190-191; Bess Myerson, "Women and the Employment Agencies," pp. 325-327; Lillian Roberts, "Union and Blue-Collar Women," pp. 345-346. See also U.S., Congress, House, Special Subcommittee on Education of the Committee on Education and Labor, *Discrimination Against Women,* 2 parts, 91st Cong., 2nd sess., 1970, esp. Wilma Scott Heide, testimony and documents, pp.

122-141; Dr. Pauli Murray, testimony, pp. 328-347; Helen Bickel Wolfe, "Women in the World of Work," pp. 172-173; Fabian Linden, "Women in the Labor Force," pp. 180-183; Sandra L. Bem and Daryl J. Bem, "Sex-Segregated Want Ads: Do They Discourage Female Job Applicants?" pp. 891-893; National Organization for Women, "Background on Federal Action toward Equal Employment Opportunity for Women" and documents, pp. 934-968; Women's Bureau, Labor Dept., "Why Women Work," pp. 916-917; Elizabeth Waldman, "Marital and Family Characteristics of the U.S. Labor Force," pp. 977-988; Samuel Stafford, "Women on the March Again—Are They Being Discriminated Against in White Collar Federal Jobs?" pp. 1049-1056. Although the 1963 Equal Pay Act prohibits paying women less than men for the same work, it has not yet had the effect of eradicating the practice; and employers often cover the discrepancy by assigning one title and rank to a woman in a job and a higher title to the man in the same job.

44. "Help Wanted," *The Spokeswoman* 2 (Oct. 1, 1971): 3; "Detroit Papers Drop Male-Female Job Headings," *The Spokeswoman* 2 (Nov. 1, 1971): 2.

45. Marijean Suelzle, "Women in Labor," in Micheal E. Adelstein and Jean G. Pival, eds., *Women's Liberation* (New York: St. Martin's Press, 1972), pp. 114, 113. For a similar contrast of myth and reality about women and jobs, see Sylvia Porter column, *Minneapolis Tribune,* May 29, 1972.

46. Suelzle, p. 119.

47. Suelzle, p. 121.

48. Suelzle, p. 124.

49. Suelzle, p. 124.

50. Helen Gurley Brown, *Sex and the Single Girl* (New York: Pocket Books, 1962), *passim.*

51. Dana Densmore, "Sex and the Single Girl," *No More Fun and Games: A Journal of Female Liberation* 2 (February 1969): 76.

52. Hole and Levine, p. 378.

53. Hole and Levine, pp. 385-388.

54. Hole and Levine, pp. 388-389.

55. Mary Daly, *The Church and the Second Sex* (London: Geoffrey Chapman, 1968), pp. 15-25.

56. Daly, p. 35. See also Phyllis Trible, "Depatriarchalizing in Biblical Interpretation," *Journal of the American Academy of Religion* 41 (March 1973): 30-48.

57. Daly, pp. 40, 42.

58. Daly, p. 37. For a similar argument from biblical scholarship, see Leonard Swidler, "Jesus Was a Feminist," *Catholic World,* January 1971, pp. 177-183.

59. Daly, p. 41; also pp. 43-75.

60. Daly, pp. 76, 83, 95.

61. Daly, p. 107.

62. Very Rev. James Alberione, quoted in Daly, pp. 115-116.

63. Daly, pp. 118-119.

64. Daly, pp. 134-142.

65. Sarah Bentley Doely, ed., *Women's Liberation and the Church* (New York: Association Press, 1970), pp. 11-14.

66. Davida Fay Crabtree, "Women's Liberation and the Church," in Doely, pp. 20, 25.

67. Rosemary Radford Ruether, "Women's Liberation in Historical and Theological Perspective," in Doely, pp. 36-37.

68. Doely, pp. 77-94.

69. Alix Kates Shulman, *Memoirs of an Ex-Prom Queen* (New York: Alfred A. Knopf, 1972).

3. The Women's Liberationist Perspective: Women Over Against Men

1. Susan B. Anthony, "Marriage Has Ever Been a One-sided Affair," in Leslie B. Tanner, ed., *Voices from Women's Liberation* (New York: Signet Book, 1971), p. 79.

2. Millett, p. 23.

3. Millett, pp. 24-25.

4. Millett, pp. 24, 26.

5. Millett, pp. 30, 31.

6. Millett, p. 35.

7. Millett, p. 36.

8. Millett, pp. 44-46.

9. Millett, pp. 49-54.

10. Millett, p. 55.

11. Millett, pp. 126-127.

12. See Robert A. Nisbet, *The Social Bond* (New York: Alfred A. Knopf, 1970), pp. 197-217; Ralf Dahrendorf, *Class and Conflict in Industrial Society* (Stanford, Cal.: Stanford University Press, 1959), pp. 3-9, 136-141; John Dollard, *Class and Caste in a Southern Town,* 3rd ed. (Garden City, N.Y.: Doubleday Anchor Books).

13. Shulamith Firestone, *The Dialectic of Sex: The Case for Feminist Revolution* (New York: Bantam Books, 1970), p. 11.

14. Firestone, pp. 46-53.

15. Fireston, p. 114.

16. Firestone, p. 132.

17. Firestone, pp. 172-191.

18. Firestone, pp. 227-234.

19. Firestone, p. 202.

20. Kathy McAfee and Myrna Wood, "Bread and Roses" (Detroit: Radical Education Project, n.d.), p. 35.

21. McAfee and Wood, p. 13.

22. Frances Beale, "Double Jeopardy: To Be Black and Female,"

in Toni Cade, ed., *The Black Woman* (New York: Signet Books, 1970), p. 92.

23. Beale, p. 92.

24. Beale, p. 98.

25. Juliet Mitchell, "Women: The Longest Revolution," *New Left Review,* November-December 1966, pp. 11, 15.

26. Mitchell, p. 34.

27. Evelyn Reed, *Problems of Women's Liberation* (New York: Pathfinder Press, 1971), pp. 72, 64.

28. Betsy Stone, "Women and Political Power," in Linda Jenness, ed., *Feminism and Socialism* (New York: Pathfinder Press, 1972), p. 33.

29. Morgan, p. 533.

30. Roxanne Dunbar, "Female Liberation As the Basis for Social Revolution" (Boston: New England Free Press, n.d.), p. 3.

31. Roxanne Dunbar and Vernon Grizzard, "Caste and Class: The Key to Understanding Female Oppression," mimeographed (Cambridge, Mass.: Female Liberation—Cell 16, n.d.), pp. 1-3. This argument is also made by Tortoise, "The Logic of Male Supremacy in Keeping Women Down," *Female Liberation Newsletter* (Minneapolis), May 7, 1970, p. 5.

32. Irene Peslikis, "Resistances to Consciousness," mimeographed (Cambridge, Mass.: Female Liberation—Cell 16, n.d.).

33. Judith Brown and Beverly Jones, "Toward a Female Liberation Movement" (Boston: New England Free Press, n.d.), pp. 19, 23, 37.

34. Ti-Grace Atkinson, "Radical Feminism," mimeographed (New York: The Feminists, May 1969), p. 3.

35. Barbara Mehrhof, "Class Structure in the Women's Movement," mimeographed (New York: The Feminists, November 1969), pp. 1-2.

36. For a rhetorical analysis of the Women's Liberation movement identification of man as the enemy and the prowoman line, see Brenda Robinson Hancock, "Affirmation by Negation in the Women's Liberation Movement," *The Quarterly Journal of Speech* 57 (October 1972): 264-271.

37. Morgan, p. 534.

38. Jones and Brown, p. 35.

39. Robin Morgan, "Goodbye to All That," in Leslie B. Tanner, ed., *Voices from Women's Liberation* (New York: Signet Books, New American Library, 1970), p. 269.

40. Marlene Dixon, "The Rise of Women's Liberation," in Roszak and Roszak, p. 200; Sally Kempton, "Cutting Loose," in Wendy Martin, ed., *The American Sisterhood* (New York: Harper and Row, 1972), p. 352.

41. Morgan, *Sisterhood,* p. 514.

42. Morgan, p. 515.

43. Morgan, p. 515.

44. Morgan, pp. 518-519.

45. Betsy Warrior, "Man As an Obsolete Life Form," in Sookie Stambler, ed., *Women's Liberation: Blueprint for the Future* (New York: Ace Books, 1970), pp. 45-47.

46. Robin Morgan, "Goodby to All That," in Tanner, pp. 366-367.

47. Dixon, p. 192.

48. Dixon, p. 200.

49. Susan Brownmiller, "The Enemy Within," in Stambler, *Women's Liberation,* p. 23.

50. Alice Stone Blackwell, "The Indifference of Women," in Tanner, *Voices,* pp. 88-89.

51. Dana Densmore, "Who Says Men Are the Enemy?" in Stambler, *Women's Liberation,* pp. 47-51.

52. Susan Brownmiller, "Sisterhood Is Powerful," in Stambler, *Women's Liberation,* 150.

53. Morgan, p. 535.

54. Hole and Levine, p. 117.

55. For the range of literature on sisterhood, see Lynette Wells, "Sisterhood," leaflet from Female Liberation—Cell 16, n.d.; Susan Brownmiller, "Sisterhood Is Powerful," in Stambler, pp. 141-155; Morgan; Gloria Steinem, "Sisterhood," *Ms.*, Spring 1972, pp. 46-49; Dana Densmore, "On Sisterhood," in Elsie Adams and Mary Louise Briscoe, eds., *Up Against the Wall, Mother* . . . (Beverly Hills, Cal.: Glencoe Press, 1971), pp. 350-353.

56. Wells, p. 1.

57. Wells, p. 1; Steinem, p. 46.

58. Brownmiller, p. 145.

59. Ware, pp. 44-45.

60. See Peggy White and Starr Goode, "The Small Group in Women's Liberation," *Women: A Journal of Liberation,* Fall 1969, pp. 56-57; Kathie Sarachild, "Feminist Consciousness-Raising and 'Organizing,' " in Tanner, *Voices,* pp. 154-157; Women's Collective, Stratford, Conn., "Consciousness-Raising," Pittsburgh: KNOW, n.d.; Jane Howard, "Is Women's Lib a Dirty Word in Milwaukee?" *Life,* Aug. 27, 1971, pp. 46-51.

61. "For Continuing Formation of Consciousness-Raising Groups," *Female Liberation Newsletter,* March, 1970, p. 2; p. 47.

62. Women's Liberation Collective of Palo Alto, Cal., "Women's Revolutionary Manifesto," in Roszak and Roszak, p. 270.

63. Hole and Levine, p. 330.

64. Tanner, pp. 242-243.

65. Jones and Brown, "Toward," p. 31. They propose celibacy as a means for some women at some times to "stop the world and get off." See, also, Dana Densmore, "On Celibacy," Adams and Bris-

coe, eds., *Up against the Wall,* pp. 358-361. She argues for celibacy as an "honorable alternative," saying it need not be the course for everybody, but that the idea of celibacy needs to be totally accepted.

66. Varda One, "Toward a Female Counter Culture," *Everywoman,* March 26, 1971, pp. 18-25.

67. Ti-Grace Atkinson, "The Institution of Sexual Intercourse," mimeographed (New York: The Feminists, November 1968), p. 1; Hole and Levine, p. 131.

68. Anne Koedt, "The Myth of the Vaginal Orgasm" (Boston: New England Free Press, n.d.) p. 1.

69. Koedt, p. 2.

70. Koedt, p. 3.

71. Koedt, pp. 4-5.

72. Ruth Herschberger, *Adam's Rib* (New York: Harper and Row, 1970), pp. 30-33.

73. Herschberger, pp. 35-37.

74. Hole and Levine, p. 241.

75. Gene Damon, "The Least of These: The Minority Whose Screams Haven't Yet Been Heard," in Morgan, p. 304.

76. Morgan, p. 304; Martha Shelley, "Women of Lesbos," in Adams and Briscoe, pp. 353-358.

79. "List of Contacts," *motive* 32 (1972): *passim*; "The Gay Women's West Coast Conference," *Female Liberation Newsletter* (Minneapolis), June 1971, p. 8.

78. "Support for Abortion 7," *The Spokeswoman,* June 1, 1972, p. 1.

79. "Rhode Island Abortion Challenge," *The Spokeswoman,* Nov. 1, 1971, p. 7.

80. "Repeal All Abortion Laws," leaflet distributed by the Women's Abortion Action Coalition of Minnesota, n.d.

81. "Abortion Is a Right!" mimeographed (Seattle: Seattle Radical Women, Mar. 28, 1968).

82. *Ms.,* Spring 1972, pp. 34-35.

83. Lucinda Cisler, "Abortion Law Repeal (sort of): A Warning to Women," in Stambler, p. 80.

84. Hole and Levine, pp. 369-370.

85. Hole and Levine, pp. 366-367.

86. "Women's Culture of Humanity," *The Spokeswoman,* Aug. 1, 1972, p. 7.

87. "Two Coups for New Feminist Art Journal," *The Spokeswoman,* Dec. 1, 1972, p. 5.

88. "Bad-Dream House," *Time,* Mar. 20, 1972, p. 77.

89. "Bad-Dream House," p. 77.

90. Alta, "Penus Envy," in Edith Hoshino Altbach, ed., *From Feminism to Liberation,* (Cambridge, Mass.: Schenkman, 1971), p. 87.

91. Alta, "The Vow for Anne Hutchinson," in Altbach, p. 19.

92. Alta, "Poem," *Aphra* 3 (Spring 1972): 21.

4. The Androgynous Perspective: Women and Men Equal to Each Other

1. Elizabeth Janeway, *Man's World, Woman's Place* (New York: William Morrow, 1971), pp. 13, 26.
2. Janeway, pp. 26, 40.
3. Janeway, p. 48.
4. Page Smith, *Daughters of the Promised Land* (Boston: Little, Brown, 1970), p. 322.
5. Janeway, p. 98.
6. Janeway, pp. 104-105.
7. Carolyn Heilbrun, *Toward a Recognition of Androgyny* (New York: Alfred A. Knopf, 1973), p. ix. The British publisher (London: Victor Gollancz, 1973) titled the book *Towards Androgyny* and lost the significance of her meaning.
8. Heilbrun, pp. ix-x, xi-xii.
9. Heilbrun, pp. 54, xvi.
10. Johanna Johnston, *Mrs. Satan* (New York: G. P. Putnam's Sons, 1967), pp. 102-103.
11. Johnston, p. 66.
12. Commodore Vanderbilt was attracted to the Claflin sisters through their spiritualism, slept with Tennessee Claflin, and taught the sisters about the world of finance. Colonel James Blood, allegedly Victoria's second husband, helped her clarify her principles at an intellectual level, and did much of the behind-the-scenes managerial work for the brokerage firm and for *Woodhull and Claflin's Weekly*. Scholarly Stephen Pearl Andrews taught her his exotic world political system of pantarchy, wrote for the *Weekly*, and contributed ideas for her speeches.
13. Emma Goldman, "Marriage and Love, 1917," in Wendy Martin, ed., *The American Sisterhood*, (New York: Harper and Row, 1972), pp. 226-232.
14. Richard Drinnon, *Rebel in Paradise: A Biography of Emma Goldman* (Boston: Beacon Press, 1970), p. 153.
15. Charlotte Perkins Gilman, *Women and Economics*, ed. Carl Degler (New York: Harper Torchbooks, 1966), pp. 238-245.
16. "Gloria Steinem: A Liberated Women Despite Beauty, Chic and Success," *Newsweek*, Aug. 16, 1971, pp. 51-55.
17. "A New Ms. at *Ms.*," *Newsweek*, Mar. 13, 1972.
18. Gloria Steinem, "What It Would Be Like If Women Win," *Time*, Aug. 31, 1970, p. 22.
19. Steinem, p. 22.
20. Steinem, p. 23.
21. Alice S. Rossi, "Equality Between the Sexes: An Immodest Proposal," *Daedalus* 93 (Spring 1964): 608.

22. Rossi, pp. 631-632.

23. Rossi, pp. 624-625.

24. Rossi, p. 637.

25. Rossi, p. 643.

26. Dwight Bolinger, *Aspects of Language* (New York: Harcourt, Brace and World, 1968), p. 253.

27. Edward Sapir, "Language and Thinking," in Charlton Laird and Robert M. Gorrell, eds., *Reading about Language*, (New York: Harcourt, Brace, Jovanovich, 1970), pp. 19-20.

28. Varda One, "Manglish," *Everywoman*, Oct. 23, 1970, p. 14; Millett, pp. 54-55.

29. Varda One, "Manglish," *Everywoman*, Nov. 12, 1971, p. 16.

30. Kate Miller and Casey Swift, "De-Sexing the English Language," *Ms.*, Spring 1972, p. 7.

31. Miller and Swift, p. 7.

32. Varda One, "Manglish," *Everywoman*, Jan. 22, 1971, p. 14.

33. "What's a Ms.?," *Ms.*, Spring 1972, p. 4.

34. Varda One, "Manglish," *Everywoman*, July 10, 1970, p. 2.

35. Varda One, "Manglish," *Everywoman*, June 18, 1971, p. 6.

36. Varda One, p. 6.

37. Robin Lakoff, "You Are What You Say," *Ms.*, July 1974, pp. 65-67.

38. Varda One, "Manglish," *Everywoman*, Aug. 20, 1971, p. 3; May 28, 1971, p. 11; Aug. 21, 1970, p. 18.

39. Varda One, "Manglish," *Everywoman*, Mar. 5, 1971, p. 12.

40. Varda One, "Manglish," *Everywoman*, Jan. 22, 1971, p. 14; Ethel Strainchamps, "Our Sexist Language," in Vivian Gornick and Barbara K. Moran, eds., *Woman in Sexist Society* (New York: New American Library, 1971), pp. 347-361.

41. Mary Daly, *Beyond God the Father* (Boston: Beacon, 1973), pp. 25-26.

42. Daly, p. 26.

43. Florence Howe, "Sexual Stereotypes Start Early," *Saturday Review*, Oct. 16, 1971, p. 76.

44. Matina Horner, "Fail: Bright Women," U.S., House, Committee on Education and Labor, *Discrimination Against Women*, 91st Cong., 2nd sess., 1970, p. 896.

45. Horner, p. 896.

46. Horner, pp. 899-900.

47. Naomi Weisstein, "Kinder, Kuche, Kirche As Scientific Law," *motive* 39 (March/April 1969): 78-85.

48. Naomi Weisstein, "Psychology Constructs the Female, or the Fantasy Life of the Male Psychologist," in Edith Hoshino Altbach, ed., *From Feminism to Liberation* (Cambridge, Mass.: Schenkman, 1971), pp. 143-144.

49. Weisstein, p. 152.

50. Weisstein, pp. 156-157.

51. Weisstein, p. 157.

52. Frances Wright, "Course of Popular Lectures," in Miriam Schneir, ed., *Feminism: The Essential Historical Writings* (New York Vintage Books, 1972), pp. 18-24.

53. Johnston, pp. 110-111.

54. David M. Kennedy, *Birth Control in America: The Career of Margaret Sanger* (New Haven: Yale University Press, 1970), pp. 127-135; Margaret Sanger, *Woman and the New Race* (New York: Blue Ribbon Books, 1920).

55. *Playboy*, January 1972, pp. 61-82.

56. Germaine Greer, *The Female Eunuch* (New York: McGraw-Hill, 1971), p. 108.

57. Greer, pp. 328-329.

58. Greer, p. 61.

59. Greer, p. 4.

60. Greer, p. 4.

61. Greer, p. 8.

62. Betty Rollin, "Motherhood: Who Needs It?," in Michael E. Adelstein and Jean G. Pival, eds., *Women's Liberation* (New York: St. Martin's Press, 1972), pp. 59-69.

63. Alice Rossi, "Family Development in a Changing World," paper presented to the annual meeting of the American Psychiatric Association, Washington, D.C., May 5, 1971, p. 7.

64. Letty Cottin Pogrebin, "Down with Sexist Upbringing," *Ms.*, Spring 1972, pp. 18, 20.

65. Pogrebin, p. 20.

66. Florence Howe, "Sexual Stereotypes Start Early," *Saturday Review*, Oct. 16, 1971, p. 77.

67. Elizabeth Fisher, "The Second Sex, Junior Division," in Sookie Stambler, ed., *Women's Liberation: Blueprint for the Future* (New York: Ace Books, 1970), pp. 89-95; D. G. Stavan, "Reducing the Miss Muffet Syndrome: An Annotated Bibliography," *Library Journal* 97 (Jan. 15, 1972): 256-259; "Feminists Look at Children's Books," *Library Journal* 96 (Jan. 15, 1971): 235-240; "Sex Stereotypes in Readers," *Library Journal* 96 (Feb. 15, 1972): 680.

68. Rossi, pp. 1-3.

69. Cynthia Ozick, "We Are the Crazy Lady and Other Feisty Feminist Fables," *Ms.*, Spring 1972, pp. 40, 41. Definitive text is in *The First Ms. Reader*, ed. Francine Klagsbrun (New York: Warner, 1973), pp. 60-72.

70. Ozick, p. 41.

71. Ozick, p. 43.

72. Ozick, p. 43.

73. Ozick, p. 43.

74. Ozick, p. 44.

75. Ozick, p. 44.

76. Cynthia Ozick, "Women and Creativity: The Demise of the Dancing Dog," in Gornick and Moran, p. 435.

77. Ozick, p. 439.

78. Ozick, p. 443.

79. Ozick, p. 445.

80. Ozick, p. 450.

81. David M. Potter, "American Women and the American Character," in John A. Hague, ed., *American Character and Culture* (DeLand, Fla.: Everett Edwards Press, 1964), pp. 67-69. Regrettably, Potter did not write further about women.

82. Potter, pp. 70-75.

83. Potter, pp. 92-93.

84. Anne Firor Scott, *The American Woman: Who Was She?* (Englewood Cliffs, N.J., 1971), p. 1.

85. Anne Firor Scott, *The Southern Lady: From Pedestal to Politics, 1830-1930* (Chicago: University of Chicago Press, 1970).

86. Gerda Lerner, "New Approaches to the Study of Women in American History," *Journal of Social History* 3 (Fall 1969): 62.

87. Ann D. Gordon, Mari Jo Buhle, and Nancy E. Schrom, "Women in American Society," *Radical America* 5 (July-August 1971): 11.

88. Gordon, Buhle, Schrom, p. 18.

Index